...ion for Australian ... Australian history at the University of South Australia, and was the winner of the inaugural Greg Dening Memorial Prize. She appears as an on-camera historian in a four-part series on Australian bushrangers for Foxtel's History Channel in late 2017.

In 2006, Kiera discovered a faded newspaper clipping describing the moment her great, great, great-aunt, Mary Ann Gill, sobbed bitterly in the witness box of Sydney's Supreme Court. She was being forced by her furious father to give evidence against the man she hoped to marry. This tantalising clipping compelled Kiera to rummage through the Australian, British and Irish archives to unearth the astonishing history of a controversial ancestor who was determined to pursue her own marital ambitions, come what may.

~

Praise for *The Convict's Daughter*

'Archives, adventures, seduction and shipwrecks—*The Convict's Daughter* has it all.'

Lucy Bracey, *Way Back When*

'This is a ripper read and a great way of dealing with our history.'

Chris Wallace-Crabbe

'Truth really is stranger than fiction. A youthful and intrepid heroine makes a daring escape down a drainpipe, is pursued by her outraged father and disappointed by her down-at-heel gentleman lover. *The Convict's Daughter* contains all the elements of melodrama or farce: love divided, love betrayed, and love triumphant. Hardest of all to believe is that these events actually occurred, in a period of Australia's history often dismissed as dull—and that no historian or novelist has ever before done them justice.'

Professor Penny Russell, Department of History, University of Sydney

'Unputdownable! I'm struck by Mary Ann's amazing audacity, and the way the book captures Sydney as a place so utterly brilliantly.'

Dr Catie Gilchrist, Dictionary of Sydney

'*The Convict's Daughter* might be called "the new history"—highly readable, in fact, a compelling page-turner, but resting on solid scholarship.'

Babette Smith, *The Sydney Morning Herald*

'Lindsey tells the story of Mary Ann Gill, the daughter of enterprising, emancipist parents, with conviction, drama and flair.'

Meg Foster, *History Australia*

'Lindsey is a potential game changer: she shows how historians can move between and beyond the known facts, weaving rich stories that reveal fresh new perspectives on the past.'

Professor Alan Mayne, Hawke Research Institute, South Australia

'In recovering this fascinating tale from her own family's history, Lindsey reminds us that "colonial Australia was much more diverse and dimensioned" than our well-worn national myths might lead us to believe.'

Sophia Barnes, *Australian Book Review*

'Lindsey weaves together a tapestry of colonial Sydney with expert archival research and clever imagination.'

Fiona Poulton, Vice President, Professional Historians Association (Victoria)

'An engaging insight into life in Sydney starting in the mid-1800s.'

The City

'Lindsey tells a cracking tale, and gives an absorbing Australian history lesson at the same time.'

Tim Hilferty, *The Advertiser*

The Convict's Daughter

The scandal that shocked a colony

KIERA LINDSEY

ALLEN&UNWIN
SYDNEY · MELBOURNE · AUCKLAND · LONDON

For my mother

This edition first published in 2017
First published in 2016

Allen & Unwin
83 Alexander Street
Crows Nest NSW 2065
Australia
Phone: (61 2) 8425 0100
Email: info@allenandunwin.com
Web: www.allenandunwin.com

Cataloguing-in-Publication details are available
from the National Library of Australia
www.trove.nla.gov.au

ISBN 978 1 76063 092 8

Index by Puddingburn
Author photo (p. i) by Brian J. Marshall
Set in Minion by Midland Typesetters, Australia

10 9 8 7 6 5 4 3 2 1

Printed and bound in Australia by the SOS Print + Media Group.

Contents

For words, like Nature, half reveal
And half conceal the Soul within

       Alfred Lord Tennyson, *In Memoriam*, 1849

Prologue

1848. Pitt Street, Sydney.

Clutching hard to the wooden frame, the fifteen-year-old girl hoists herself up, knees first, onto the windowsill then through the open window and onto the third-floor ledge of her father's hotel. Carefully negotiating her precarious position, she twists her body this way and that until finally she comes to standing. Next, she places her palms flat against the sandstone wall and shuffles along the wet ledge until she finds a spot to stop.

She peers out at the darkening city harbour, then up at the night sky—chest rising and falling as steamy scuds of her breath burst into the night. Already her gloves are damp with drizzle. If the rain sets in she will be soaked through before she gets to The Sportsman's Arms on the Parramatta road, let alone the coachman up on York Street.

She must hurry. The town's streets are unsettled at the best of times—worse still at night. The darker it is, the greater the chance of trouble. She is wearing her street boots, and a good thing that is, for the drainpipe looks more difficult than she had previously assumed. She squints into the dark, trying to trace the path of the rusty piping onto the street below, but from where she is standing it seems to disappear into a pool of black. Suddenly, the prospect of scrambling down the unstable structure seems absurd and she glances behind her uncertainly.

She should turn back. Climb inside and shake the damp from her dress, slip into bed. No one other than James would know any different. Only she has made a promise. Just the night before James had been standing under an arc of gaslight right below this very spot. She had heard him whistling soft and low and hurried from her bed to the window, still in her night bonnet, face aglow with the impossible thrill of it.

Straightaway she noticed he was rocking on his heels, and when he finally asked her she detected a slight slur to his words—but she didn't care. This was what she had been full of for months. So she had answered him, nodding fast and full of breath, 'Yes, James. Yes.'

Now, however, Mary Ann feels rooted to the spot. She pats her skirts about her legs and fixes her bonnet, trying to steady her thoughts as she teeters a little on the ledge. An image of her father's pistols comes to mind and she remembers how he thrust one of them under her nose just a day or so ago. 'If what I hear is true,' her father had muttered, thumb tight under her chin so she had no choice but to look him square in the eye, 'there will be trouble.'

Mary Ann had been sure to warn James that night. 'If you take me from my father's home,' she had said, swallowing to steady the tremor in her voice, 'there can be no turning back.' But the gentleman settler only brushed her fears away with a flurry of his hand. 'There is no fear to it, Mary Ann,' he had said, 'you shall be mine.'

The convict's daughter nods to herself and peers below. She has come this far. The carpetbag she has stolen from her mother is already in James' carriage. The coachman is waiting. She must to it. So, Mary Ann straightens each glove and reaches for the drainpipe and when it is firmly in her grip, she begins to fumble in the dark, searching for a foothold with which to commence her descent.

Introduction

This is the story of Mary Ann Gill, a little known Australian woman who was born in Sydney in 1832 and died in 1902, a year after the Federation of Australia. Mary Ann's parents were Dublin convicts who had very different ideas about their daughter's marital future than her own. Like many girls of her age and class, Mary Ann was allowed a little learning as long as it served her role as a helpmate within the family business, which included several well-patronised confectionery stores and a number of hotels. Mary Ann's parents, Martin and Margaret Gill, were capable and canny and by the early 1840s had assumed management of a large three-storey hotel on Pitt Street. This solid Georgian mansion occupied the position where Martin Place stands today and soon became known as one of the best hotels in Sydney.

In 1848, just months before Mary Ann's sixteenth birthday, Gill's Family Hotel became the site of a romantic interlude between this young currency lass and a gentleman settler named James Butler Kinchela, who also happened to be the son of the previous Attorney General of New South Wales. When Martin and Margaret Gill found out about this intimacy, a domestic drama erupted that spilled into the courts and newspapers where it became one of the great causes célèbres of that year. More than 40,000 words were published about Mary Ann's 'Parramatta Romance', ensuring that her 'strange and eventful history' was widely circulated throughout the Australian colonies, even as far as New Zealand.

I first became fascinated with Mary Ann's story in 2006 when my mother showed me a clipping from *The Sydney Morning Herald* of 5 June 1848. It was, she explained, an excerpt from a larger newspaper article that described the moment when my great, great, great aunt, Mary Ann Gill, stepped into the witness box of Sydney's Supreme Court. As she took to the stand, the report noted, this fifteen-year-old girl was 'too agitated to be sworn for several minutes'. No wonder—for she was being forced by her father to give evidence against the man she hoped to marry. Her testimony could condemn her to social ostracism and him to prison, but with the pressure of the court and her family upon her, what choice did she have?

Mary Ann's romantic scandal occurred during a crucial period in the colonies when people like the Gills were insisting upon their rights as British subjects, while 'Regency gentlemen' such as her suitor were finding themselves increasingly at odds with the new middle-class sensibilities of the Victorian age. The year of this scandal, 1848, saw dramatic change throughout much of the world and eventually became known as the 'Age of Revolutions'. Each week, it seemed, newspapers were reporting upon fresh uprisings in France, Italy, Germany and Hungary as well as the Netherlands and Denmark as, one by one, feudal systems began to crumble under the pressure of a new and defiant democratic temper. In Sydney, radical colonists used this European unrest to stir up social and political change. It was, after all, an election year in New South Wales, and men like Martin Gill were keen to secure their position within the colony.

The trouble unloosed upon the world in 1848 had, in fact, been brewing for some time. In Australia this might be traced to the late 1830s when thousands of free British immigrants flocked to the colonies eager for a better life. After the cessation of transportation in New South Wales in 1840, many saw their chance to establish the foundations of a new and free society better suited to their personal and professional interests. These men and women were energetic and ambitious and their often single-minded pursuit of these objectives helped to make the 1840s a time of activity and enterprise.

This decade was also a time of rapid European expansion that led to the establishment of numerous fledgling outposts beyond established townships throughout Australia. In many the male population outnumbered their female counterparts by as much as twenty to one. Such rough and ready settlements were also frequently marked by ferocious frontier conflict. Indeed, an atmosphere of brooding violence seemed to permeate colonial society in ways that provoked a vigorous assertion of European manners from those wanting to assuage their unease about these conditions.

Such complex conditions make the 1840s a time of intense tension and tribulation, and yet this period remains something of a forgotten decade in Australian history—a time often dismissed as little more than a drought and depression-afflicted lull that occurred after the precarious beginnings of penal settlement and before the glittering madness of the gold rush. For me, however, the 1840s was a thrilling threshold period. A time when everything was up for grabs and anything could and often did happen. Eighteen forties Sydney often resembled something of a miniature Dickensian London. It was a place where fortunes could be made and lost in a heartbeat and reputations were vulnerable to vicious vicissitudes. In the streets could be found Regency rakes and military men as well as scurrilous entrepreneurs and drunken debt collectors. There were also 'flashmen', native-born idlers and shabbily clad sailors from the South Seas. And there were women, such as Mary Ann and her mother, Margaret Gill.

Mary Ann's story allows us to see the colonial world through the eyes of a young Australian woman. We travel through the streets of Sydney at a time when both she and this town were on the threshold of a new era. We meet the influential people whose lives intersected with her own and who helped to shape the colony during this period. Hers is a story that spans from transportation to Federation, from the excesses of the Regency era to the high ambitions and petty peccadillos of the Victorian period. It confirms that women's lives were controlled by constraining ideas and attitudes, but that there were nonetheless numerous ways that an enterprising woman might become, as one newspaper wrote of Mary Ann, 'the Mistress of her own Actions'.

Mary Ann's story also travels far beyond the British world to tropical villages and goldfields, ranches and plantations in America and the French Pacific. In so doing it confirms that Australia has always been part of a much larger world and that Australians, or colonists as they were then most commonly known, frequently travelled the world with curiosity and confidence. As such Mary Ann's story reminds us that colonial Australia was much more diverse and dimensioned than the well-known narratives of discovery, convicts, gold and bushrangers sometimes suggest. Like Mary Ann, colonial Australia was contested and contradictory—shaped not only by uncertainty but also by a growing desire for greater freedom and self-expression. Perhaps then we might consider Mary Ann's story not only the biography of a little-known colonial adventuress, but also a fresh way of charting the transformation of Australia in the nineteenth century.

CHAPTER ONE

High-Growing Fruit

The Gills had made good. Little Martin had come a long way from the wind-shocked cobblestone lanes of North Dublin where he had learnt to live off scraps once the weaving work died after the war had finished. He had had nothing really. A ma he couldn't remember, and a da who had passed him onto an uncle who sent him over to a man who ran the workshops. It was there he had been left after the boss cleared out during the slump when everyone who could leave, did.

Twelve-year-old Martin Gill had watched the carts and coaches piled high with trunks—twisting this way and that as they crawled out along the road to Dun Laoghaire like a giant wooden caterpillar. Those who remained in the winter, hunched up against the cold, were lucky to survive. Or were they? All the while more cast-off soldiers kept drifting into town where they haunted the inns and markets with makeshift weapons beneath their filthy army coats.

In this brutal universe Gill fossicked and stole, using his fists and teeth to rip food out of the hands, sometimes even the mouths, of others. He was small, even for a Dublin desperate. A sharp thing, all bones and tight skin with a bold shock of greasy black hair. Just seventeen when he was caught with an iron griddle he slipped up his shirt while begging at one of the big kitchens off the park.

1

The prison book said his eyes were hazel and his complexion pale. No wonder of it, standing only five feet and two inches and lucky to get something in his belly each day. Actually, it was something of a relief when they finally hauled him off to gaol in the winter of 1819. Once a day, they threw something like food at him, however foul. He had to fight for this, too, but at least he usually ended up with something.

By the time they took him from the city cell and dragged him down into the hull of the boat, ready to sail, six months had passed and Martin Gill was almost animal. Living off his senses more than wits. Feeling into the dark wet spaces, trying to anticipate the next thwack, shove, thud or bludgeon. Most of the time, the boat rocked and groaned in the heaving black and he was too weak to move. A day or so from Dublin, they docked again and picked up another crew of felons who slurred their curses and smelt of animal shit. With not much but instinct to keep him alive, he slumped back into the shadows. Nonetheless he noticed things. And again he stole. Bits of rations the others didn't finish and which were small enough for him to take with no one seeing. Once, when he was mad with hunger, he chanced a chunk of green meat hanging above a tub. When they found that on him they flogged him on deck, then locked him down below in hand irons. No food for days. Shat his pants.

He had been lucky, the ship's doctor told him; things used to be tougher. But in the last few years there had been so many complaints in the newspapers that the captains were now keen to keep the men alive. It wasn't worth the cost, let alone the noise from do-gooders who put about pamphlets and wrote flowery, high-minded letters about the rights of British subjects. It was also generally understood, the doctor said, that there were useful men among the criminal classes and a hungry boy stood a better chance than most of coming good. Out there, there were all sorts keen to make a fortune from the grunt work of government men, he explained, and a young man was considered a commodity even if he was not much more than a runt. So the doctor fed the boy and sent him down below where the captain of the

2

City Boys gave him a solid thumping and Gill kept quiet for the rest of the voyage.

That was 1820; seven years later Martin Gill was twenty-five years old and out of the gangs. Regular food, time working the roads and the audacious sunlight of a new country added almost three inches to his scrawny frame. He had had his run-ins—a stint on the treadmill for starting a fight on York Street and another for trying to steal a Spanish dollar from his boss while in government service. But after the Dublin thief had earned his ticket-of-leave he got a better sense of how things worked. He began to stand a little straighter and develop a way to him. Being a thief in the bleak of those early years had caused him to see things sideways and slightly upside-down. He even had a certain turn of phrase that made some fellows look twice.

One of his first jobs was assisting the Barnetts of Pitt Street. They had a kitchen that backed onto their inn and the young ticket-of-leaver ran errands and helped with the fires. When the cook disappeared Gill got the job making pastries and it was not long before people were saying they were better than those of the old cook.

He met Margaret the same year, just as he was starting to make a name for himself. She had come out on the boats, too, although they didn't talk about it much. She was a domestic and one of her jobs was collecting supplies from the same store Gill visited. One time after work he spotted her standing with a man he fancied must be her father. A balding, burly sort of bloke with a scar under his right eye. Margaret was short and stocky but Martin could see that she knew what she was about and in a way that made it clear it was no one's business but her own. He watched her eyes follow a half-dressed urchin weaving through the auction crowd, the lad no more than six or seven, testing pockets for loose tin.

She knew. That was what it was like. You saw a lot but you didn't say much. He liked her complexion, natural and fresh with a splattering of freckles across her broad nose. Margaret was seventeen and had only been in the colony for a few months after a stint as a hand to the Lord Lieutenant's pastry chef where she had learnt the right way of

3

doing things. You suffered if you forgot when you were in his kitchen, Margaret would recall, but it paid off in the long run. Even as a young girl she was proud of her craft and what she could do.

Margaret had kept to herself when Gill first greeted her, but once he had told her what work he was doing at the Barnetts' she had looked him up and down with interest. Over the next month or so she had come past his kitchen during the busy hours. Just outside the door, mind. 'You need to fold the mixture faster,' she had said when he spied her in the market one afternoon a few weeks later, 'get it rolled and into the trays quicker, too, if you want to keep the lightness to it,' she finished with a curt nod before moving off. Gill grinned, he liked the way she could tell him but not hold it over him.

Margaret's da had been a tailor, but he had had a thing for selling certain items that weren't exactly his. When things had got desperate after the wars, when the prices soared and no one wanted to buy Irish butter or linen anymore, McCormick had little choice but to train his daughter up in the sly craft of fencing. They had done all right for a few years until she was found with a handkerchief from one of the ladies in the house. They were both sent out for that. First her father, and then when nothing came of the petitions from the local priest, Margaret had been sent out too. For some reason no one could quite work out, Dublin Castle allowed McCormick to bring his wife, Margaret's stepmother. Not many got that chance, they knew, but that was the way with Mary Riley. She often had a bit of luck on her side.

And so here they all were, the Dubliners. A girl with her da and a thin slip of a stepmother and a man who had never been a boy but was not much bigger than one, and who hadn't known his own family since he was nine or so but knew how to make things go his way wherever he was and whatever was required. It made sense for them to throw their lot in together, Gill had explained to Margaret once he had made up his mind. But they had to do it properly, McCormick insisted when the young man sounded him out on the matter. 'We are not like those slovenly Proddies, who slip in and out of each other's huts, rutting whatever moves.'

4

Martin and Margaret were married at St Mary's Roman Catholic Cathedral in the spring of 1831. The first of their children came nine months later. Almost to the day. It was around dusk on the shortest day of the year, during a winter solstice that might have been a long balmy summer's day back home, but was a wet whinge of a day in Sydney, with a cruel wind that blew right off the bay and straight into your bones. Margaret pushed and sweated with as much poise as a woman in her first birthing could, and eventually Mary Ann entered the world in the tiny back bedroom of the George Street confectionery shop where Martin and Margaret started their business life together. It was Margaret who decided on the girl's name and Gill was happy to grant her that for he had been clear he would name the boys. 'Who knows,' the new mother said as she watched her stepmother wrap her newborn in a rough grey blanket, 'she might get some of your luck, then.'

From the moment Mary Ann gulped air into her baby lungs, she was about it. For Gill, the noise of her breaking into the world was unbearable. But, next moment—there she was—blinking back at him with unfocused eyes and a tuft of fly-away brown hair. Having nursed the bundle for less than an awkward minute Martin Gill handed her back to Mary Riley with a nod. He had no idea. He had never been around babies and could barely remember his own father's face. He just knew that now he had a child of his own to provide for and he was going to do better than had been done to him.

Fate was on his side in this matter, for now anyway. By the time Mary Ann was six months old the government bowed to pressure regarding the fact that George Street was barely fit to carry a coach on wet days. They paid a number of shopkeepers proper sterling pounds to move on until the street was fixed. With the flush, Gill bought a hotel on York Street, and named it The Donnybrook after the fight he had had there while he was still in government service. There were already too many squalid drinking spots about the town, so the Gills decided they would make their establishment more refined. That way they could bring in some of the better sorts about town. Margaret had firm ideas about how to fit it out and McCormick helped find curtains and such. Gill spoke to a mate down at Market Wharf where there were always good prices to be had. Soon the family were in possession of the types of goods they had once stolen from the big homes around the Green.

From looking about and watching others, Gill quickly worked out that you didn't make money by keeping it in your pocket. The opening of The Donnybrook happened to coincide with the Christmas season so Martin took his wife's suggestion about making a splash. The pair worked in the kitchen for days putting together a gigantic fifty-pound Twelfth Night cake, thick with dried fruit and spices. They displayed it in the window on the night before Christmas Eve and raffled it for a good profit. Early windfalls like that helped the couple get a toe and then a foothold, and there were days when Gill thought that his wife and daughter were some sort of charm that had come to bring him his fortune. How could it be, he would ask himself as he stood across from his hotel admiring the solid shape of The Donnybrook, that a man had to steal to survive on one side of the world and could end up making cakes and selling them for a profit on the other?

But with Mary Ann getting older and another baby on the way, Gill was going to need all the good fortune he could get. Luck and pluck, he thought. It didn't take long for him to realise that the biggest part of making good here was bluff. His new hometown had just about as many people as the Dublin of his childhood, but the mood was something else. Here the air was thick one day but could then suddenly shift, just like that. Sometimes when things had been sticky for a few days the whole town felt like a keg of powder about to explode. Where the cold had made people tight and sharp in Dublin, here the heat made folks unpredictable—like the molasses Gill used to watch the old cook heat up to make boiled sweets. You had to have your wits about you in Sydney. Just about everyone was making and shifting. It wasn't like home where you were told where you fitted and got whacked if you stepped out of line. Here, you had to be always on the move so they couldn't get hold of you.

6

It was McCormick who came up with the idea of placing regular advertisements in the news-sheets. He had done it in Dublin with his tailoring and it had served him well enough, for a time. His son-in-law took the idea further though. But he didn't want meek supplications like the sort his wife read to him from *The Gazette* in her stop-start way. He was keen to impress the city's better families as well as certain 'gentlemen from the interior'.

'Martin Gill', the advertisements would typically announce in bold capital letters, 'begs to inform his friends and numerous customers' of the new 'Genteel Parlour for Refreshments' he has recently opened 'opposite the Treasury'. In this new establishment, he boldly declared, 'ladies and gentlemen' will be pleased to find 'a large and varied stock of bottled fruits: Lawson's gooseberries, cherries and damson plums all of which have been recently selected for him from the first houses at Home'. If customers 'called to the store', he continued, often with Margaret chiming in her two bits' worth, customers could also enjoy caraway comfits and, of course, Gill's famous pastries. 'Always baked twice a day to guarantee freshness.'

'Those who continued to bestow their favours upon Gill's Victorian Confectionery Establishment,' another advertisement announced a few years later when Gill informed his customers of a new property he had taken up on George Street, 'could be assured of fruits, confectionery and cake ornaments of a style superior to that which has been done heretofore in the colony.' The proprietor and his canny wife, who was no doubt responsible for the finest of these sweets and treats, also hastened to reassure their 'numerous friends' that such provisions would 'be suitable for all manner of balls and routs'.

This was all flourish and pomp, sometimes so grand that Margaret would make a few subtle adjustments before her daughter ran the ad to the newspaper office. But Margaret liked a bit of flair, too. It reminded her of her days in the Lieutenant's kitchen when everything was done right. Later the Gills opened yet another confectionery stall, announcing this with an advertisement that began: 'Strictest attention will be given to those ladies and gentlemen who patronise the new and extensive premises of the Victorian Confectionery Establishment at the city's new Royal Victoria Theatre, which the Gills have fitted up at great expense and in the latest London style.'

But the Gills were not just solid buildings and sweets. Martin Gill was also around and about, busy supplying the very best private occasions in the colony, attending the Five-Dock Steeplechase and other races, where he was pleased to provide for his patrons in a 'spacious booth and large marquee' in which he served 'excellent luncheons' as well as a 'generous array of wines, spirits ales &c.'. Gill discovered that if you became a regular advertiser, the press looked after you, and that could be handy. Having his name in print on such a regular basis also meant that people began to know who he was.

These were years of expansion both for the business and the family. All up, Margaret gave birth to twelve children, although only six of these were to survive. Baby Margaret was born less than a year after Mary Ann but died two days later. Ten months after that came William. He survived, but was small and needed a nurse most of the time. Even as he grew and became a devoted companion to his older sister, the boy was thin with weak lungs that wheezed. William was followed by five more infant deaths before finally Isabella was born around the time the family opened The Donnybrook. After Isabella came Harriet and Thomas Edward. By early 1848 there were six dead and five living children with another due to arrive at any moment. Two of the dead ones were consecrated and put in a local churchyard but some of the younger ones, born and lost when money was tight, were buried quickly and quietly out the back of whatever house they were residing in at the time.

In the early days the store had been most of what Margaret liked to talk about in the evening, but once the babies had started coming, there had been a stop to that. But that was alright for by now Gill had a handle on it anyway. He had staff in his employ, a number of establishments, and was looking at one or two bits of land down south. These days he was all for getting out and about with others of his sort. Men like him, who had come from grim circumstances and were now enjoying a much warmer reception than those who had once preferred to show him their whip or throw him in the lock-up. Many of Gill's associates were men who rarely accepted a sideways glance and were quick to deal with any sort of slight, real or imagined, and they were also handy for teaching him a few new tricks.

These were the sorts of things that helped the Gills close in on their most sought-after goal. It was something he and Margaret had needed to joke about when they first discovered they shared it. Respectability. And all that came with it. Not so much the money as the feeling. Although it was clear to them that you needed the former to secure the latter. They both knew that they wanted to be looked upon in a certain way. Spoken to and greeted with the right tone. Referred to in the papers as people of substance and colonists of standing. This was the high-growing fruit both husband and wife hankered after, and they had a hushed way of talking around and about it, trying to work out which branches might be easiest to pull down and where the fruit was ripest and ready to taste.

But for now Mary Ann loomed large in Margaret's world and her happiest times were taking the girl out to her father's farm along the Punchbowl road. Once he had been freed from working for Major Mitchell, Surveyor-General of the colony, McCormick had put away the box of threads and scissors he had brought with him from Dublin. He even agreed to Mary Riley's prompting and procured a patch of their own—something simple with a few pigs and one or two crops to keep the soil. It was manageable for McCormick and he soon discovered it could be more satisfying than the tailoring work. At least he didn't have to get down on his knees before the high and mighty. 'Your own land gives you dignity,' Mary Riley insisted. He doubted they would make much money, but he liked it well enough for now.

While her girl scratched in the garden with her grandfather, Margaret liked to talk about home with Mary Riley. It was a lighter world without the endless demands of the town and the sense of always being on show that came with living and working in the hotel. Margaret was often shocked at how big the plants could grow at her father's. Some of them were so tall and lush that they looked vulgar. She wondered if it was the same with the people, too. Considering some of the big, red-necked men who came into the hotel. The southern sun seemed to be brash enough to make a mockery of them all. Even the young ones looked old and leathery to her. Not her Mary Ann, though. Margaret would keep her eldest apart from such things. Mary Riley was for the same thing, too. They wanted the girl to have things they had not even thought to dream of at her age.

By the time she was ten, Mary Ann was well and truly the boss of her siblings and considered old enough to take on certain duties. She was sent to the small local seminary twice a week and sometimes, if she had done her writing for the day, was also allowed to accompany her father to the Royal Victoria Theatre at the top end of Pitt Street. Gill had recently taken a lease of the refreshment rooms at the theatre and had these fitted up 'in splendid style, no expense avoided', of course. It was the girl's job to stack the confectionery boxes under the shelves, and Mary Ann loved to stay there in the dark below, peering out through the gaps in the wooden booth and watching the well-dressed couples choose their treats for the matinee performances. Sometimes she also caught a glimpse of the actors rehearsing on the stage in their street dress.

The Vic was all gilt and velvet. She loved the way the actors tipped and bowed, flourished and fancied, although she was a little scared of the low-voiced men with coarse moustaches and claret cloaks. Most of all, she loved the well-dressed women. They were delicate and exotic like the birds that flitted about in the bamboo cages which hung above the doors of the George Street stores. She loved to hear them sing, for their voices transported her into a world of pure enchantment.

One afternoon she watched a boy in pantaloons and sailor's cap make a pair of white horses dance backwards across the stage. Another time, men in chains and helmets thrust long blades at one another, forcing each other back and forward across the stage until an awkward-looking boy pulled something thin and gleaming from a papier-mâché stone and the audience exploded in triumph. Sometimes

Mary Ann would tell William and the younger ones about the performances she had seen, although she knew that only William could really picture what she was saying.

There was one play she never told William about, and which stayed in her mind much longer than the others. She had seen it one afternoon while she was helping her father set up jars of blackcurrant drops. Unlike other melodramas and burlesques from 'home', this rough and ready musical was a local story titled *The Currency Lass*. It was a frothy farce that seemed rather bold and at odds with the turgid melodramas most often performed at the Royal Vic. It was all poke-in-your-eye fun, too. Mary Ann was sure she could recognise the characters on the stage from the people who came into her father's hotel and others from the streets and thereabouts. There was Harry Hearty, a thick chested, native-born hero who bounded onto the stage at the play's opening boasting that the local skies and seas far outstripped all the beauteous lands of Europe. There was his best friend, Edward Stanford, a handsome but naïve new chum, who had fallen in love with his best friend's sister, Susan Hearty, a fifteen-year-old native-born girl he longed to marry, but for a fat fool of an uncle, a boastful thespian named Samuel Similie, who had arrived from London, determined to stop his nephew's match.

This girl, Susan Hearty, was a pretty and quick thing, whose vowels sounded just as flat and nasal as Mary Ann's own. The audience cheered each time she appeared on the stage. She seemed to take particular delight in outsmarting everyone, particularly her fiancé's uncle, whom she tricked and teased, coaxed and cajoled with dazzling song and dance routines. Susan Hearty reminded Mary Ann of one of the older local girls she sat next to at the school, the sort she hoped she might one day become. In the play Susan Hearty got into all sorts of larks with an Irish servant called Lanty O'Liffey who wore a green peaked cap and shoes with giant gold buckles. He made sly, funny asides similar to the ones Mary Ann had seen her own da do with certain customers from time to time. One minute Lanty played the humble servant to the fat old thespian and the next confounded him in such a way that made the audience erupt with laughter. He also danced the sorts of steps that Mary Ann had seen performed on Saint Patrick's Day.

For weeks afterwards, Mary Ann turned that play around in her mind marvelling at how much it was like her own world. The old fool of an uncle was like those guests who spoke in high tones when they first came off the boats and who made her ma sniff and mutter 'airs' under her breath after they walked away. Mary Ann rejoiced at how the young girl repeatedly thwarted the uncle's attempts to stop her marriage to Edward Stanford and how, by the play's end, she had so baffled and bewildered the old uncle that he had no choice but to surrender to her charms. Indeed, at the play's end, the pompous old uncle had thrown his arms about the Currency Lass and declared 'Advance Australia! Blessed be the Land who gives existence to so bright a gem' before consenting to their marriage. Mary Ann wondered if one day she might have to sing and dance like Susan Hearty. She could be every bit as clever, and she hoped that one day she might also be as pretty as that girl.

But that was a moment in time. The Gills didn't keep the rooms at the Vic Theatre for long, and the sumptuous delights of that establishment dissolved like one of the greengage fancies her father sometimes gave her as a reward for a good day's done.

Next Mary Ann began helping her father at his various race meetings and private parties, for now Gill was not only running two hotels and a couple of stores, he was also judging flowers at agricultural shows, leaving little time to tend to his various businesses. Gill had a feeling that he was finally on the brink of becoming a person he most desired—a prominent colonist. Indeed, he was even described in this way when he was invited to join 'a select number of well-known Roman Catholics' who called upon the mayor. Thereafter, whenever his wife questioned certain decisions he had made or dared to side with her father over a business matter, Gill would remind Margaret, 'Old McCormick is off playing in the mud while I'm shaking hands with the best men in the land.' He would add, 'This is your family now.' To which Margaret would nod, then look away.

By late 1846 Martin Gill was ready for his grandest ambition thus far, a highly respectable establishment where he could welcome the very best clientele in the colony. After months of looking about he finally found it, on the better side of the Tank Stream and no more than ten minutes from the quay. It was, in fact, the only three-storey hotel in town and this allowed it to perch above the other buildings on the street and to also command something of a view of the harbour, at least from the north-facing rooms.

This solid Georgian mansion had been built in 1835 for Saul Lyons, the free brother of the wily old emancipist and auctioneer, Samuel Lyons. The ambitious free settler had lived in it for close to thirteen years until he finally tired of what was becoming an increasingly litigious life. By 1846, Lyons was so keen for fresh pursuits that he handed the matter of finding a tenant to his mercantile nephews, Saul and Lewis Samuel.

It was young Lewis who took the matter in hand and he and Martin Gill soon came to a reasonable price. A few weeks later the Gill family were out of their York Street property and set up on the third floor of their new Pitt Street establishment, the lower floors being part of the main hotel and the second storey reserved for eleven large guestrooms. The move seemed to stir something in Margaret, who was determined to have a say in all the furnishings—not only in their own quarters, but the entire hotel and restaurant. What would it be like to be the mistress of a house that was every bit as fine, if not finer, than those around the Green back home? she wondered. The very sort of place where she had once been a humble employee and not allowed past the kitchen door?

The truth was that the proposition made Margaret anxious, as if the family were pushing beyond their lot, and she wanted to be about it, keep things in check, so they didn't stir up reprisals in this world or the next. She had a feeling that while they were going so big, they had to also keep things modest. More and more it looked like the wealthy in this town were splashing their fortunes about only to find themselves dragged into the debtor's courts the following season. From what she had seen, the most powerful didn't flash their money about. But if you looked closely you could see they had it in the way their coats were finished or how they held their knives when they were dining. These were the sorts she wanted in the hotel and to do that she needed to set the right tone.

Both Margaret and Martin agreed that the kitchen needed to match their patrons' growing expectations. It had to be bigger and better than anything they had known, as it would be the centre of all their operations within and beyond the hotel. And so it was. A huge spacious room with two long wide benches that ran along the whitewashed walls, where you could set up all sorts of dishes at different stages of preparation without worrying that someone might send the plates flying during serving time. The windows were square and wide and placed up high in the tall room, and when the cooking began in earnest each morning clouds of flour would float up into the shafts of light that slanted in from outside. There were two generous stoves and another section just for the fire so that there was little risk of running short of hot water during service. The kitchen also came with a separate pantry and a larder, both the size of the first bedroom the Gills had shared on George Street—where Mary Ann had been born. Once they had lit the huge kitchen fire a few times, the damp dried out of the upstairs rooms, which had stunk badly of old wet when they had first moved in. After a few more baking sessions, the upper floor seemed to lift with the sweet juices of baked ham as well as the sticky promise of Margaret's much-loved pastries.

The kitchen was the heart of the Gill's Family Hotel. In fact, it was the centre of their entire lives. Often Margaret would get up first thing before the fire boy arrived and rub down the wood benches with walnut oil, while Martin liked to come in after his staff had finished for the day and spend the better part of an hour sharpening the carving knives and shelving the supplies. Margaret insisted on keeping all the trimmings in the new hotel within a certain range. The carpets and the curtains would be fine but not showy. The brass would be polished each day, twice, if there was an idle moment, and the wood panels around the bar and the dining room would be varnished at least once a week.

Modest management was what Margaret was intent upon and it made her feel more in control of the grand mansion as well as the staff of sixteen she and her husband now employed. The only other indulgence Margaret was prepared to concede to her husband was something that they both felt certain would attract the right clientele. Running the advertisement down to the paper's office on the morning before the opening of their new Pitt Street premises, fourteen-year-old Mary Ann had to agree: It was indeed a great luxury, particularly in summer, to have 'a beautiful bath' like the one which now adorned the second floor of Gill's Family Hotel.

For the adolescent girl, however, the best thing about her new abode was the fact that she had her own bedroom. It was still located next to the nursery but it had a door of its own. One bedroom window looked out onto the filthy Tank Stream on the western side of the building, but there was also a tall thin window that looked down the tail end of Pitt Street, out across the quay and over the harbour. Often, after Mary Ann had finished her writing lessons for the day, she would sit in front of that window savouring the exhilarating snatch of freedom, hoping no one would find her.

The window was her shimmering threshold. Directly below there was a line of cottages and office buildings that ran all the way down to the quay where she could just see the great expanse of glistening water and sometimes, early in the morning, also hear the chink of the masts. Here and there the horizon was punctuated with squat wind-mills, sometimes furiously spinning, other times listless in the still air. Mary Ann would watch the various carts and carriages pushing up and down Pitt Street as loose loud groups of women loitered about the gangs of men who slouched in the doorways, faces concealed by the broad brims of cabbage-tree hats. But it was the better-dressed folk, particularly the women, set up high in their phaetons and tilburies, who most captured Mary Ann's attention.

Tucked away in her third-floor bedroom watching everyday life from that tall, thin window, reminded Mary Ann of the times she had spent within her father's confectionery stall at the Royal Vic watching the actors from her safe and invisible distance. Like then, she could see it all but she was not part of it. Sometimes she would catch herself leaning forward, as if she was on the brink of entering the scene. Other times, she realised she was talking aloud—caught in some imaginary conversation with one of the strangers on the street.

A little time after her fifteenth birthday Mary Ann began to acquire a growing sense of curiosity about what it would be like to move around the town according to her own inclination and without any sort of permission. To be like the people she saw through her window. But how? Mary Ann's life was insulated and defined by specific tasks and errands determined by her father according to her position within the family business. Recently, she had also heard her mother talk, more than once in fact, of putting her to work as a nurse for an elderly lady. If this happened Mary Ann knew there would be even more order and obligation. But home was no longer much respite now that her mother had given birth to yet another child, little Martin, who had been born in the first month of the year.

Spun tight within this close domestic cocoon, Mary Ann came to savour the few tantalising moments she was able to snatch for herself. And that was how it was and how indeed it seemed that it might always be until one particularly sticky afternoon in the last week of summer in 1848, when a gentleman settler just off the Moreton Bay steamer arrived at her parents' hotel, attracted, no doubt, by the promise of a soothing soak.

CHAPTER TWO
Decline and Fall

There was a yellowness to the man's eyes. Although he dressed with the right neckerchief, wore a well-tailored coat and carried himself like a gentleman, there was something in the lines on his 33-year-old face that spoke of sickness and disappointment. He could conceal his vulnerability with a certain turn of phrase, which sometimes made his brown eyes glint with wry amusement, but more often than not it depended on the audience.

Others of his class were likely to overlook his deficiencies and cast forward to better times. They saw a man with a well-connected past and understood the need to keep his sort in position as a way of ensuring a stable future for their kind. But there were others coming up the ladder who smelt weakness and could barely contain the urge to attack. Out on their stations many of his sort had shown more compassion to the blacks than their own countrymen. That was probably the greatest insult of all. That and the fact that well-heeled settlers like himself had done everything they could to keep their grip on land grants, the justice system, in fact, the whole bloody colony.

And so, most of the townies looked at men like James Butler Kinchela and saw the end of an era. They considered his sort as little more than relics who relied upon a set of increasingly implausible references to make up for a string of failed speculations that were longer, some said, than the southern road to Port Phillip. There was always a reason for these misfortunes. Some trick the land had played on them. A drought. A bad river crossing. Fires. The blacks. Or some blight that had ruined the stock. But the truth was—more often than not—it was the grog. Once it had been the only alternative to water, easier to find and more popular round the camp. They had all used it to assuage fear when they were out there the first couple of times, but it didn't take long for it to become their consolation for *every* fear and failure and then, after a time, their only constant companion. Complexions ruddy, livers shot, hands unsteady, the grog had got many of his sort.

The truth of it was that James Butler Kinchela, the gentleman settler of Moreton Bay, was not much of a hero. His liver was spent, his family were not as they once had been and nor, for that matter, was he. But for a fifteen-year-old girl, and one who had been watching life through her bedroom window, the well-turned, weather-beaten man with a non-chalant air was intriguing. He looked like he knew about life and even more importantly, for Mary Ann, about adventure.

She watched him from just inside the kitchen. He was standing with his back against the bar resting one elbow on it. His hand was tucked into his kerseymere waistcoat and one of his riding boots was pushed up against the foot railing as he gazed out the window to where two men on fine geldings were making their way up Pitt Street. What was he thinking?, she wondered as he lifted the glass to his lips, then chucked back its contents with a swig before downing it on the bench. And then the gentleman settler turned his head and looked straight to where the young girl was standing in the gap of the half-opened door. 'And what is your name?' he called out, light and teasing, a slight lilt to his voice. Mary Ann was so shocked at being noticed, let alone addressed directly, that she darted behind the door and then bolted upstairs. Next minute she was back in her bedroom, fingers pressed against the windowpane, wondering what had just happened.

Or should we say who had just happened? James Butler Kinchela was born in Dublin, around the tail end of the Napoleonic Wars, in one of the big houses on St Stephen's Green. The very sort that Margaret had worked in and Martin Gill had stolen from. James had not lived there long. When he was still in lace tunics, Kinchela's father, a man of the law known as the doctor, had moved the family back to his hometown of Kilkenny. There the family took up residence in a fine thatched house named Ormonde Hall, perched just under the shadow of the Duke's great grey castle where they kept company with an extended family of millers and merchants.

James was named after his great grandfather's patron, the second Duke of Ormonde, a haughty-looking wigged and armoured Protestant who had been up to his eyeballs in Jacobean conspiracies when he became the Lord Lieutenant of Ireland in the early eighteenth century. A generation later, when the Protestants were securing their place in Ireland by imposing their ruthless penal code upon the Roman Catholics, another Duke of Ormonde intervened to change the fate of the Kinchelas. The family were old Irish and had been Catholic for centuries until they shifted alliances to suit the Duke in the mid-eighteenth century. There were still a few Roman Catholics in the family closet but what the Duke didn't know wouldn't hurt him. 'I'll ask God to take care of my soul and not bother him about my land', was the way converts like the Kinchelas responded to those who challenged them about their religious convictions. Whatever others might think, it had been the right choice for the family, for the Duke rewarded them by sending their second son, the bright one, to Kilkenny College and then, when he showed a talent for the law, on to Trinity. There he became part of a society of promising men and when he graduated Dr John acquired both a town house on the park and a wealthy wife named Elizabeth Thornton.

The couple had a son together, who they named Lewis Chapelier. By the time their boy was in trousers, Elizabeth had died and John Kinchela married again. The doctor's second wife, Anne Bourne, was all blonde ringlets and sweetness, and John Kinchela was devoted to her. She gave birth to her first two children, Anne and John Junior, during the Napoleonic Wars, but of these, only John was to survive. Matilda was born the year the British were finally declared victorious. James came a year later and finally, several years after that, Mary was born. For a time the Kinchela family flourished on the fortune of the dead Elizabeth Thornton and when Anne's two boys were both very young, Dr Kinchela was made mayor of Kilkenny, an event that was celebrated with a succession of banquets. Within a few years, however, the doctor had divested almost all of his first wife's fortune upon friends and family. By then Lewis had been sent to Edinburgh to study medicine which was just as well, for the family situation was increasingly unstable. John Kinchela Senior was simply too kind and also hopelessly uncomfortable with his dead wife's fortune. Whenever it was time to do the books, for example, Anne would find her husband fussing about, dashing his hands through his hair, claiming all was well before hastily handing out bank notes to the very next person who asked for them—and some who hadn't.

By the early 1820s things had got so grim that Anne told her husband he would have to petition the Duke for an appointment. It didn't matter where, really, just as long as it would keep him from the debtor's prison. It was during that dreadful year, while they waited upon the government's charity, that the Kinchela family were compelled to open their home and witness their precious items being dragged into the town square and sold at public auction. So great was the shame that the doctor went to Dublin and didn't come back until the business was done. Young John and James sulked about the house for a bit and then borrowed some horses and went calling. Anne took to the parlour with her two young daughters and refused to take visitors.

When the Colonial Office finally sent news of an appointment, there was much relief but little excitement. The Kinchelas were to sail to the West Indies where the doctor had been commissioned 'to inquire into the state of captured negroes'. To console the boys, who were now in their teens and particularly aggrieved by the family's dwindling circumstances, Dr Kinchela promised the pair proper fittings with a London tailor. What with the collars and cuffs, buckskins and hessians, neckties and waistcoats, the pair ran up a pretty bill, but what was the doctor to do? In his youth, he had passed as a bit of a buck himself. It would have been wrong to deny his boys the same.

From this time on, Dr Kinchela was hounded, almost night and day, by two great devils: debt and deafness. The debt he brought upon himself and couldn't keep at bay, while the deafness dwelt within and seemed to consume more of him with each passing year. The learned doctor had had a fortune, and a healthy one too, but he had given it away—without a second thought and with all the goodwill in the world.

The West Indies experience was unpleasant to say the least. From the start the Irish family had been confronted by the sweet stench of the place and a sea breeze thick with the scent of fermenting fruit and cane. This rotten odour may have been an omen for the ensuing corruption they witnessed, for the entire family saw things in the Indies they would prefer not to remember. Anne and the girls, for example, had been confined to the worst sort of female society. Indeed, several of the colony's 'better women' delighted in relaying ghoulish information about the Creoles and the astonishing 'reprisals' their husbands exacted in response to the uprisings. Such women would describe the floggings with great relish before calmly finishing that this was simply 'the way things are done here'.

There was, in fact, more to it, as the doctor knew, for he was out there, week after week, in the heat of the day, observing the plantations from his government gig as he carefully collated his findings. There were stirrings, he reckoned, all about the island and for good reason. He had presided over one hearing, for instance, in which a planter had coupled with a woman while the poor creature was still in her leg irons. But somehow—whatever the circumstances—the Kinchelas had to make the West Indies work and to do that, certain alliances—however uncomfortable—were necessary. So the doctor asked his family to endure a little longer and promised they would soon be back on their feet.

Despite all the careful sidestepping, the West Indies brought few rewards for the Kinchelas and when the family returned to London in the late 1820s they were still encumbered with debt, and had little notion of what to do next. There was no way a gentleman could live within his means, Kinchela tried to explain to his wife, particularly with two spirited sons as well as a couple of daughters who would need to be settled soon enough. The family simply had to keep extending their line of credit and hope that someone might help them honour their debts. The Duke had been willing, twice, but the Colonial Office took a grimmer view these days. Nor did those underlings employed by the colonial secretary appreciate the unpleasant missives they continued to receive from a most aggrieved London tailor demanding compensation for a long list of cuffs and shirts and jackets and trousers for the Kinchela boys.

Such matters continued to dog Kinchela, and by the time the news of a second and much better appointment as the Attorney General of New South Wales arrived it was received with great relief. The doctor arrived in the colony in early 1831 ahead of his family. He was blessed with a reputation for being a careful judge, particularly when it came to criminal hearings, although it quickly became apparent that he cared less for civil matters. Still he went about his new appointment with renewed vigour and when his wife and children stepped ashore several months later they found the doctor energetically engaged in his new position and happily ordering everyone he could into line.

Within a year, however, there were rumours. And even with the support of a sympathetic governor like the Irishman Richard Bourke, the tide was beginning to turn. The doctor could manage administrative matters quite ably, that was true, but how on earth could a deaf and debt-ridden man preside in court? Even in a colony of felons, scoundrels and imposters, the prospect of a deaf judge seemed too great a mockery of Blind Justice. Stories of Kinchela's various courtroom confusions spread like wildfire and the sniggers and asides became such that several of the colony's better men determined that something had to be done. But because Dr Kinchela was so well liked, it was agreed that it would be best to move him sideways—without too much discomfort to his family. By the mid-1830s things were falling nicely into place when suddenly Major James Mudie made that all quite impossible.

Mudie was a nasty sort. Years earlier, while still in England, he had been discharged from the marines for thieving and then after a failed turn at selling fake medals commemorating war heroes he had been declared insolvent. 'Major' Mudie, indeed! He had been lucky to avoid transportation. Most marines crossed the street to avoid 'the Major' when they saw him coming. But such was the lack of good men in the colony that Mudie not only got free passage but also a generous land grant. Within a few years he had established Castle Forbes, which he ran like a tyrant, flogging convicts at whim and guarding his home with half-starved Newfoundland dogs.

Mudie was like one of his own dogs, snatching lame prey and then tearing at their limbs until the life leaked out. Most men sensed this about the Major and kept away. Except those who couldn't, like the convicts at Castle Forbes, who were caught in Mudie's ferocious grip, try as they might to escape. Which many did, God help them. Rumours began to circulate that Mudie had captured one such party of runaways and then—without so much as a trial—strung them from makeshift gallows outside his gates. Those in the upper ranks of colonial administration—John Kinchela, John Hubert Plunkett and Roger Therry—were convinced that Mudie had violated British justice. They went to Bourke and insisted he take a closer look. But even though everyone knew what had happened at Castle Forbes, none of the convicts were prepared to speak. So the colonial administration was left with mud on their boots and Mudie walked free.

From that time onwards, the Major nursed a lethal grievance against Dr Kinchela and his friends—and he set to writing a book that would bring down not only that administration, but also the entire colony. In London there was a market for anything about the colonies. Some authors made an attempt at accuracy, but most books and pamphlets were rife with salacious froth about hoary whores, rampaging blacks and murderous convicts who ate one another. Many of these embellished versions were written by people who had never set foot on colonial soil and few bore even a passing resemblance to reality, but even so, they titillated the prim and the perverse alike and—more importantly—they sold like hot cakes. While most colonists were intent upon elevating the reputation of New South Wales, Major Mudie persisted with his crude distortions and lewd ridicule and his new book, *The Felonry of New South Wales*, scaled new heights of personal malice. When the first copies arrived in Sydney, replete with sneers about many well-known colonists, including the Attorney General, people began to bay for Mudie's blood and by the time the Major returned to New South Wales in the spring of 1840, he was well and truly *persona non grata*.

From his magisterial seat in Wellington Valley, Dr Kinchela's second son, the bold and resolute John Junior had been waiting. The young man had read the offensive book and stewed and steamed throughout that winter, plotting his revenge as well as the restoration of his family's name. He had even chosen the thick stock crop he was going to use on the old blackguard when he dared to show his face in town. John's mood was made worse by the fact that his poor father had been suddenly 'attacked by paralysis'—a stroke so cruel that he was forced to leave public life—and with nothing more than a modest pension. Once more the family's fortunes hung in the balance and this time Anne Bourne determined they had no choice but to satisfy their creditors by leaving the fine two-storey property they leased on the South Head Road and named Ormonde House in memory of their beloved Kilkenny home. The family was forced to move to a modest cottage in Liverpool where Anne nursed the afflicted doctor in significantly reduced and now also greatly aggravated circumstances.

It was a spring morning in 1840 when John Junior finally spied the Major in the George Street market. 'Brimming with Hibernian blood and courage', the 'stalwart son' stepped forward to teach the old rogue a lesson. It was far from a fair match, the local papers crowed, John Junior not yet thirty, while the red-haired Major was somewhere in his sixties, and not at all in good health. The doctor's eldest son smacked Mudie about the chops with his crop and then chased him down the street, whacking the older man about his hat, ten times, twenty, and on and on until there was blood about the Major's mouth and he finally fell cowering to the ground. 'Not such a fan of floggings now, are you,

Mudie?' someone jeered as all of Sydney stopped to watch. 'Where are yer dogs now, Major?' another sneered.

The Major took the matter to the civil court, insisting John Kinchela Junior pay £1000 for the injuries inflicted upon his person. Their father's friend Roger Therry came to John Junior's aid and the tiny Irish lawyer was all flourishes and fancy words in court, expounding upon the various ways that Mudie had offended the honour of both this noble Irish family and the colony itself. Therry provoked such a steady stream of laughter that in the end Mudie came out worse than those he had lampooned in his vindictive book. The court resolved John Junior should pay only £50 and the doctor's second son was also deeply gratified when the Major's many enemies came crawling out of the woodwork, eager to pay for the pleasure of Mudie's public humiliation.

But then, within a few years the doctor died and to make matters worse, John Junior suddenly went to London on business, robbing James of his closest companion as well as the man in whose shadow he was happy to reside. When John returned a year later, he had become quite earnest and also entirely preoccupied with restoring the family name. Indeed, from this time on, John was so engaged with his enterprises that James came to feel that he had lost a brother as well as a father. Sure the two men still travelled and worked together, but more often than not John made a point of distinguishing who was earning what. He also refused to adopt the light banter that had been their way together as boys. John was also dismissive of his younger brother's sense of fun and made it quite clear that he would henceforth confine himself to the serious business of making money.

From this time on, when John wasn't on one expedition or another he was superintending someone's property so he could bring in money for his next big investment. As well as pastoral runs in Bathurst and the Wellington Valley, where he had done a short stint as a magistrate, John had also acquired a parcel of land in one of the most remote parts of the colony. And so, in 1845, the Kinchela boys—along with a number of well-heeled Irish Protestant lads—pushed north in that direction taking with them thousands of sheep. They were looking for a tract of land that was large enough for them to manage as a series of runs within one giant landed estate—a sort of Protestant empire in the north, if you will. After several months of pushing their stock through the swamps and stone country they eventually found it—about 300 miles north of Moreton Bay in the Upper Darling Downs Region. John called the run Hawkwood and for the best part of the last three years he had been up there—wrestling with the country and 'warning off the blacks'. As James had no other means of inheritance, he had little choice but to follow his brother into that mosquito-afflicted territory.

So it was that James now followed in the great man's wake, but it hadn't always been that way. In their early years James had shared much of his older brother's zeal, although he had always been less prone to sharp thoughts and fast action. Nonetheless, the two boys had been united in their pursuit of gain and glory, until the last few years when James had found it increasingly difficult to muster up the energy to care as much as his earnest elder brother. It had been those three overlanding expeditions to Adelaide that had done James in. Back then, in 1838, their father was still around and the two men had been younger. The more James looked back to that dreadful spring associated with their last expedition, the more he was convinced that he should never have agreed to overland cattle with William Thornton, their cousin who had just got off the boat brimming with his own brilliance. By then James had already done two runs with John but in early 1840 his brother had just raised some extra capital—£4000 in fact—which he had borrowed from his sister's husband, Thomas Gore—and he wanted to stay in town to work out what to do with it while he waited for the return of Major Mudie.

John was willing, however, to finance another expedition, as long as James was prepared to take the lead and give Thornton second in command. James had been champing at the bit. He had never been one for the books, nor that position in the office his father had arranged for him. He wanted to be out and about, preferably on a good mount and with something to do. This was his chance to prove himself. He knew he had a good sense of the land and that he could see things most of his brother's friends missed, like which way a river would flow and where they would find feed for the stock. A final run would set them all up, James was certain, and also show them all what he was made of.

But from the start, the expedition had been a disaster. The sheep were sickly, the weather vile, the land parched and the party at odds with one another. The worst of all was Thornton. James had some idea how to handle the blacks, but his cousin was trouble, especially when grog and women were involved. There were too many times out there—in that flat dustbowl of the interior—when the native fires had surrounded them and they couldn't find their way through the smoke, that Thornton had created more trouble than he was worth. And then, when the party eventually got back into Sydney, boots worn to shreds, horses just about bone and their best dogs dead, his damned cousin had turned on his heels and married some older widow with a good estate. Why not? All the money was gone. Dried up on the road to Adelaide somewhere. James shrugged when his brother came asking questions in an accusing tone, clearly still smug about his recent victory over Mudie. At the time, James had been so sick he could not leave his home for nigh on three months let alone explain the matter to John. His liver had been shot ever since. Shortly after that, a sort of stiff silence had descended upon relations between the brothers and James had lost most of his ambition.

❧

The whole experience still left a nasty taste in his mouth, Kinchela realised as he leant against the front bar at the Pitt Street hotel. He took another swig of his drink to push the memory away. Gradually, however, he became aware that someone was looking at him. From the corner of his eye he noticed a young girl standing in a wedge of late afternoon sun at the place where the kitchen door had been left ajar. She was small and fresh, with dark brown hair and hazel eyes and seemed to be watching him with some intensity. Well, he thought, scratching his top lip as he sought to conceal the slightest of grins. He could stay here a few nights. Cool his heels for a bit and take a look at the stockyards. That might be a start.

CHAPTER THREE

The All-Seductive James

Little by little the gentleman settler from Moreton Bay began to notice an improvement in his health and disposition. 'Must be the turtle soup,' he had joked to the personable proprietor once or twice. At first the hotelier had been entirely genial, but then a little later he became less cordial, and recently, about the fourth week of his stay, James had noticed a distinct cooling in the older Irishman. 'The broth does wonders, sir, for those who look after themselves,' the woman of the establishment said, perhaps a little curtly, in reply to what was becoming a rather predictable performance of affability, which Kinchela kept up in the dining room most evenings. He made a note to give up a few extra bills to keep them happy.

James had grown more comfortable with his mother's new house at Liverpool and the obvious pleasure it gave her when he called for dinner most Thursdays. He had meant to stay in Sydney for only a fortnight and return to Moreton Bay before pushing onto Hawkwood with some stock and a crate of Swan Drop for the firearms, but after a few weeks of good meals in Sydney, James Butler realised that he was not relishing a return.

When he and John had first travelled up to Moreton Bay in the mid-1840s, a few years after their expedition to Adelaide, other men were still making their gunyios down by the lagoons, using tea tree bark to create the makeshift shelters when the rains came. Back then the township of Moreton Bay was not much more than a few buildings clustered about half-finished streets. Those who settled after the convicts had left often brought their favourite blackfellows with them from down south. They learnt quickly they needed local men to find out where things were but that there could also be trouble in that too. Things could turn quickly—like what happened to the sawyers up at North Pine who had been speared by Dundali and then finished off with a few good blows of a waddy. You had to be on your toes. Sure, there were a few good men like that fellow Petrie who kept things as steady as possible, but the potential for trouble was greater than anything James had ever known. And that was just in Moreton Bay.

After a few slow weeks forcing their way towards the Upper Darling Downs—thrashing through the undergrowth and clambering over rocky outcrops with their stock—Moreton Bay had seemed positively civilised. But it was worth it, for the two brothers found a land of steep-sided gorges, massive water-sculpted granite boulders and miles after endless miles of salmon-coloured sandy plains punctuated with winsome hardwood through which their sheep and cattle could easily graze. They knew they would need money and lots of it if they were going to make Hawkwood work, so John took a job as a station manager and James stayed behind to mark out the boundaries and keep an eye on the couple of old lags they had brought with them to watch the stock. That had been James' lot over the last couple of years—building fences and boundary riding, moving stock to avoid skirmishes with the local blacks and pulling water from the river they had named the Boyne when things got too dry. Sometimes riding a day or so to take company with the other Irish boys on the nearby runs. That and the occasional visit to Moreton Bay for settlers' meetings or down to Sydney to sell stock.

But now, despite all the hard work, both brothers were coming to the conclusion that the Hawkwood run was an impossible proposition—perhaps the whole of the north was—what with the mangroves, mosquitoes and diseases. If the blacks didn't get you with their spears and waddies then it would be one of their fires. Kinchela had heard stories that would silence the boasters in town. The things that had to be done up there were not the sort of thing anyone wanted to talk about. Swallow it down with a quart of rum and be done with it.

But that was up north and things were different down in the south, particularly about town. These days Sydney was one of the few places where you didn't have to keep your wits about you because now things were more or less settled. Sure there were a few stragglers about—and a good many knew the ropes and could be useful, as well as those who camped behind the barracks where the Kinchela boys had regimental friends among the 39th brigade. But Sydney was not like Moreton Bay or the far north country in the Darling Downs, where things were particularly grim. There had been quite a few days over the past couple of years when Kinchela considered himself lucky to have woken up alive. He had heard of men found dead in their beds, although most of them were asking for it, he reckoned, or at least that was what some of the ex-convicts who lived among the blacks said.

These days few city folk cared to know that there was a war going on out there beyond their fancy coffee rooms. They were pleased for the sugar and meat on their tables and didn't care much about how it got there. In fact, many preferred not to know. They were two very different worlds. And right now, for the first time in a while, Kinchela was in town. He began to splash his family name about the better establishments to secure a little credit. He was a Kinchela, after all, and the name counted for something. Within a week he had chummed up with Jim Davidson, a magistrate mate of his brother who had a taste for rum and fun, and by April James was actually beginning to enjoy himself for the first time in a while.

And there was the girl to play with. He had a feeling he might be making a little mischief, but he thought he could string it out a bit longer for, surely, there was not much harm to it. The way she looked at him, though, and the considered nature of her questions, made him wonder otherwise sometimes. He had never had that sort of careful but direct attention from a woman before. On the whole, women were a rather awkward proposition for James Butler Kinchela and, in general, he couldn't understand their simpering games. Women made him nervous—the way they could snap just like that. For the most part, and like many a good Irishman from country parts, Kinchela preferred horses. You could ride them fast and feel the wind rushing past you as you thundered along, lifted by the horse's generous gait and that exhilarating sense of freedom. The young Gill girl was not like the women in his family circle and he found himself looking forward to his chance encounters with her, like the one they had on the first night just before the dining room opened.

By the second week they were both seeking each other out around the time of the first dinner sitting—and each time they were together they committed some new observation of one another to memory. He had black hair, like her da's, Mary Ann thought, only his had a little more curl. He was taller than her father, but not by much. He was, however, much stouter around the chest and where her father's eyes were mostly hazel, his were a deeper brown. Most of all Mary Ann sensed in the gentleman settler an expanse of life that made her feel that he must know about the places she wanted to learn about. Places like the fine rooms where her father visited, but only to oversee the evening supper for a rout or a ball. When she went with her father she was always watching but never watched. These were some of the places where Mary Ann sensed that Kinchela was probably at home and where she wanted to go. With him. But there were other places, too, wild places where you would start riding on your horses but end up having to push forward on foot. She had heard about such places but had never spoken with anyone who had actually been to them. Each day the gentleman guest would offer up more details and she would muse over these throughout the day, trying to make them last as long as one of her father's boiled sweets, until she saw him again, that evening, standing by the staircase just outside the dining room, waiting for an evening meal and ready to recount more of his adventures.

Kinchela saw the girl's appetite. Initially he found it flattering and then a little daunting, but after a few more weeks he came to see that this inquisitiveness was intrinsic to who she was. This was a girl who could hardly contain her questions, as if curiosity possessed her very being. He could see that much from the light that brimmed in her hazel eyes and the way she leant forward and grew still as she listened to him. And yet, somehow despite her thirst for knowledge, the girl managed to maintain an appropriate level of decorum and composure. Not too much, not too little. The hotelier's daughter had ambitions, he picked up that much, and yet in contrast to some of the grasping girls he had come across in good society, her questions did not repel him. She was gauche, that was true, and had few of the manners and accomplishments so prized among his sisters and their friends, but she was never vulgar. Once or twice he had been confronted by her forthright disposition. Like many of the native-born girls he had met in his travels, she had no qualms about being direct and it gave him a curious sense of lightness. If they had been at home, particularly in Kilkenny, she would have known her place and been incapable of thinking beyond it, but this one, he thought, had her own head. He liked that in horses, and, it seemed, James Butler Kinchela also liked it in this girl.

Nonetheless, her questions were revealing. 'How does it feel to ride out and not know where you will stop for the night?' Mary Ann asked towards the end of the second week of his stay, when they had, without actually conferring on the matter, contrived to meet at the dining room stairwell before serving. These stairwell encounters were no more than five minutes, if that, but the intensity lingered. Her questions became something that James mulled over the following day. 'Do you think it right to whip a man?' was another question she had asked, which left him wondering. But it was this one: 'Did your father beat his daughters?', which stopped him dead.

Kinchela had stepped back and blinked. Put his hand to the back of his ruddy neck and held it there as he inhaled. He tried to imagine his soft-voiced father turning on anyone. He recalled the trembling hands and slack jaw of the old man after the stroke and tried to remember when he had been a boy and his father the mayor of Kilkenny. Kinchela could remember no such incident. Had he and John ever been cropped?

At school, yes and often they had deserved it. But he had no recollection of any beatings at home. Let alone one of the girls. Perhaps he would have benefitted from a few more thrashings, but there it was. He shook his head. No, his father had never beaten anyone. But she had got him wondering and he began watching the hotelier differently, detecting a propensity for something in the man's sharp features and grandiose gestures. The man wasn't cruel, Kinchela sensed, but he was unpredictable and perhaps also bloody-minded.

For a girl not yet sixteen, Mary Ann's evening interviews with the gentleman settler were an unknown experience of such potency that she could not draw back from them even though she knew she was courting trouble. Certainly, her father had rough handled her a number of times when she was a child, and she had also felt his hand more than twice. And more recently there had been some terrifying displays of authority, particularly after he had seen her talking with the gentleman settler one evening. There had also been that recent visit to her grandparents' when she had failed to seek permission before leaving. Her father had set off after her in such a panic, and when he arrived at McCormick's farm he had threatened the entire house with his pistols, shoving both hard under his girl's nose to let her know who was boss. The situation seemed to be building to a crisis, but even so Mary Ann could not pull back.

Margaret watched her daughter and wondered what to do. She, herself, had been a work girl and then a felon. After that she had been lucky to be 'freed' into marriage. In contrast to her own life, her daughter's was one of great advantage. People petted the child as a way of finding favour with her husband, who was, after all, a man on the rise. Margaret and Martin had agreed to give their daughter something of an education. There would be better opportunities for a girl who could read and write and it would also assist the business. And so, as the Gills consolidated their position, Mary Ann had reaped many advantages and could, quite reasonably, be described as 'a respectable female' who was 'competent in every respect'. At least this was how Margaret described Mary Ann in *The Herald* a few months ago when she had placed an advertisement that informed the public that her daughter was 'desirous' of engaging herself as a 'monthly nurse' to an 'invalid lady'. It was time to put her into work, particularly with conditions in the colony looking so uncertain. But the advertisement was not true; Mary Ann did not want to do anything of the sort. Mother and daughter were now in a standoff about this and Mary Ann had somehow managed to undermine every opportunity presented to secure gainful employment.

It was beyond the range of Martin Gill to imagine a daughter having her own ideas. When you were fossicking for food around the backstreets of North Dublin, you didn't have ideas, you did what had to be done or you died. But now, there was his child, a daughter even, being obstinate about earning a living for the family. He did clip her round the head, and box her about the ears, too, and he was not ashamed to say that he had also shown her his pistols. But that was the most of it, really. In contrast to other men of his position he had been eventempered. He knew men, a number of his associates, for example, who put their children to work much earlier and would think nothing of horsewhipping a disobedient daughter. The girl needed to bring in money, both he and Margaret agreed. They were counting on it, in fact, particularly with the drought drying up the land and talk of more trouble to come. They couldn't rely on the rich pastoralists to feather their nests. He had already seen a few of his associates go under in recent months and was aware that the family needed to play a careful set of cards if they were to come out on top.

If Martin Gill had struggled with the natural affections of fatherhood when Mary Ann was an infant, his daughter was an even more inscrutable mystery to him now that she was on the brink of womanhood. And the way she was behaving with the well-heeled Irish settler gave him a feeling that she was playing with something that would bring them all down. He would not have it—particularly not with the sort of man he had watched about the Green as a young half-starved boy. The type he had seen lording it over others when he had first come to the colony. But he was still uncertain about how to approach the matter. As a consequence of this, Martin Gill found himself decidedly agitated whenever he thought about his daughter, let alone when he had to be in the same room as her.

Her husband was one of those men who needed his own head, Margaret knew that much. He had a heavy hand and a simple way of seeing things, but although he was intent upon putting himself on top of every circumstance, he was not particularly driven to make others feel worse. When it came to his daughter, though, Margaret had learnt to leave off or she would wear the cool edge of his contempt. He did have an affectionate side, particularly when things were going well, but under pressure the street rat in Martin Gill came out with plenty of fight and he was not one to be beat.

Margaret, now a mother of six, with the young one still on her breast, was trying to work out what to do to keep things steady. She had tea with her daughter most afternoons, after she had put the baby down, and watched carefully for an opportunity to say something right, but the phrases didn't come and her daughter kept up a light banter that seemed to discourage Margaret from finding a way in. Well, no need to make life too complicated, she thought. There is usually another way if you keep a look out for it.

And so there was. The opportunity presented itself in the dining room of the Gill's Family Hotel about a fortnight after the Saint Patrick's Day celebrations. The gentleman settler was there, as he was most nights except Thursdays. He tended to come in early for dinner, now, and on that particular day she sent two of the staff out into the kitchen to help with the pots and another off to the yard until she was alone with him. He looked up, suddenly aware of it. At first he was a little surprised and then, as she calmly made her way to his table, he began to process the situation. 'Sir,' Margaret said, her fingers just touching the linen tablecloth as she tipped her head in a manner that she hoped would secure his attention. Kinchela put down his cutlery and looked up at his host. 'This situation won't do,' she said quietly. He coughed awkwardly and took a swig of his claret before looking away. 'It can't be,' she continued, fixing him with a look that forced him to meet her gaze even though he was unable to find a reply. 'We need to ask you to leave,' she finished firmly, 'and to pay your bill in the morning, if you please, sir.' Margaret Gill didn't want a reply and she didn't wait for one. Instead she bowed her head and walked back to the entrance of the dining room. Kinchela watched her for a moment and then nodded to himself. Then carefully, but perhaps not quite so calmly, he picked up his knife and fork and resumed his meal. So that was it, he thought. He was to leave.

CHAPTER FOUR

The Parramatta Romance

James Butler Kinchela considered the dalliance between himself and the hotelier's daughter an amusement. It took several weeks back at Hawkwood before he realised he was thinking about the girl who lived in the hotel on Pitt Street. First he considered that he might be simply concerned for her wellbeing, given her odd question about the beatings. But frankly a bit of rough from a father was not frowned upon, quite the opposite in fact. It was also considered indiscreet to interfere in the private lives of other families. Kinchela tried to imagine what his older brother might do in a similar situation and realised that he had never heard John express concern for any particular woman. So John was no good. He would have to sort out the matter on his own.

Next thing, a month had passed and Kinchela was back in Sydney again. This time he had come down on the *Tamar* to get materials for the fences. It was good for his mother too, he reasoned, he could meet up with her and his friend, Jim Davidson and also make some enquiries. Kinchela booked into the Adelphi Hotel on York Street, a solid establishment that had been known as the Donnybrook when Martin and Margaret Gill managed it a few years back. Kinchela had no intention of going anywhere down *that* end of Pitt Street. And yet, somehow one night in early May, about two o'clock in the morning, he found himself standing beneath a third-floor window that looked out over the night-time swell of the city harbour.

He began to whistle. Soft and low. And then, suddenly, there she was. Sleep-swollen, perhaps, and definitely more of a young girl than a woman. But she was thrilled to see him, and the funny night bonnet on her head kept bobbing up and down in a way he found endearing. 'Shhhush,' James cautioned, staggering back on his heels—clearly more than a little bosky after a night out with Davidson.

Davidson had been in fine form that night and, after listening to his brother's friend over a couple of jugs of something pretty strong, made a suggestion that shocked Kinchela with its daring. 'Marry her, James, and be done with it,' he had said. 'If the father doesn't agree, get a special licence and do it anyway.' The proposition intrigued Kinchela. She was young enough to learn and seemed to have a taste for something different, although he was fairly sure that Hawkwood would not be what she had in mind. He grimaced a little at the thought of her out there. But some part of the idea was taking hold. A wife.

After Davidson bade him farewell, Kinchela wandered the wet streets of the darkened town, mulling it over. It wasn't as if he had a fortune to lose; in fact it was likely that her father had been more careful with his money than had his own. It would get her out of that home and if her father was sensible he would see the advantage of Kinchela's connections. By now, his own mother might be pleased with any match he made, provided it produced grandchildren, and he could go about it in a way that would avoid embarrassment to John and his sisters. Both girls were safely matched anyway. He would ask Gill first, but before he did so, he wanted to know if she was amenable to the idea herself.

He was a little taken aback by Mary Ann's response. Sure she was light and breathy with it but within a few minutes he could see that she was surprisingly measured and composed as if she had thought the whole thing through already. She even made her concerns perfectly clear: 'If you take me from my father's house,' she had said, swallowing twice before she continued, 'and don't marry me, James, my father will murder me. You understand, don't you?' Mary Ann asked, holding him with her look. But he wanted no more of that sort of talk for he had a clear sense of how it was all to be. 'Give me a week, Mary,' he responded, for he preferred the shorter version of her name, 'and we will know which way to go.' And then caught up in the improbable thrill of the moment, he had added, 'There is no fear to it, you know, you shall be mine.'

After Kinchela left, Mary Ann slipped back beneath her bed sheets and listened to the fast rhythm of her breathing. This was exactly what she wanted, what she had longed for, in fact, for several months. But now he had finally asked her, the whole thing felt like yarn slipping through her fingers and unravelling beyond her grasp. What would happen? How would her father reply? She had no say in any of it. The whole thing felt like a game where anything could happen.

It went like this: James Butler Kinchela found Martin Gill three days later as the older man was standing outside the Waterloo Stores supervising a selection of ales and porters for the hotel. The two men nodded curtly at one another and Kinchela advanced. 'A word, sir, if I may.' Gill turned away and thought straight out of snubbing the man who had been too friendly with his daughter, but he stopped himself just in time. The long and short of it was a flat 'no'. Gill was having none of it. He had plans for Mary Ann and they didn't involve his sort, thank you. 'It is best you don't come near the hotel again,' he finished, before stepping back to where his men were securing a cart piled high with barrels.

And so, on 19 May 1848, in the middle of a particularly wet and unpleasant evening, Kinchela appeared again beneath the third-floor window of Gill's Family Hotel and whistled until Mary Ann appeared. Since she and Kinchela had spoken the young girl had wrestled with what she was about to do. Her father had come to her the evening after his street conversation with Kinchela and stepped up to her, too close for it to be anything but untoward, holding her chin with one thumb so she had to look up at him. He had hissed through clenched teeth,

'If what I hear is true, my girl, there will be trouble.' Mary Ann had made a shocked sound and stepped back. 'There is no truth to any of it, sir,' she had lied with wide eyes. Then Martin Gill had showed his daughter the two pistols he had crammed down the front of his belt for the occasion. 'There is no error in this,' he warned with his finger pointed, 'I'll not have it.'

Mary Ann knew then that she was riding a knife's edge. The whole thing could go either way and when it did, whatever happened, there would be consequences. But when that night she saw Kinchela standing in the arc of gaslight with a long double-breasted coat fitted and his top-boots well polished, if a little worn, her fear slipped away. They agreed upon a plan with quite precise instructions. She was to pack a bag of clothes and send these out to the Adelphi. On the night in question she was to make her way to Somerville, the cab driver in Kinchela's employ, and then they would head out to Parramatta separately. Kinchela would organise for someone to perform the ceremony by special licence. And then it would be done. They would be husband and wife. On the day in question all Mary Ann needed to do was send a note to James confirming everything and then they would proceed as planned.

When, however, the day finally arrived James was almost done with it all. He had expended such attention on the various parts of the forthcoming episode that he was, in truth, already a little tired of it. He imagined heading back to the *Tamar* still docked in the harbour, slipping away and leaving this moment of folly behind. But her note came in the late morning. Mary Ann sent with it a humble-looking carpetbag comprising some garments as well as several combs and two dresses that she thought would last until James fitted her in the standard appropriate for the wife of a gentleman settler.

That night Mary Ann and her mother took tea in the parlour near the nursery, a custom they had maintained since moving into the hotel. As the pot brewed, Mary Ann tried to imagine herself through her mother's eyes. She must give nothing away. She encouraged her mother to talk of future plans and how Mary Ann might now be ready to do as another girl from her writing school had recently done and find suitable employment. Margaret mentioned an old widow who lived out towards her grandmother's way. 'You could visit their farm more often,' Margaret suggested, and Mary Ann smiled and nodded, trying to imagine what her grandparents would think of their Mary Ann married to an Irish gentleman.

Thomas McCormick and Mary Riley had certainly encouraged Mary Ann over the years. It was also true to say that they were rather restrained in their praise of Martin Gill, particularly after the incident when he had come in pursuit of the girl armed with pistols and talking to his father-in-law in a fury. 'It's a father's job to keep his daughter straight,' he fumed at the old man, 'and what would you know when you trained your own one to steal. Keep away,' he finished up short with a snarl, 'and don't put yourself as the head of my family.'

The old woman had warned Mary Ann that she was courting trouble when she told her grandmother about the gentleman at the hotel. 'These sort of matches don't work,' she started before recounting a well-known story from back home about 'a girl named Ellen Hanley, who had married up, to a rich man who knew about the land and such. But, only four days after the wedding,' her grandmother continued, 'the girl's new husband learnt that his well-to-do family would never accept his new bride. Next day,' she said, nodding to herself as much as to Mary Ann, 'he paid a servant to shoot his pretty wife full of lead then dump her body in the Shannon. Six weeks after that the dead girl's corpse was found, stripped naked and floating in a sea pool near Moneypoint, a huge rock still tied to her legs. She was your age.' The old woman stopped and peered out to where a crop of beans was beginning to push through the earth. 'This is what happens when you go beyond your lot. It never works.'

With both hands gripped around the drainpipe that travelled down the back of her father's hotel, and well out of sight of the main thoroughfare, Mary Ann stopped and cast another glance back at her bedroom window. She was contemplating climbing back inside and staying there. Actually, she wanted to step inside and find herself back in her York Street bedroom at the Donnybrook, the one she had shared with William and Isabella when she was still a child. Just days ago, the smell of her younger siblings had annoyed her, but now the sound of William's uneven breathing and Isabella's soft inhale made her long for her childhood.

But instead Mary Ann fossicked about in the dark and when she found a small niche in the brickwork for her boot to grip onto she eased herself off the ledge and then put her whole weight onto the drainpipe. She made a horrible job of edging herself down it and halfway through she caught her calf on a bit of nail that was jutting out. A few clumsy minutes later it was done. A tear of blood trickled towards her boot. She knelt and dabbed at it with the inside of her petticoat and, for a second, an image of the Hanley girl flashed to her mind, legs bound and floating in the pool of seawater.

It was about nine o'clock on a Saturday night and the street around the hotel was unsettled from the windy mess of the day before. It was growing darker. She would need to walk quickly if she was to get to Somerville in time. Her father had friends all along Pitt Street and up on George Street, but she and Kinchela had agreed that she would stop for a few minutes in the front parlour at Mrs Kelly's, off Castlereagh Street, so a note could be passed on to James at the Adelphi. Then she would head behind the police station, of all places, to the coach yard where Somerville would be waiting.

Down this end of town, Pitt Street was so wide that her only hope of not being seen by the shop owners and hotel men who knew her father was to hide herself within a crowd. But for some reason—other than a few stray dogs—the street felt curiously empty. Mary Ann pushed on until she arrived at the Vic Theatre where a cluster of Cabbagers were mingling about the front gates, clearly intent upon mischief. She knew well enough to keep her head down. One boy called out, but before the group could get organised she was off, too fast for them to bother. After another wretched ten minutes or so she knocked on the appointed door and a buxom woman, older than her mother, appeared, her hair piled high above a face that was both tough and flabby. 'Miss Gill,' she nodded, offering the girl's name as a statement rather than a question before ushering her inside.

Mrs Kelly's place was not pleasant. Mary Ann could see that, even from the front room. She had no business in a place like this and if her father ever found out she had been there he would be right to belt her. Some sort of smoke hung low and heavy in the corridor. She shuddered as she sat down. The plush and lush of it. It was like nothing she had ever seen before. Low and dark with muffled laughter elsewhere— but inside the room—heavy quiet.

After what seemed an eon, a girl, younger than Mary Ann, with loose plaits and a stiff walk, came in and asked for the note. Mary Ann had not thought to write anything in advance so she requested some paper and ink. This elicited an expression of irritation from the girl, which Mary Ann assumed had its origins in Mrs Kelly. But eventually the paper was presented, the note written and sent on to the Adelphi. Then she waited, trying not to look at, to even be in, this place. Why had James sent her here? What was he thinking? Surely this was not fit for a gentleman's wife, she thought as something began to stir inside Mary Ann's stomach. Already this was not the sort of adventure she and her school friends would have recounted to one another from the stories they read in books.

It was a relief when she finally left Mrs Kelly's, even if it did mean heading back out into the night. Another downpour had made the street wet and it was also much darker than when she had arrived at the house, but Mary Ann was glad to be free. Mrs Kelly's girl had given her a drink. Something brown and sweet in an etched glass that was meant to keep her warm and steady her. After a few sips Mary Ann felt lighter in her step and somehow also dazzled. To keep herself steady she trailed her fingertips along the rough brickwork of a low wall that ran along part of George Street, before turning into Bathurst Street. She had to walk a strip that was known to be particularly rough. There was a broken cart parked on one corner where someone could be hiding so she made sure to take the other side of the street. Mary Ann knew her way around town from running errands, but everything looked different in the dark, especially when she was stepping beyond her father like this. She turned her head to look into one of the tumbledown shops and was startled by a brace of rabbit carcasses hanging from a window hook. Again she imagined the Hanley girl. The same age on the day of her wedding as Mary Ann and then a week later, dead.

Once more Mary Ann thought of turning back, but then the grey orb of the police station appeared through the night clouds, its weathercock spinning in soft arcs with the wind. She shoved her doubts down and made her way into the coach yard. 'Well then,' said a corpulent man when he saw her standing beneath the entrance to the coach yard, 'there you are.' The man had been working on his letters while waiting for the girl. He wanted to get Kinchela's job done so he could get off the wet night road and back to his slate.

'You are Mr Somerville?' Mary Ann heard herself asking, and when she received confirmation of this she moved further into the yard. 'And you know where you are to take me?' she followed. Somerville replied by hauling his great hulk from the chair and pointing out into the dark. 'I'll fix up the horses and we can be on our way.' She refused his offer of a seat and instead stood counting the revolutions of the weathercock while she waited. Once, twice, three times it spun in the wet night air and then to her surprise it was not Somerville who spoke next, but James Butler.

Mary Ann turned in surprise. They were meant to arrive at Parramatta by different drivers. So why was he here? Wasn't this bad luck? She could hardly breathe let alone speak, so she found herself nodding in response to whatever he said. 'Yes,' she agreed, 'Webb's Inn, the Sportsman's Arms, out along the Parramatta road. Yes,' she agreed again, thinking he must be planning to stop en route before they arrived at their final destination for the ceremony. 'Ask to speak to a man named Healy and tell him about your father.' She nodded, blood surging through her head. 'I'll be there within the hour,' Kinchela reassured her as Somerville opened the door and beckoned her into a poorly lit and rather damp carriage. Then Kinchela slapped the coach with the palm of his hand and stepped back. 'We are just an hour or so behind,' he said lightly. 'All will be well.' With that he closed the door and the vehicle lurched forward on its wheels as Mary Ann began her journey off and up and out along the open street towards the Sportsman's Arms.

The truth was Kinchela had been drinking. What had started as a celebratory jug with Davidson had become two or three more jugs, and after Davidson left James found himself considering his options over another bottle of something stronger. He was now steaming with it, sweating around the neck and unsteady on his feet. He hadn't got round to securing the licence because he had figured it wouldn't be too hard to get one, and, as Jim had said when Kinchela had asked for his help, there were plenty around who would be prepared to produce the document quickly for a good price. Davidson himself would pitch in but he needed a few days to get something like this sorted, even if he was a magistrate. The delay had put a dint in Kinchela's plan and made it easier for him to keep putting everything off until the very last minute and then he let a few *more* minutes slip by. It was getting hopeless, and, to use the sort of racing metaphor Kinchela best understood, the horses were now well and truly out of the gate. Had long bolted in fact.

Kinchela had asked Somerville to come back after he had dropped the girl at Webb's, pick him up from the Adelphi and take him out to Webb's. By then he should have a plan as well as a way of explaining the situation, which would put everything right. So he staggered back down Market Street towards York Street, trying to sharpen his thoughts. He did genuinely like the girl. There was something in her character, but he couldn't stand the thought of her seeing the truth about him. It was now a case of when to disappoint her. He felt feckless and angry and considered a visit to Mrs Kelly's to lighten his spirits.

But, when he got to the Adelphi, instead of entering the hotel he found himself suddenly hailing a coach and heading out along the

Parramatta road. He was blowing it. Come to think of it he had been mad to send her to Mrs Kelly's, but there it was—he really wasn't much crack at this sort of thing. He had a feeling that he was going to make a mess of it. James sucked his breath in through his teeth and took himself in hand. He was going to get this right, he decided.

By the time Mary Ann alighted the coach at the Sportsman's Arms she was trembling. Not only from fear but also sheer frustration. She had followed James' plans precisely—but now it felt like the earth was opening up beneath her. On and on the coach had driven into the dark taking her, she felt, to her doom. She had smelt the grog on James and had a sickly feeling that everything was going to unravel.

Nonetheless, before she entered the establishment Mary Ann regained her composure so she could seek out the proprietor, Mrs Webb, and ask for Mr Healy. Mrs Webb pointed through the curtains to a private parlour and then went back to the bar, where she had a good view of the young buck and the girl. As she watched them talk, something about the young girl began to nag at her. And then she got it. She was the daughter of another licensed victualler, that fellow Gill, with the fancy establishment down towards the quay on Pitt Street. 'Best let Mr Gill know straightaway,' Lydia Webb told her corpulent husband, who nodded obediently and, despite the late hour, saddled up and headed into town. They could not afford to be caught up in an intrigue, his wife reminded him.

Healy told Mary Ann to take a room and that Kinchela would be up with her soon enough. With few alternatives, Mary Ann did what she was told. She made sure, however, that there was a girl on hand to help her out of her travel dress and to stay with her while she waited. She was in bed, the lamp down low and the maid in the corner chair, when Kinchela burst in, twenty minutes later. 'Your father is on his way, Mary,' he said, sounding strangely animated. 'You'll need to get dressed and mind yourself.' Her father? Something plunged inside Mary Ann. She was done for. Kinchela had said he was to marry her and now she stood a large chance of being murdered by her own father or even worse—left to hang in the wind.

Kinchela was ashamed of himself. He had to do the job properly or he was no better than his cousin William Thornton, probably worse. He thought of his own sisters. She was not of their class, that was true, but still the girl deserved better. 'Listen,' he continued desperately, 'I'll have the licence by the morning, so say you will come again.' He swallowed. 'Promise me, before dawn, and we will have it done by noon.' Mary Ann looked at him as a mingling of rage, pity and something more physical stole over her. She had no other option and she knew it. 'He will be here soon,' Kinchela continued, imploring her, 'promise me you will go to Somerville in the first light. He will bring you to me,' Mary Ann nodded, twice so he could see, and then once again after he had shut the door and was long gone.

Mary Ann kept the maid in the room after she had dressed so that when her father came into the room he would see that she was in her travelling clothes with another girl nearby. Martin Gill was apoplectic. Even more so when he found her sitting there, primly waiting, as if she was a step ahead of him. He did want to thrash her, then and there, but thought better of it with the servant in sight. Instead he beckoned to his daughter with his finger. Mary Ann followed her father downstairs, out of the hotel and into the coach he had organised to take them home. Back they travelled over the same potted road. Mary Ann focused on her gloves as she tried to keep herself to herself and control her breathing. Meanwhile Martin Gill muttered insults at her, and promised, with his riding crop clasped tight between both hands, that there would be a world of trouble for her soon enough.

How Mary Ann got through that night and what exactly happened is hard to say. Did Margaret intervene? She had gone in to check on her daughter, only minutes before Webb arrived at the dining-room door, panting hard and with his hat off and no collar. Margaret was coming down the staircase and was about to tell her husband that their daughter was gone, when Webb broke it to her husband first. Margaret saw the wildness in her husband's eyes and watched as he went behind the hotel counter to get his pistols. Margaret had stepped into his path and stopped there for a few seconds—all the while keeping her head low. Quietly, Martin Gill put the guns back, but, on his way out, he picked up the thin, black crop he kept by the coach yard door.

Now the girl was back home and in one piece. It was almost two in the morning. Margaret had stayed awake, looking into the court-yard below their bedroom window. She had seen her husband drag their daughter out of the vehicle and across the yard, into the kitchen. She had heard muffled yelps like a dog under the wheel of a cart and decided it was best to turn in to bed. The girl had brought it upon herself, Margaret thought. She could not be helped now and perhaps this punishment was for the best. Scare her properly once and for all and then it will be done for good. Through the bedroom wall Margaret heard her daughter's muted sobs and when her husband came to bed an hour or so later, Margaret pretended to be asleep. Her plan had been to go into her daughter's room first thing in the morning and have a word to put the matter to rest, but when Margaret stepped in there, just after dawn, it was clear that things were going to go from bad to worse. The girl had gone again.

If Mary Ann had harboured any doubts about keeping the promise she had made to Kinchela in the upstairs room of the Sportsman's Arms, her father's energetic assertion of paternal authority must have strengthened her resolve. The curtain blew in from the window Mary Ann had left open after climbing through it a second time. The bed sheets were dishevelled but it was impossible to miss the smattering of blood on the girl's pillow. Martin was right behind his wife. He had followed her to put a stop to any tenderness, but when he saw the empty bedroom he turned on his heel and was gone, bounding down the staircase, two, three steps at a time and still in his night-shirt. He shoved his feet into the boots he kept by the door and was away. Margaret heard horse hooves clatter across the yard and from the window glimpsed her husband dashing past, reins hardly in his hands as he spurred his horse up Pitt Street.

No sooner had Kinchela seen the coach with the girl and her father in it drawing away from the Sportsman's Arms than he went inside again to ask Healy to assist him with a licence for the morning. Things were getting desperate and he needed to come up with something quick smart, only Healy was not making any promises and the hotel owner was also proving a little troublesome. He was even forward enough to give Kinchela a piece of his mind when the gentleman settler asked for a drink. It was nearly three in the morning, Webb said, and he wanted upstairs with his wife. Still, a gentleman's money was tempting and he was curious, too, so he agreed to one. Even then, he made his point. 'You have no right, sir,' Webb said, crossing his arms across his chest after he had put a glass of rum on the bench, 'bringing a girl in here like this.' Kinchela looked up and shrugged, 'There is no harm to it,' he said as much to himself as the innkeeper. 'Why not do it proper then?' Webb followed on. 'I have tried,' Kinchela shook his head and muttered. 'I asked her father and he'll have none of it. Flat.' Then Kinchela lightened, 'There is no fear of it, you two,' he said as the two men looked doubtfully at him. 'It will be done first thing in the morning.'

Mary Ann was hoping the same thing as she sat once more inside Somerville's cab making her way back along the Parramatta road towards Homebush in the early hours of Sunday morning. They were now racing against time, she knew, but Somerville sounded confident. He knew where to go and what to do, he said, before closing the door and stepping into the driver's seat, she was to sit back and think about her wedding day.

But when Somerville pulled up at the Homebush racecourse, Kinchela couldn't be found. He didn't want to unsettle the girl so he got back on the coach and continued on to Cutt's Hotel where he had a feeling he might find the gentleman in question. He walked around to the kitchen, where a boy was splitting wood for the fire. 'Is Cutt inside?'

he asked. The boy pointed to the front verandah where the owner was tending to his guests. Somerville took his chance and went right up and explained that he was in something of a delicate situation. Cutt, a rough old Scotsman, who was in the habit of protecting his wealthy clientele, took a note from his waistcoat pocket and handed it over with a curt nod. The old driver brought it back to the young girl in the coach's cabin. Mary Ann took the note from the old man and read it. Once, twice, and then after the third read she tore the letter into three pieces and threw it out of the coach window where it lay dissolving in the dew. 'Take me on to Mrs Beaton's Inn,' she commanded in a voice thick with disgust and resignation.

Kinchela was biding his time and betting on a break. He had put a lot on the hope that Davidson would help him put all the pieces together. After all, it had been his idea in the first place. He planned to meet Jim for an early breakfast at the track out at Homebush and get the licence as soon as they could after that. Only they would have to head into town to do that, Davidson explained, and there was a horse he wanted to watch first, so they would have to go up together in the afternoon, after the race. Davidson was starting to feel sorry for Kinchela, who was looking particularly queasy. Hadn't had much sleep, Davidson suspected, and there was a hint of stale grog on his breath. 'We can go by gig,' the magistrate proposed as they found a breakfast table on the verandah, 'get it done in the afternoon and be back tonight. I'll even be your witness. How's that?' Kinchela nodded, looking a little desperate as he went off to pen a hasty note for Somerville to give to Mary Ann, which he left with the proprietor. Then, as advised by Davidson, he ordered a meal to fortify himself for the day ahead.

It was a crisp bright morning and the fresh air, along with the fusty residue of last night's drinking session, encouraged Kinchela's appetite. He dug into his baked eggs, and was thinking about how to set things right with his soon-to-be-wife when two nearby guests began making such a ruckus that he felt compelled to ascertain the source of their excitement.

Off in the distance, on the flat land of the plains, just beyond the racetrack about half a mile away or so, a man was galloping towards them on a large, dark brown mount. A mare, Kinchela thought, and in good nick. The rider was hardly in control of her, he noted, but seemed to be going at a cracking pace. You could hear the rumble of the hooves thudding along and this kept up even when the pair disappeared into the winter morning fog. There they were again. Then gone and then back again and now much closer. Closer again.

Some of the guests were up on their tiptoes, trying to make out what was going on, and there were two young lads in cabbage-tree hats leaning against the railing, cheering the rider on. 'He's got to be drunk,' the younger one snorted. 'That or pretty bloody mad,' the other replied. The two lay-abouts seemed to have laid a bet on how long it would take the rider to get to the track and if he would fall before he arrived. Kinchela half-listened. He contemplated tossing a crown into the bet and was feeling his pockets for coins when he stopped short. The man and his mount were in sight again and straightaway James could tell. It was the girl's father.

The hotelier's boots were not strapped up and it looked like he might even be wearing his nightshirt. 'Good lord,' Kinchela swallowed as he looked about for heaven-knows-what—a way out, perhaps. He was trying to think about what to say to Davidson, but before his thoughts were even partially formed, tough little Martin Gill was pulling up hard out the front of Cutt's Hotel. Next minute he was off his mount and bounding up the stairs leading into the verandah. Everything seemed to stall as Kinchela watched Mary Ann's father push through the crowd and hurl himself towards his table, a pistol in each hand. There was a clatter of plates and a shove of chairs as the rest of the breakfast crowd rushed inside.

Suddenly, there was only Gill and Kinchela facing one another in the autumn dawn. Kinchela stood and asked for a quiet word with his assailant, but Gill was having none of it. He cocked his weapon, 'Will

I give you time, sir?' he growled, before he pointed it at the younger man's head. Kinchela deftly grabbed hold of the muzzle with one hand but this only provoked the gunman further. 'Let go, sir,' he barked, 'or I will blow out your brains.' No sooner had Kinchela released the weapon than a generous portion of powder exploded from its mouth, bruising Kinchela on the side of his forehead before skidding along the verandah. There was a stir and whinny of horses and then all was still.

'My God,' Gill groaned, dropping the finished weapon to the ground. 'I can't believe I missed you.' The gentleman settler raised his hand to his forehead where the powder had left a black smudge. 'Come now, sir,' he said, but the gunman shook his head. 'I will finish you, Kinchela,' Gill snarled as he struggled with shaking hands to cock the second weapon.

As he did so, the settler took a step away from the table and then another until finally he was standing inside the entry of Cutt's Hotel. He was looking about for Davidson but spotted another of his brother's friends, a fellow named Graham Hunter, who had been the Commissioner for Crown Lands in Wellington Valley when James and John had first started there. Hunter was having his breakfast in a corner of the dining room and hoping to keep out of it all, but when Kinchela advanced towards him he acknowledged him reluctantly. 'Hunter,' Kinchela insisted, 'I'll not stand by and be shot at like a dog.'

Hunter nodded and stepped from the table before proceeding to where Gill was furiously pacing the verandah, his second pistol at the ready. 'Sir,' Hunter coughed at the agitated fellow, 'we will have to apprehend you.' Gill shook his head and lifted his pistol, pointing it at Kinchela, who was standing right behind Hunter in the dining-room doorway. 'I am sorry I have not killed you,' Gill spat as he took aim at Kinchela's head.

At that moment, Davidson, who had been watching the whole thing from the corner of the verandah, saw his chance, seized the weapon and somehow also managed to wrestle Gill to the ground. Seconds later, Cutt was on the gunman, too, and in a flash the two lads wearing cabbage-tree hats also jumped in, hooting as if the whole thing was a great lark. Minutes later, the Commissioner stepped forth to formally arrest the hotelier on a charge of shooting with intent. Kinchela shook his head, 'No, Hunter,' he protested. 'I don't mean to lay charges.' 'Too late, old boy,' Hunter responded without even turning to look at him. 'It's not your decision, disturbing the peace and all that, don't you know?'

Minutes later the crowd returned to their tables chattering with considerable excitement. One or two turned to consider Kinchela who was standing with Davidson and watching as Hunter and Cutt led the handcuffed Gill to a small outhouse. 'He will be able to cool off there for a bit,' Davidson said with a smirk, but James shook his head. He was in no mood for jokes.

⁓

Meanwhile, as instructed, Somerville had driven Mary Ann Gill on to the establishment of yet another friend of James, a woman named Mrs Beaton, who ran an inn near the Parramatta racecourse. The middle-aged woman was attempting to soothe the young girl with a cup of tea. Neither knew what had just transpired at Cutt's Hotel, but after the great anxiety of the night before and this second terrible disappointment Mary Ann was close to giving up. Despite their careful plans and her great daring, Mary Ann was still not married, and if James didn't come through very soon she would have no choice but to return home to her father's guns. She would then have to face the ignominy of having stepped out with a man who clearly lacked the enthusiasm or ability to see her properly wed. An indignity of this sort, once it got out, could be a hundred times worse than death, Mary Ann thought, particularly in a town like Sydney where her family were well known and a woman's respectability was everything.

Mary Ann was still trying to work out if there was any way she might still believe the best of James, when, suddenly, old Somerville came thumping into the front room leaving a trail of mud across the rug. 'Police are on their way, girl,' he bellowed, shoving the young girl down the corridor. 'You best be out and quick smart,' he said, pulling a window open and forcing Mary Ann through it as quick as he could. One leg, two legs. Out.

Then, thwuck, thwuck, the girl began running across the wet lawn, her skirts heavy with morning dew as she pushed on, desperate to make a dash for it. Twenty yards or so from the house, Mary Ann turned to see a slim young man in police uniform jumping out the window after her. She pushed off again—faster than before—and was thrashing desperately through the dewy lawn with all her might when suddenly Mary Ann felt her skirts snag and she found herself toppling head first into the long wet grass.

CHAPTER FIVE

Shooting With Intent

Eighteen forty-eight was like no year before it and few that followed. When the first steamers arrived at Circular Quay in early May carrying with them London newspapers bursting with bloody tales of winter revolutions in France then Italy, Germany, Poland and Hungary, the unsettled state of the old world suddenly became a matter of 'vast importance' throughout the colony. One local newspaper declared with alarm that 'in less than a few hours . . . a throne had been overturned, a monarchy crushed and a republic established' in Paris. The 'heroic people' had risen up, another proclaimed, and hurled 'their trembling sovereign from the giddy eminence of his throne'. Suddenly, all over 'Milan, Berlin and Budapest' the people were taking to the streets.

France had sneezed, it seemed, and the rest of Europe had caught 'the great contagion of liberty'. The entire thing was more of a dream than a reality, another news-sheet mused, although they were just as astounded that it had taken only eighty-five days for the news of these European insurrections to arrive in New South Wales. From what the press were saying, everything had begun in Paris. With winter sharp in the air, the desperate and diminished had pushed through the snow-thick streets, dragging behind them bits of dismantled omnibus and city gigs, which they threw onto blockades already stacked high with trees they had cut down from the city's parklands. Once news of the poor grain supplies and empty government coffers became common knowledge, thousands more took to the streets and within a few days 'every gate, every street, lane and court' was blocked with 'enormous barricades'. Yet again, French historian Alexis de Tocqueville observed, 'young France was simmering like a live volcano'. And when Louis Philippe, the Citizen King, fearing insurrection, decided to ban the banquets that had been established to feed his starving citizens a 'terrible conflagration' ensued and great plumes of smoke rose from the barricades, colonial readers learnt, fuelled by hunger, rage and desperation.

Some were saying that it was 1789 all over again. Or 1832. Mobs rallied, palaces were stormed and within hours the King's troops had all but capitulated. A few days later a man mounted upon a fine black horse trotted along the periphery of the palace to where a throng of hungry people had gathered about their bonfires. 'The last King of the French has abdicated,' he called out, only moments before the so-called Citizen King—dressed modestly in civilian clothes—passed along the *pont tournant* in the company of his ageing wife. All the way, the royal couple were heckled by starving subjects. 'Vive la Reform' and 'Vive la France' they hissed, except for a lone voice, which dared to call out 'Vive le Roi' as the last king and his wife slipped quietly away.

England, of course, had its own problems. At the Monster Rally on Kennington Common that April, the banners had made all sorts of brazen statements such as 'Ireland for the Irish' and 'Politics for the People'. Some said 300,000 had marched through London for the rally, although the conservative press had been instructed by the government to put the number at no more than 15,000. The same was said about the petition that mad band of ideologues dragged up the stairs of Parliament House. Their leader, the half-crazed Irishman Fergus O'Connor, boasted that they had secured well over six million signatures. Stuff and nonsense, the papers retorted—less than a million, if that—and some of the names were clearly fraudulent, one paper fumed. Still, there was a general concern that the Chartists were growing uncomfortably bold. Change was in the air—even in England, even after the workers had been given a ten-hour work day. Just as well the young British Queen and her ever-expanding family was of sufficient interest to quell much of the unrest that the French nonsense was stirring up throughout the rest of Europe.

What a year. From France to the Netherlands, Italy to Hungary, Poland and Denmark, monarchs and aristocrats were dragged from their thrones and driven from their estates as articulate artisans took to the streets, inciting workers and students to march against corruption. In Ireland things were as fractious as ever. Yet another potato blight had crippled the country and there were now 800,000 starving and bedraggled Roman Catholic paupers in the village streets and town squares, most too weak to catch whatever crumbs fell from Protestant tables. And with the soil still soft around the graves of more than a thousand emaciated corpses, the spectre of cholera also roamed the land, plucking fresh victims from those who dared to survive.

These were events of 'astounding importance', one rather radical colonial paper wrote, and surely signalled the end of absolute power. It would not be long before ancient edicts, royal decrees and elite privileges were replaced by a forthright press as well as public squares bustling with well-read workers ready to change the world.

For most of the colonists in the increasingly respectable town of Sydney, the news-sheets were both appalling and enthralling. It was impossible to avoid the fact that *something* was going on and yet few were certain about what that was and how to respond. No sooner had news from the first of the May steamers arrived than it became a common practice, for a time at least, for the streets outside the city newspaper offices to throng each daybreak with crowds of men desperate for the latest European intelligence.

The majority of those in the crowd were the sort of idlers who thought it a lark to knock the brown beavers off the heads of new chums making their way onto colonial soil for the first time. They were tough men, typically much bigger and stronger than those coming in off the boats. Their insolent pride showed in their uniform—rough calico working pants with a striped shirt of some description, often finished with a red or blue kerchief and a cheap hat made of cabbage-tree palm that had a tall crown as well as a wide brim. It was better at keeping the sun out of their eyes than those silly brown felt things the 'Jimmy Grants' arrived in. True some of the Cabbagers, as they were known, had only been babes when they came in the last of the prison boats, but the biggest number were currency lads and the sons of convicts. They nursed their parents' shame and added to this a longer list of real and imagined insults. With little learning and even less luck, these Cabbagers were all pent-up fury and seething resentment and most of them roamed the streets like a pack of surly farm dogs.

The factory and ship bosses were only marginally better. Most were canny and knew how to smell opportunity quicker than a change coming through the Sydney Heads. Many had come in chains them-selves and were usually smart enough to keep the younger men and the troublemakers tight. They were wont to make a bit of a show of reading the paper aloud over smoko. As if to themselves, but always within earshot, so that those who wanted to could linger in the corners, slouched over, looking away, but still able to hear what was going on. That was Sydney all over. It was a town built upon unspoken assump-tions and tacit agreements. You never asked a man about his past and you used careful courtesies to navigate certain embarrassments.

Across the road, a good husband would be recounting the key points of interest from the news-sheets to his wife over supper, and in the hours after serving and before it was time to retreat for the night the better house staff would pass on certain tidbits to the less learned staff. Meanwhile, men from the clubs and among the legal fraternity had the papers as well as a host of other official and less official sources at their fingertips. They were well placed to keep abreast of all the news—local and abroad. And so it was, that from washtub to horse trough, coffee house to tanning room, the colonists of Sydney and its surrounds came to learn about the extraordinary events of 1848. The same papers also contained dire warnings about the weather, how drought was drying up the best of the country blocks and more and more men were being forced into town rather than watch the last of their wretched stock die.

Things were looking grim and some of the townies were also starting to sniff the dry dust coming in on the city winds.

Not a good time for a local election, but what could you do? It was all set to start in a month or so, and, being only the second election in Sydney, those in possession of sufficient property would have another chance to elect a few of their own men to the Legislative Council of New South Wales. Few wanted the date to change now. Well, not the townies anyway. Bit by bit parliament was being righted, they reckoned, and if those intent upon changing things once and for all played their cards carefully, this particular election might well prove the very moment that the people, or at least those who could vote, finally wrested power from the governor and his landed associates.

But there was also some anxiety, for five years earlier the first elections had been spectacularly shambolic, with mobs to rival the current European madness ripping through the streets of Sydney with their own idiosyncratic expression of colonial violence. All down George Street and across Hyde Park, gangs armed with whaling harpoons, sabres and clasp knives had charged through the campaign tents, burning down the blue bunting for that native-born turnabout William Charles Wentworth, before tearing along The Rocks, where they clashed with crews wielding barrel staves and fence palings. Shops were looted and innocent civilians assaulted before the mounted police finally thundered in and read the Riot Act to a brawling mass of Cabbagers and ex-cons.

Thereafter, voting had been suspended and the town engulfed in a spirit of drunken carousing and wanton destruction. This not-so-distant memory meant that there was a fair bit of excitement about the forthcoming political contest. A chance to do it better this time, some of the new chums said, and in a way that would prove that the colony was ready for further freedoms. Others shook their heads and said the election wasn't worth it. But for the emancipists and the bounty migrants as well as any others who had been desperate enough to arrive in the colony with insufficient capital and connections, these elections felt like their first real chance to break the squatters' hold.

And so, among the shop folk and the new men of town, people were holding their breath and waiting hopefully.

The whole mood seemed to see-saw, this way and that, with old settlers stomping about in a stew and firing off verbose epistles to the papers and other officials while smart and shabby newspaper editors alike pandered to the artisan and emancipist set by publishing droll sketches about the various candidates likely to take a crack at an elected seat. One jolly spark was sure that it would be a case of the 'bland leading the bland' if Wentworth and the old fusty doctor, William Bland, teamed up to run for the two coveted seats of Sydney. There was also a lot of talk about Wentworth's policies, but no one was quite certain either way. Sure he was a native-born, but he seemed to have foolish ideas about a local aristocracy made rich on the toil of government men. For that to happen the colony, of course, would have to resume transportation.

Never again, was the hiss that followed any rumours the Colonial Office was thinking about sending out convicts again. As long as there were men in chains on the town streets, the colony was bound in servitude and no one back home would take them seriously. The presence of 'white slaves' had been a stain upon them all and it wasn't until the boats had finally stopped in 1840 that Sydney-siders had been able to hold up their heads. Not long after that they had also begun to sue for more of a say in local affairs. And there were now plenty of vigorous musings from those who called themselves radicals. Men like Captain John Lamb, for instance, who had been talking about running for one of the Sydney seats, and who had wild stuff to say about Paris. Some down the tail end of Hunter Street, where young Henry Parkes ran a toyshop, were also murmuring about a possible partnership with the great demagogue, Robert Lowe, who had already torn strips off a few governors since arriving in the late 1830s. Quite a few were also wondering what would happen if Lowe did lie down with Lamb.

There were, in fact, a lot of mixed opinions about the curious albino lawyer Robert Lowe. Indeed, it was fair to say that with his splayed hips, white hair and shaded spectacles as well as that vicious wit he was by far the most contentious figure in the colony, which was something considering the numerous crackpots and conmen, imposters and improvisers who had made their way to New South Wales. No one could quite determine the nature of Robert Lowe and, as he confided to his imposing and athletic wife, Georgina, one morning, he preferred it that way. He wished to function as a law unto himself and this is precisely what he had done.

Without remorse the brilliant whirligig had taken on the courts, the newspapers and even a few governors. Despite his original sympathy for the settler set, he quickly decided he must undo the 'squattocracy' and he set to fearlessly clashing blades with several of the wealthiest families. Among *that* set much had been muttered about the lawyer's 'low' methods. But the same victories had also seen Robert Lowe crowned the People's Idol by the likes of Henry Parkes and his friends.

Throughout the colony, the lawyer was loved and loathed, feared and admired and no one was entirely sure if he would actually run to become an elected representative member for the Legislative Council. He had already served a term on the Council as the governor's appointment, but when he bit the hand that fed him by destroying the governor's name and then refusing to present anything by way of an olive branch it seemed unlikely that he would receive another appointment that way. Rumour had it that Parkes paid a visit to Lowe, and the great man had told the toyshop owner that he was considering his options. They would make an unlikely pair, most speculated. The angular and incisive intellect that was Robert Lowe and the thick-headed, rocking-horse vendor with a propensity for insolvency and Chartism. But Parkes was intent on forging an alliance. With his florid waistcoats and striped trousers, as well as the riding crop he insisted on carrying with him everywhere, Lowe was not only eccentric but also a highly lethal weathercock. He could heap lavish praise one minute and then, depending on his whims and fancies, execute an exquisite humiliation the next. 'Better to have him with rather than agin' you,' Parkes confided to one of the newspaper men, who called at the toyshop to discuss the current political climate. 'He is the only one who can stop the squatters,' Parkes added with conviction, even though he still found himself quaking before the imperious intellect each time he was permitted to visit Lowe's Macquarie Street chambers.

Those who preferred their news more bloody, skipped the news of trembling European monarchs, country drought and local elections and turned directly to the Law Intelligence pages, where they could feed upon a feast of local felonry. As well as the sordid details of James Thompson, who had bludgeoned a man behind the ears on his walk home through Hyde Park, there were reports about William Woods who had a crack at horse stealing, and Timothy Duffy who was up for two accounts of 'attempting to murder Aborigines'. There was also the 'quiet and industrious' Henry Porter, who had shot a friend named Daniel Budge in both wrists after he learnt the devil had ill-used his daughter.

There, among the colonial carnage of violence and vengeance was our Pitt Street hotelier, Martin Gill, indicted for 'unlawfully, maliciously and feloniously' shooting at James Butler Kinchela with the intention of murdering him. Gill was also called to answer a second charge of attempting to commit 'grievous bodily harm' against those who apprehended him at the racecourse. The Gill case was stirring up considerable excitement, not only in the coffee houses and city hotels but further afield in the Maitland and Bathurst districts and even as far away as Moreton Bay, where James Butler Kinchela was well known.

Some papers expressed sympathy for the thwarted lovers. That irreverent publication, *Bell's Sporting Life*, was clearly amused by the guileless Miss Gill and her runaway romancer. Others expressed their astonishment at the 'very frantic state' of Martin Gill on that fateful morning when he had arrived at the Homebush racecourse with murder set upon his grim countenance. Many were appalled by the gall of an upstart emancipist taking on a gentleman, but already the majority had sided with the unfortunate father—a man who had only done, they asserted with indignation, what was required of any red-blooded fellow facing familial indignity. In this day and age, they fumed, fathers deserved to have their feelings and their property protected by the courts, whoever they were and wherever they came from, particularly if the offending party was a gentleman who should have known better.

No lesser personage than the current Attorney General, John Hubert Plunkett, was representing the Crown in this case against Martin Gill, and to counter this threat, the ambitious hotelier procured none other than the Great Gyrator, Robert Lowe, to defend him. The white-haired toff was at the peak of his game, Gill knew that much, and commanding a pretty fee thanks to his popularity and the promise of the election close at hand. But Martin Gill knew that if anyone could get him off, it would be Robert Lowe.

Gill certainly needed assistance, especially if word got out about his previous preference for resolving differences with his fists, or a crowbar as had been the case a few years earlier when he last stood before the criminal court charged with a serious felony. Back then he had got off due to a lack of witnesses, but this time the evidence was much more compelling. There had been many people at Cutt's Hotel that morning and the Commissioner, Graham Hunter, had made the effort to send both pistols to a blacksmith to confirm that shots had been fired. The consequences of a conviction for Gill would be considerable, and with his background he faced not only the prospect of a stint in a local cell but perhaps even a term in one of the worst gaols in the colony, where it was rumoured men were eaten by the blacks or otherwise left to starve. It could have been worse, too. If he had done what he meant to do, Martin Gill would have ended up swinging in the breeze on Woolloomooloo Hill, with his wife and children watching as his corpse danced at the end of a hangman's rope.

Margaret dealt with the vexing circumstances in a spirit of irritated compliance. It was enough to be keeping an eye on a newborn and his wet nurse, let alone her disobedient daughter. Now she also had that matter of her husband's criminal charges to consider. She was, in truth, furious beyond words, but Gill didn't particularly care. He had a feeling—what with the election and the mood currently in favour of middling men of hard-earned respectability—that things would go his way. More and more the old set were on the nose and popular sentiment was with the enterprising middleclass and those intent upon improvement. He could feel it, whenever he made his way about town. In addition to that, most of the men on the jury were fathers like himself. There was even a good chance that he would know a few of them. No one wanted their daughters running around thinking they could do whatever they liked.

Lowe suspected the same. Having finally relented to Parkes' supplications and consented to run for one of the elected Sydney seats, Lowe quickly determined that the story of a father wronged would hold just the right appeal for those members of the voting public he most needed to woo. Given the pastoral activities of the defendant, this case could also be useful in his tug of war with the settlers and their upstart sons. So Lowe was relishing the opportunity for yet another stoush, particularly when he realised he would be able to fight this one out not only in the courts but also at the polling booth.

He needed to make quick work of defending Gill if he was to have a crack at prosecuting Kinchela, Lowe decided. He needed the first case finalised so he could ensure that the much more interesting abduction trial coincided with his election run. If he got it right, Lowe smiled with satisfaction, he could be everywhere. In the evening he would entertain audiences in the city theatres as he expounded upon the abundant evils of the squatters, and during the day the lithe and limber legal wit would be able to regale the court with the wily antics of a certain so-called gentleman, who seemed to think he was fit to take whatever he wanted whenever he liked. It wouldn't take much to ensure that both performances found their way into the papers, Lowe reckoned, and before long he would be lionised as the true defender of the public good. Or so he hoped. Much as Lowe held a certain disdain for the middling men of the colony, he shared with them a loathing for men like Kinchela. Those well-to-do squatters and settlers reminded him of boys from his school days who had considered it their right to menace and mock anyone they considered sufficiently feeble. They had certainly subjected him to diligent and daily persecution.

And so the Modern Gloucester, as he was known in some circles, pushed on towards his prize, all the while delighting in what appeared to be a series of coincidences that gave him every confidence that providence was on his side. Lowe took pains to prepare his defence carefully and was pleased when he arrived in court with Martin Gill, who was reassured that the men in the jury were 'his sorts'. 'Enough said,' Lowe said, brushing his client's confidences aside and pretending not to understand. But he could see that circumstances were lining up for him.

Lowe was deterred only by the fact that the prosecution's key witness, the blackguard in question, appeared to have disappeared from the face of the earth. The police had, in fact, done the rounds of Kinchela's favourite haunts, but it was not until Sydney's beleaguered Police Magistrate, Captain Joseph Long Innes, went out to the home of Dr Kinchela's widow in Liverpool, that anyone laid eyes on Kinchela for the first time in over a fortnight. Innes saw a man much changed. Kinchela's usual affable disposition had been replaced with a truculent sullenness. He lurked in his mother's garden and refused point blank to come to court when Innes asked him to do so. It wasn't until Lowe's assistant Bob Nichols called by a few days later that Kinchela finally agreed to do the right thing. He felt he could speak straight with the native-born lawyer, even if he was working for Lowe in this instance. Kinchela had never wanted Gill charged in the first place, he explained, and was done with it all. He began to realise, however, that as things stood he would not be free of the matter until it was sorted. So yes, he finally reassured Nichols, he would go to court, and no, he would not lay a trap for Gill.

'Watch out there, though, James,' Nichols warned Kinchela once he had the gentleman's agreement on the matter. 'Word is that once Gill is free he plans to come after you, and that he has paid Lowe to lead the attack.' Kinchela shrugged, but he was a little taken aback. He had hoped that his absence would show the girl's father that he meant no ill will. He was beginning to sense, however, that there might be no limit to the man's vengeance. The whole thing was completely out of proportion with what had in fact been a rather tentative romance. He hadn't even kissed the girl, for pity's sake. Such an interlude was common enough at home and should have been treated with even more lightness here. What a folly, Kinchela thought. He desperately wanted to head back to Hawkwood and get out and about on his prize stepper so he could forget about it all. That would fix everything, he mused, but as things were shaping up he could see that he would have to face the matter. Still, he knew his mind. He would not be part of that man's conviction, and he kept true to this even when he finally stood in the infernal witness box, answering a volley of impudent questions with a quite deliberate, even taciturn, indifference.

Lowe's court performance was an exercise in political persuasion which Kinchela watched, gritting his teeth and loathing the wily cleverness of the man even as he admired his skill. Lowe coaxed and petted the jury of shopkeepers and middling property owners with such earnest respect that none but his own wife would have detected his veiled contempt. And then, when Lowe called the men of real position, such as Kinchela, the portly Graham Hunter and Jim Davidson, who was clearly put out by the proceedings, Lowe was sly and condescending. The jury lapped this up as if they themselves had inflicted the slights and insults upon these men.

William Cutt, the Scotsman who ran the inn out at Homebush, was called to the box and stood firm in his boots as he answered both lawyers with an air of irritability. 'Of course Kinchela was a regular customer,' he replied tetchily. 'Never once had he had any problems with the esteemed esquire, little trouble at all, in fact, at his establishment,' if anyone wanted to know. 'He had no business to know why Kinchela was there that morning, nor was he in the habit of prying upon his guests.' Although he had a mind to suspect it 'might be to attend the races,' he finished, provoking a titter of laughter from those in the upstairs gallery of the court. He had 'never seen Miss Gill before'. He had 'heard, though, that she was something of a wee thing, even if she hadn't yet learnt it was her duty to do what her father bid,' to which there was another flurry of muted laughter from upstairs. 'I did see

Mr Gill that morning but I could not say for certain if the pistols were fired. I heard a crack of something, but while I did see some powder smoke the air for a bit, it is hard to say.'

Stepping lithely back and forth along the length of the jury box, Lowe presented the court with his concluding remarks. The only real difficulty in this case, Lowe advised, was that 'the esteemed jurymen must divest from their minds the grievous wrong that had been inflicted upon the prisoner, which, as men with fathers' hearts might be a natural and noble response to such a wicked grievance'. This final flourish did the trick. After less than five minutes the jurors returned their verdict. Despite the evidence of the blacksmith, several witnesses testifying to seeing Gill shoot at Kinchela point blank—and the powder on the pistol—the Pitt Street hotelier was found innocent of both charges.

No sooner was the verdict announced than the court audience erupted in a 'most unequivocal demonstration of applause', which continued, the papers said, until the judge finally ordered 'the restoration of decorum'. Quick as a wink, the defendant was up, bouncing about the court with a tight grin on his face, shaking hands with his legal team and even one or two of the jurors.

What a farce, Kinchela noted with a measure of dry contempt as he stepped outside the court and leant against one of the columns waiting for his coach and driver. He watched as Gill and his team bundled out of the courtroom boisterous with triumph, then watched, shocked, as Gill turned back from his party, caught Kinchela's eye and spat at the ground. The settler sucked in his breath and shook his head but said nothing. Lowe saw it all and looked aghast, before he quickly recovered and set off down the steps of the court with a great bundle of papers under one arm and that damn crop in the other. The whole thing was beyond the pale, Kinchela thought, taking his seat in the coach and feeling in his pocket for his snuffbox. And there was probably worse to come, he thought, for it was clear that Gill had the bit between his teeth, and there was no saying if he could be pulled back from the brink.

CHAPTER SIX

The Deposition

Business continued at Gill's Family Hotel in the final weeks of May and throughout June 1848 because Margaret Gill made it so. If Martin had showmanship, and, with it, a lot of hot and bluster, Margaret had craft and common sense. She was generally sensible, although a little tetchy if pushed. When her husband failed to return home after he galloped off to the Homebush racecourse in pursuit of his daughter and that man, Margaret sent a messenger out to the track and before lunch she knew what was what. She sent the same boy off to Punchbowl and asked him to come back with Mary Riley, who would need to supervise the kitchen while she took over the dining room.

Just after lunchtime a rather pleasant looking policeman called to the servant door of the hotel and asked to speak with the mistress of the house. Mary Ann was in the cabin of the wagon and watched as her mother, hands clasped in front of her, stood and listened to what the young constable had to say. Their conversation was economical, for that was how Margaret Gill preferred words, and shortly after that Mary Ann was escorted inside. Margaret followed her through the kitchen, up the back stairs of the house and then directed her into the room where mother and daughter took tea most afternoons. Then Margaret bade her daughter sit and asked their girl Rebecca to bring some tea.

Mary Ann was pale and the sight of her looking so tense made Margaret feel grave. This was a bad business and there was worse to come, no doubt. Margaret sat down in her usual seat opposite Mary Ann and both women looked at their laps then out the window, not knowing what to do. Tea came, and with it all the comfort of fond familiars. The old silver tray Margaret had picked up on the cheap when she first married Gill, the pot that her father and Mary Riley had gifted her one birthday—a sweet, floral thing with a rather prim spout. Family things, Mary Ann thought, looking about the table and noticing that even though she was home again there was a sense that somehow, perhaps, it would never be in the same way again. As she did every day, Mary Ann picked up the pot and poured the brew into her mother's cup and then her own. Only this time her hands were unsteady. Her mother added milk to her own cup and placed the jug just where it had been when she picked it up, so that Mary Ann would have no choice but to ask for it.

Mother and daughter sat in this awkward silence for a time, Margaret sipping her tea and Mary Ann not yet able to form words. Eventually Margaret realised she needed to help her daughter just a little. She poured a slip of the thick milk into her daughter's cup and then, as the girl stirred the blend into a soft brown steaming liquid, she finally spoke. 'You will need to collect yourself, my girl.' Mary Ann carefully took the cup and saucer and brought the cup to her lips. Thirsty. It was the first thing she'd had since she was at Mrs Beaton's much earlier that morning. The warm tea travelled down into her hollow centre. It made her feel empty and sick. She wondered if she would ever feel right again.

'Your father is in the goal house now,' Margaret Gill continued, 'and I will need you in the kitchen with Mary Riley.' Mary Ann's mind began to race. What had her father done to be imprisoned? Was James dead? Was that why James hadn't come to her? Mary Ann tried to make sense of it. What on earth had she unleashed? Margaret watched her daughter's face. She wanted the girl to take in the full measure of her actions and to be apprised of the consequences therein. The girl's breathing increased and her skin seemed to drop another shade of pale. 'You will need to mind yourself,' Margaret said, drawing her body up and making sure she sounded stern, 'you have stirred up a lot of trouble for us, and worse is to come, if I am not mistaken.' She fixed her daughter with a look. 'You must be on your wits, Mary Ann, and keep out of your father's way when he gets home.'

'When he gets home' echoed in Mary Ann's mind. So it can't be murder if they are going to let him out, she thought. Perhaps, then, James is safe. But as soon as she considered this, Mary Ann was filled with foreboding. Her father would no doubt flog her, and probably within an inch of her life this time. At least they would have taken the guns off him in gaol. 'Keep in the nursery,' Margaret instructed, 'out of the way. And for all our sakes,' she finished tersely, 'do what you are told from here on.'

Mary Ann nodded. Every part of her was done. She knew she was going to pay a price for her boldness and for what? All the courage she had shown scrambling down the drainpipe, and then the shock of Mrs Kelly's front parlour, those few fleeting encounters with James, followed by their frustrating meeting at the Sportsman's Arms and that dreadful flogging she had received from her father after they returned home that night. And then, despite all this, she had the courage to slip away a second time—in the early dawn—only to receive a note that spoke of still further disappointment and delays and that also carried in it her downfall. It had all been too much. She was exhausted. Tears came and the young woman let them roll thick and fast down her cheeks as mother and daughter said nothing. Eventually Margaret started again, this time a little softer, 'Now girl, go and clean up, for goodness' sakes. I need you in the kitchen before your father gets home. We must push past this business and keep it from the servants if we can.'

But by the time Margaret had gone out to her father's farm to ask for £200 in sureties so that she could bail out her husband, it was clear to everyone concerned that any hope of discretion was lost. The story of Mary Ann's Parramatta Romance was in *The Sydney Morning Herald* the very next day and the day after that and then just about every day thereafter one colonial newspaper or another seemed to find some fresh tidbit to report regarding this incident. Much of it was fantasy, but it fed the public's appetite and ensured that news-sheets otherwise devoted to the forthcoming election or the mayhem in Europe had a little more colour to them. Despite the fact that both Margaret and Mary Ann came to loathe those papers, the girl was still grateful for the few morsels of information she could glean about James. It had been a job to get her hands on one of the papers, but the few times she could she was able to learn that even before her father's trial was done, James Butler Kinchela had been asked to attend an interview behind closed doors at the Parramatta Police Office, where he had been summoned to answer a charge of abduction.

It was then determined that her sometime suitor should be committed to take his trial at the next sitting of the Supreme Court after the trial at which her own father was made to answer the charge of shooting with intent. Kinchela, she realised, had not been charged directly by the Crown, but by Martin Gill. Mary Ann was not at all surprised when she read that. She knew her father well enough to believe that he would take this to the end. Hell or high water, as he often muttered under his breath when someone tried to cross him. She registered even more alarm when she read that the man who was heading up the prosecution was the same man who had been all over the papers: 'the Loathsome Lowe', she remembered James calling him one time when he had talked about the need to push north because of the change in tone about land grants and such. This was news, but in no way was the news of Lowe coming after Kinchela good.

Mary Ann had spent the first day back home shrouded in shame and terrified of her father's imminent return. But when he eventually did step back across the threshold of his establishment the next morning, Martin Gill said nothing. In fact, he refused to even see his daughter. He simply looked around, checked that the pantry was provisioned and the front rooms prepared, and then after sharpening several carving knives in the kitchen he took himself upstairs.

Gill was no stranger to a prison cell but it had been a while. Time in the Parramatta lock-up had reminded him of other places he had long put away. He had forgotten the squalor. Or perhaps back then he had been so brutish he hadn't noticed it. Could it have been that his filthy desperation had transformed the bucket in the corner and the fetid lay of hay on the floor into some kind of a reprieve? Now, however, Martin Gill was completely repulsed by it all. It also made him realise how far he had come since his childhood on the bitter streets of North Dublin. He would not let anyone take away all that he had since achieved. Not his daughter and certainly not that so-called gentleman.

He had been about the girl's age when he had been hauled into the Kilmainham Gaol in Dublin and he thought, for a moment, that a day or two cooling her heels in a cell would probably do his daughter the world of good. If not for the shame it would bring upon them all, he might even have seen to it himself. He suspected, however, that his new plan for Mary Ann would probably be just as good and not bring the family down. But for now he really didn't want to think about her anymore. He had simply wanted the grime of the entire episode gone. And so, while his wife managed the lunch crowd, Martin Gill took possession of the second-floor suite of his hotel and ordered himself a bath. He was going to soak in it all day if he had to, or at least until he worked out what he needed to do. There was a way to turn things to his advantage, he was sure, he just had to think it all through.

Meanwhile, Gill decided that he would invest more in his eldest boy, William. He had been so caught up with the girl and that way she had of agitating him that he had passed over his eldest son. William could be useful, he decided, and he would speak with the boy about what was required. A son, after all, stood to benefit more. First, he would get his son to keep an eye on Mary Ann, in the interests of them all, of course, and see how he handled that. William was close to fourteen now and old enough to take on some manly tasks. Gill would build him up and make him useful. He would also need to get a gauge of the mood from his customers this evening, too. He had to assume a clear position as soon as possible and act as though he was on top and in the right from the start. He had *The Herald* in his pocket, just where he needed them. They liked his money too much to turn on him, he reckoned. His wife was tricky, though. He couldn't quite work out her play although he would make sure he did soon enough. Meanwhile Martin Gill needed to make sure that public opinion favoured him for he had absolutely no intention of going back to gaol.

He was also prepared to expend considerable energy to ensure that Kinchela met with justice. The thought came to him initially as an amusement, but once it had caught his imagination it began to shape itself into a distinct possibility. Over the years he had heard stories from home about men who had been hanged for taking a wife without asking for her hand in the right way. There were quite a few too who had come on the boats lucky to avoid the swing for such a crime. After all it was just another form of property theft in the eyes of the law. One such felon was a blacksmith who went by the name of Captain Rock. Gill had heard many an Irishman speak of the Captain with hushed admiration. Around the time that Gill was finishing his sentence, the Captain and a gang of twelve Limerick boys had ripped a fifteen-year-old Protestant heiress from her bed and held her captive for nigh on three weeks. All that time they had hidden her in the mountains while they tried to force her to marry some lazy squireen so that he could take her land. But the girl wouldn't have it and eventually the Captain lost his nerve, abandoning the wretched creature in an empty cabin, but only once the squireen had well and truly ruined her. Gill had a mind Kinchela was not far from those sorts—a squireen who thought nothing of taking what wasn't his.

He had been something, that Captain Rock. Smart enough to disappear after the legal officials had rounded up the rest of his gang. No one could catch him for months, even with men scouring the mountains and trying to bring him in on charges of arson, stolen arms, secret oaths, threatening notices and eventually even murder. In the end, Captain Rock surrendered on his own terms and pleaded guilty but only to the charge of abducting Honourah Goold. He was set to swing for this when for some mysterious reason his sentence was suddenly commuted to transportation. No one knew why but some suspected the blacksmith had friends in high places. Next thing, the great Captain was working at a forge somewhere in Campbelltown, only a few miles from Sydney.

Gill knew all this because when he was still working on the roads, some fellow working beside him had pointed to a boy who could not have been more than fifteen, 'That's Daniel Doody', he whispered, 'the youngest of Captain Rock's men'. 'The devil in his eyes,' someone else had muttered and when Gill took a look at the stunted thing and saw the gleam about his visage, he had to agree. There was something bold and bloody to the boy. For weeks after there was talk among Gill's crew of nothing else—how the Captain had one of Napoleon's war coats as well as a white feather in his hat; how the Captain's crew had been within a breath of taking Southern Ireland in the winter of 1822. 'Held the whole country on a knife's blade,' one of Gill's mates had said.

At the time Gill had thought the Captain a great lark. But now that he was a man with property of his own as well as a father he didn't feel the same. The thing was, Gill mused as he lowered himself into the bath he usually reserved for his guests, it wasn't just *squireens* taking *maydens*, or old knights stealing spinsters, but sometimes a gentlemen of real standing would also try his hand at taking a wealthy widow who he wanted for no reason other than her easy fortune. Only a few ever found themselves before the law, although those who did sometimes left all sorts of tales for others to tell: the popular gent who got hanged twice after the rope snapped the first time and the two half-mounts who took the Kennedy sisters and were hanged when they were caught. How the town divided over that particular abduction, and one side so hated the girls that they dumped the corpses of their two dead boys at the Kennedys' door.

Everyone knew about Sir Henry Hayes, too, the old knight from Cork who had been one of the first to come to Sydney at a time when the colony comprised little more than a church and a few half-finished drinking inns. Sir Henry should have hanged, too, it was said, and probably would have but for the fact that the 'cock would not stand' as one of the London papers said, when he tried to consummate his marriage with the rich spinster Mary Pike. Well, Gill thought, if court was good enough for Sir Henry, it was certainly good enough for Kinchela.

~

Less than a week from the wet evening that Mary Ann had scrambled down the drainpipe and onto Pitt Street, Martin Gill was in a coach travelling out along the Parramatta road in the company of his wife and daughter. They were going to the Police Office to give evidence in the forthcoming trial of James Butler Kinchela, who had now been officially charged with the crime of abduction.

Mary Ann had not left the house since she had returned the previous Sunday. While her father was in the lock-up, she assumed kitchen duties, which entailed her standing mutely in the corner until ordered to do otherwise by her grandmother who remained tight-lipped throughout it all. After her father returned home, Mary Ann was confined to the nursery. There would be no more school for her, no more needlework lessons, no more books, and, of course, no chance of running errands about the town let alone visiting the hotel dining room. From now on Mary Ann would be the family nursemaid and perform these tasks with a meek countenance. Her penance would be the care of Isabella, Harriet, Thomas and little Martin but there would be more. After several days of waiting for her father's wrath to erupt Mary Ann began to wonder if, perhaps, his silence was crueller. She longed for some word, anything that might release all the pent up forces pulsing within the upstairs floor of the hotel where the family resided. But instead there was stony silence.

The girl Rebecca was the only exception to this cool indifference, but she was careful. She said nothing directly to Mary Ann. One evening, however, just before bed, the awkward servant girl came into the young woman's room and quickly laid a comb and a ribbon on her pillow. They were from the carpetbag Mary Ann had taken from her mother and given to Rebecca to pass on to Kinchela with the note, the day before she had slipped away. Somehow Rebecca had salvaged them. The two girls exchanged the briefest nod and then Rebecca left Mary

Ann to her bed. No sooner was the girl alone than she picked up the ribbon and began to weep. It was a mawkish, sentimental thing to do—the action of a girl from one of those books—but it gave Mary Ann some sort of release and she eventually fell asleep on top of her bedclothes.

When she woke the following morning, Mary Ann felt a little lighter. A few hours later, however, she was out on that dashed road again. Once more towards Parramatta in that coach, this time with her parents. She should have been married by now, enjoying the fresh pleasures of a good dress while sitting in a handsome gig with her new husband on their way to the races or some other fancy. Instead, here she was. Still Miss Gill. It also looked like Mary Ann had little choice but to give evidence against the man she had hoped to marry. The situation was sickening and, what was worse, it was in large part all James' doing.

The welcome Martin Gill received as he stepped through the doorway of the Parramatta Police Office on Friday, 26 May 1848 was a source of considerable surprise to both his daughter and his wife. Having been detained overnight in the very same station only a few days ago, both women assumed that Gill would receive a measure of cool contempt from the sergeant on duty. But instead, it was 'Mr Gill' this and 'Mr Gill' that. 'Allow us to find a seat for your wife' and 'Is that to your satisfaction, sir?' Gill was obviously enjoying himself and at the very least this allowed Margaret some respite from the grim mood that had descended upon their relations. She had decided it was in her family's best interests to back her husband, but she was not going to roll over easily. Gill had been a fool and she was not going to let him lord it over her, as he was wont to do.

Mary Ann, however, was completely taken aback by the behaviour of the policemen. Since she had been in James' company she had taken to looking at her father as she imagined that men of James' class looked at all ex-convicts—although James had not used this particular term nor schooled her in this matter. She couldn't make sense of what was going on. Were the policemen mocking her father perhaps? Was this a set-up before they pulled him down in a final humiliation? Whatever was going on, it soon became patently clear that she was not in favour. When the family arrived, two policemen came and stood at the desk in front of her, one with his arms folded tight across his chest. Both men sized her up and muttered under their breath before turning to her father. 'There you are then, Mr Gill,' the elder of the pair said breezily, 'I see you have brought the serpent's tooth with you.' Gill cast a cursory glance at his daughter and then nodded before pointing to the room off to the side. 'Would you like us in here, for the questions?' he asked. 'Quite so, Mr Gill, if you don't mind,' the podgy constable answered lightly, beckoning the family through.

Mary Ann was made to stand throughout the proceedings, which took the better part of the day. While her parents were served tea, she was deliberately ignored and given no option but to stand in silence. And that was not the end of it. While her mother's evidence had been reasonably straightforward and received without query or qualification, every sentence of Mary Ann's statement was subject to scrutiny. The recorder questioned the time of events, made her spell the names of each person and the places where things had occurred. He then went back and double-checked each fact. 'And Kinchela wasn't there when you got to Henry Webb's?' the balding policeman asked. Mary Ann shook her head. 'And then the next morning, when you went to the track, he weren't there neither?' he continued, squinting up at another policeman who suppressed a smirk as Mary Ann shook her head no.

This went on all afternoon, and neither parent came to Mary Ann's assistance. She was almost faint, but somehow she remained composed until it came time for her to read over her account before signing it. 'No,' her father insisted after she had looked over the written document, 'you must read it out to us, girl, so we are all satisfied with the truth.' He gestured to the policemen who were now leaning against the wall, each with their arms crossed. Mary Ann looked around desperately but her mother's gaze was fixed upon the floor. It took Mary Ann twenty horrendous minutes of starts and stops to read out the written account to her parents and the four policemen, and when she was finished she was most efficiently apprised of what a fool she had been.

But still her father was not done. Gill leant forward, 'No, girl, that is not the way it went,' he said, pulling her wrist up sharp while he gestured with his chin to the recorder. The policemen helped Martin Gill tear up the first of Mary Ann's evidence and then waited as the girl swallowed and started again. Once more she recounted the hateful events, this time altering things so that James appeared the protagonist, and she, significantly more modest. When Mary Ann had finished this second testimony, her father made her read the policeman's written account out loud again. Then he signalled to give the girl ink and pen with which to sign her name.

Mary Ann knew she was condemning Kinchela and the better part of her was aching with it, but there was now another part of her that wanted him to suffer. He had led her on, made her make a promise to him even after she had warned him about her father. She had gone out after him and trusted him, just as he had asked, not once but twice, and both times he had failed her. Now she would suffer shame—not only behind closed doors but also in court and in the papers. Where once she had hoped to be the envy of her friends now she would be reviled. Where she had wanted to prove her grandmother wrong now she would have to swallow her pride and think Ellen Hanley lucky to be free of such shame. Where she had planned to make a better life for herself now she would probably die a spinster. Worse still, a nursemaid to an old woman. And before then she would be confined to years of hard work and humiliation in her father's home.

Still she was torn. There would be no recovery from such a betrayal, as her father knew. This would spell the end for James and all she had dared to hope for even after she had returned home in the policeman's cart. But with her father bearing down upon her, it was impossible to think straight, let alone know her own mind. Once more, the fifteen-year-old girl began to sob and as she put her shaky signature to the hateful legal document a flurry of tears dropped onto the parchment leaving three inky blotches where they fell.

CHAPTER SEVEN

To Court

There were cows and sometimes even a few goats milling about the new Darlinghurst Court House. It didn't matter much to them that the building was a superb example of Greek Revival or that it housed the supreme court of the land. They were looking for respite from the ferocious winds that blew about Woolloomooloo Hill during the winter months, and the imposing Doric columns and masonry of the colony's first purpose-built courthouse offered refuge. It was just like the gospel parable, Lowe mused as he picked his way up the stairs, tapping his trusty crop against his thigh along the way. 'We are assigned the task of separating the guilty from the innocent, the sheep from the goats.'

While it was still being built in the early 1840s, the new court-house had been a site of churchly activities and numerous other celebrations. A few fairs had been set up there during that time and the earth outside the building had been quickly trampled flat by the colonists and their cows. Margaret and Martin Gill had been among those who had come to the new courthouse on one of those more joyous occasions. They had set up a stall at the Saint Patrick's Day ball that was hosted on these grounds when Mary Ann was no more than eight. Margaret could still remember the lanterns lighting up the sandstone edifice that night and how the building seemed to shimmer and float high above the town. Mary Ann had been with them that night, helping her father with refreshments. She had behaved so well that towards the end of the evening her father had taken the girl for a stroll among the stalls scattered about the fair. The girl had been mesmerised, Margaret remembered, as she watched the pair slowly weave their way through the crowd, with Martin pointing out things to his daughter that reminded him of home. After a time, father and daughter had stopped and leant against the court wall so they could watch five or six boys dancing to the pipes—their sharp kicks flouncing high into the air as the music grew wilder and faster.

They were happier times, then. That night it had been splendid to feel the green flowing through your veins. It was not, however, always so easy and some of the new Irish coming to the colony certainly made matters worse. Of these, it was generally agreed that the girls were by far the worst. Their filthy dress and strange talk seemed abhorrent to just about everyone and the colony was soon referring to them in a certain way. Margaret and Martin heard enough to decide it would be best to keep their own apart. Particularly Mary Ann. She was Irish, of course, just as her parents were, but she was growing up somewhere else now.

James Butler Kinchela had been at the ball that night in 1840, too, but only for half an hour or so, and all that time he had remained tucked inside his mother's tilbury, shaded from the falling cool and the cruel scrutiny of colonial eyes. It never paid to be seen looking poorly, his brother reminded him, especially not in town. 'There are too many who will take you down for your weakness,' he had cautioned. Nonetheless, Kinchela's mother had insisted that her two sons go and take a look. James had been cooped up in the house for more than two months, as she nursed him back to health after his shocking return from Adelaide.

By early March there had been signs of improvement but Anne Bourne had detected a cooling between her two sons, particularly since John had lost all the money he had borrowed from Mary's husband and James had come back from Adelaide with little to show for himself. They needed something to lift their spirits, she decided. 'A bit of dancing is not to be missed. But mind, you two,' she said, checking John's necktie as they stood at the threshold of Ormonde House. 'Be gentle with yourselves and go easy on the whiskey.'

In 1840, the Darlinghurst Court House had been no more than a façade emerging out of the great pit that the convicts had dug for its foundations. It looked, James thought, like an ancient ruin. 'Quite impressive,' John agreed as they sat in the confines of the family vehicle, looking out at the crowds threading their way through the darkening evening. Convicts had dug the guts of this building out of the earth, that was true, but it was said to be one of the first where there would be no chained men involved in the laying of the bricks. No wonder it was taking so long, James thought to himself. Although he also remembered his father's satisfaction that the time had come when the colony would finally be free of the shame of white slaves.

That night Kinchela had also seen the boys dancing to the pipes but, for him, the familiar strands of those well-known songs had caught him in the shadows of his gig and filled him with a strange jerky melancholy. Perhaps his brother felt the same, for after a time the elder boy turned his face to the side window and mumbled as much to himself as to his brother, 'We won't be lifting our heels tonight, J.B.,' before tapping the carriage door twice with his ring so the driver knew it was time to head for home.

About eight years had passed since then. Now, once more James was sitting in his mother's gig as it pushed up Oxford Street towards the courtrooms, although this time, his brother was elsewhere—preoccupied with certain affairs in the Orange district, no doubt. Winter was shaping up fast and the few trees that punctuated the distant paddocks had only a few leaves and most of those were already curled brown and ready to fall. James felt forlorn. He had read the papers: it was going to be a hard case. It was not going to be like his brother John and Major Mudie. The mood was different. Things were against him. He wasn't too sure about his lawyer either. Arthur Todd Holroyd was a smart man, but he would need to be formidable to take on Robert Lowe, Kinchela thought.

As Robert Lowe prepared his argument for *Regina v Kinchela* he found himself thinking back to the Shrigley abduction case from the 1820s. He had been a boy at the time but it had been impossible to live in England and not know something of it. Lowe had kept an interest in the events as a way of distracting himself from his gruelling life at Winchester College, where he was subject to incessant attacks from the older boys, who found his splayed hips, white wispy hair and tiny, flickering eyes detestable to say the least. What was crucial to that abduction case, Lowe recalled, was the way the girl had conducted herself. Certainly the accused, Edward Gibbon Wakefield, had been a villain and something of a dandy, too, but if the girl had been 'on-the-nose', the public would have turned on her.

Those proceedings had been carefully staged, he mused, and it was a tactic that ensured the case had been won in the press well before it even entered the court. It had all come down to questions of dress. Of this Lowe was certain. While Wakefield and his simpering brother had paraded the streets of Manchester in the latest styles from Paris, his victim, Ellen Turner, a fifteen-year-old schoolgirl and the daughter of one of England's wealthiest silk manufacturers, had been the very model of modesty. She had arrived at court on the first day of the trial dressed entirely in black with a thick veil obscuring her face. Indeed, the way the press wrote about it, there had been no flesh showing on the young woman at all, other than a sliver of skin on her wrists where her tailored gloves gave way to the cut of her dress. As she stepped from the carriage on the first day of the trial, Miss Turner had been escorted by her father, uncle and three servants. This party formed a barricade that made it impossible for the huge crowds that jostled about the carriage to catch more than a fleeting glimpse of the girl. The shock of the great outrage had confined Miss Turner's mother to her bed and news accounts repeatedly updated the public about the poor woman's failing condition. The combined effect was that Miss Turner rapidly became a most compelling figure of sympathy and mystique. Throughout the trial, Lowe recalled, Miss Turner remained veiled, which the judge accepted because of the girl's youth and evident distress. By the time it was her turn to take the witness box, three weeks had passed and the entire country was mad with fascination about the appearance of their heroine. Nor were they disappointed when Miss Turner finally took to the witness box and slowly lifted the dark netting to reveal a sweet, supple face with a most anguished expression.

As Miss Turner's star rose in the estimation of the public, Wakefield's plummeted and each day the offending dandy looked increasingly crestfallen. By the third day of the trial, he and his brother had given up their afternoon promenades through town and by the beginning of the second week the defendant exchanged his outlandish Paris fashion for more modest English attire. As the press became more vicious in their condemnation of Wakefield and his family, the defendant seemed to collapse altogether, and by the end of the third week Wakefield simply slouched in his chair, head buried in his hands. His guilt was a foregone conclusion, the press concurred. The only remaining question was whether or not he would swing. When the verdict came down, the general opinion among the press and public was that three years in Newgate Prison was exceedingly generous and perhaps they were right. In truth, Lowe was less interested in the sentence than the stage-craft of the Wakefield trial and he passed his remembrances on to his client. 'There are clues in this, Gill,' he said airily, 'so make sure your girl is dressed with discretion and that you come to court as a united but deeply slighted family of modest and honest means.' Gill understood exactly what was required and as Margaret was now the only one who spoke to the girl he passed this advice on to his wife, word for word.

A dress was organised for Mary Ann. This had been specially tailored for the occasion and was fashioned from a heavy dark blue silk with a thread of brown that gave only the subtlest of sheens. A veil was out of keeping, Margaret insisted, but a bonnet with a broad brim would serve the same purpose. Her costume included tight mustard-coloured gloves to match the ghastly bonnet ribbon that made her otherwise youthful skin appear sickly and sallow. The outfit was finished with a dark calico parasol, which Margaret instructed was only to be opened the moment she stepped out of the coach to enter the court. Mary Ann felt imprisoned in this dreadful garb and suffered even more when she thought of all the gay colours she had hoped to wear as the wife of a gentleman settler.

This was but one element in the production that the Gills orchestrated under the direction of Robert Lowe. Lowe was looking for the sort of spectacle that would keep him in the public eye and ensure that his name was in every paper and on the lips of every man with sufficient property qualifications to vote for him at the forthcoming election. He was keen to win the trust of the middling set, who might otherwise regard his cleverness with suspicion. Many would see this scandal as an insult to the colony and Lowe was determined to fashion events in a way that would make the girl the unfortunate victim of a careless wastrel.

If all went well he might even be able to suggest that the innocent creature was as vulnerable to the wanton whims of these settlers as the colony itself. 'Only decent men, such as those who do their duty as members of the jury today,' Lowe mused to himself as he began practising his opening address, 'might be brave enough to take a stand against those who have assumed the right to take whatever, whoever, whenever they wish.' The words slipped effortlessly into place as the great demagogue stood before his mirror, imagining himself coaxing the jury first into a state of righteous indignation and then agreeable compliance. 'Only sensible and solid men can resist those who think they have a right to rob not only a woman of her future and a family of their dearest prize,' and here he imagined himself pausing before the jury and fixing them with a look that would allow his words to assume their full potency, 'but also a respectable people of their hard-earned reputation.'

CHAPTER EIGHT

A Sporting Affair

Arthur Todd Holroyd was a man with many interests. As a young lad he had studied medicine and quickly became prominent in several of England's most respectable medical associations. By the age of twenty he had been made a member of the London Zoological Society and also married well. Upon settling into his London practice, however, he discovered that his prospects were less than he hoped. So Holroyd turned to the law and was called to the Bar at Lincoln's Inn. To temper the tedium of this period Holroyd undertook regular visits to Rome and Egypt, where he perfected his Italian and also became proficient in Arabic. These language skills assisted Holroyd during his tours to Sinai, Palestine and Syria, and before the age of thirty this promising son of a London merchant was celebrated as one of the very first Europeans to cross the scorching sands of Bayuda before arriving in Khartoum, just a few years after the town had become the capital of the Sudanese possessions in Egypt. The young explorer's writings about this desert crossing and the disease-ravaged Sudanese capital were of great interest to the Royal Geographical Society, who promptly elected him a fellow. But within a few months Holroyd was restless again. A year later he embarked upon a new adventure, travelling this time with his wife to the infant colony of New Zealand. Affable and exceptionally well-educated, Arthur Holroyd was no slouch. Indeed, with his flourishing sideburns and sharp blue eyes, he was a worthy opponent for the remarkable Robert Lowe.

Only Holroyd was off his game. Since arriving in New South Wales several years ago he had been making money but his heart was not in it. He had had a short stint at Kororareka in New Zealand en route to New South Wales, thinking he would make a name for himself in banking, there, but the place had been hateful. Holroyd had been mortified by the savagery he had seen unleashed upon the native women. On one occasion, the conduct of a ship of American and Scottish whalers had so horrified him that it had caused him to withdraw into a place within himself that even his wife had since been unable to reach. Holroyd was no stranger to violence or, indeed, to the squandering of life. He had certainly expressed himself most effectively on the matter of slavery in Sudan, but there was something about the behaviour of the whalers in that cloud-heavy part of the new world that continued to gnaw at him. The carnage they had wreaked looked to Holroyd as if some cruel child had taken paradise and sliced at it with a whip until it was shredded to pieces. Five years later and Arthur Todd Holroyd was still unable to shake off his disgust for humanity.

Still, here he was, set up in the tight little town of Sydney, intent upon building his legal practice and furthering his prospects and, who knows, if all went well in the forthcoming elections he might even run for a seat in the not-so-distant future. From his point of view, the Kinchela case looked clear enough. An easy win, in fact. Holroyd was reasonably familiar with the 1557 Act concerned with taking away 'maydens that be inheritors', otherwise known as *Phillip and Mary*, from which all laws pertaining to the crime of abduction had since derived. Even though such cases were no longer common in England, he had sat in on several trials. As he listened to his client recount the events associated with these recent charges, our man from Khartoum felt quite certain that the entire episode was little more than a comedy of errors. Indeed, he was confident he could restore not only common sense to the court but also his client's reputation.

Only, Holroyd did not know Sydney. He had been here less than four years and much of that time he had been so busy setting up his practice that he had not soaked up the tepid stench of the place nor scratched beneath its sandstone edifices. He had been relieved that the town was more settled than Kororareka. He was also curious about the native fauna. But other than that he was yet to engage. To him the town felt like an amateur, toy-kit London, with overweening pretensions and none of the grandeur of his hometown. The gaudy carriages inhabited by coarse businessmen and overdressed women were an anathema to his high-minded sensibilities and he found the meanness of even the better families intolerable. Holroyd could not take the place seriously. But, as others might have warned him had he condescended to seek their advice, such an attitude was likely to bring trouble. And probably sooner rather than later.

In the half-finished judicial chambers of the new courtroom, 37-year-old William Montagu Manning was finishing a pot of tea before putting on his robes for the day's hearings. He was quite a different fish from Holroyd and had quickly invested in his adopted home, partially because portions of the harbour reminded him of the coasts of his Devon childhood. He had been in the colony just over ten years and already had fingers in numerous pies. Quick as he could, Manning had bought up and brought in. He had land along the Lachlan and a good quantity of shares in a shipping venture. All the while Manning had also been working his way up the ladder of the local legal fraternity. He had been delighted to relieve the Chief Justice, Alfred Stephen, of his duties on the Supreme Court bench when the judge felt the need to do a stint of reading abroad. Not only was the invitation an excellent opportunity to demonstrate his legal intellect, but, as Manning's wife had recently died, it also afforded him a pleasant and productive distraction.

And so here they all were. The tenacious and terrifying radical, Robert Lowe, opposing the exotic and erudite world-traveller, Arthur Todd Holroyd, presided over by William Montagu Manning, the affluent and ambitious conservative with a taste for guns and hunting.

Supporting Lowe, although somewhat reluctantly, was the tall and handsome native-born lawyer, Bob Nichols. He was keen to strengthen his alliances and have a tilt at representing the Northumberland Boroughs in the forthcoming election because, even with his brother Charlie at the helm of *Bell's Sporting Life*, it was obvious to him that elected representation was the only way forward for the native-born of New South Wales.

Reporters from the various local papers were also in attendance. Well before the session started a few could be seen loitering about the court steps just out of the June drizzle, as they waited for the protagonists to arrive and looking, Kinchela thought as his gig pulled up, like a bunch of dogs waiting to be tossed a carcass. You could tell who, or rather what they were, by their dishevelled attire. Kinchela knew one of Charlie's mates from *Bell's*. They had drunk together down at Shaw's Racecourse and the two had a word together before the defendant stepped across the threshold into the courtroom.

Kinchela had equipped himself with a cane and was pleased to have it with him for it contained a secret compartment that promised some consolation during the long day that lay ahead. As his father had shown him years ago, the gold-plated lion's head that served as the hand grasp unscrewed to reveal, inside the wooden stick, a long, thin, cylindrical tube that could be filled with spirits. That morning Kinchela had poured a good drop of whiskey into it and the thought of it by his side armed him against what he knew would be a frosty courtroom. And so Kinchela entered the court and took his seat next to Holroyd, crossing his legs and tilting his chin at a slightly defiant angle as he thrummed the lion's head clasp of the cane with his fingers. He would show courage today, he thought, come what may.

There was something of a stir outside as the Gills drew up in their highly respectable carriage. Martin Gill was dressed in a tailored suit that sat unevenly upon his small frame despite its well-considered cut. 'Mr Kemp,' Gill said crisply as he tipped his top hat at the *Herald* court reporter he had visited in his office earlier in the week. Then Martin Gill took his wife's arm and assisted her from the carriage. Margaret appeared stone-faced in a suitably matronly dress of deep mauve. The couple stepped from their carriage and various reporters scurried about them. Of the young girl in question they got no more than a snatched glimpse of her mustard-coloured gloves and the sweep of a heavy dark dress as she alighted from the coach and made her way up the steps of the court, face perfectly obscured by her parasol.

Mary Ann stepped into the packed courtroom and then stopped in shock. Despite the fact that much of the interior was still unfinished, the public seating was filled to capacity in both the court and the gallery, and the room itself was bustling with a throng of people jostling against one another for seats and standing room. There were a number of knock-about Cabbagers who must have come for the entertainment, as well as several shopkeepers on familiar terms with her father. In the front row of the stalls there was also a collection of middle-aged women including Mrs Kelly who had a large bag on her lap from which she was eating her breakfast. Mary Ann spied her grandparents sitting quietly amidst the commotion. They shouldn't be here, she thought glumly, before she cast a hasty glance back to the gallery where she spotted several workers from the hotel, including one bumptious-looking boy who had been sacked by her father two weeks earlier. Was that Rebecca sitting with the boy, she wondered? Mary Ann could not quite tell but the court seemed to be buzzing like a nest of angry wasps.

The young woman followed her mother's cue and took her seat directly behind her father, who was sitting at the edge of the table occupied by Robert Lowe and Bob Nichols. Her legs trembled but she took pains to fold her hands in her lap and focus on those loathsome mustard gloves. Kinchela was nearby, Mary Ann sensed, but she did not dare to look his way in case their eyes met. Instead she stole a furtive glance at her father's legal team. Lowe was looking pleased with himself, deep in conversation with Mr Nichols. A little further off, sat Kinchela's counsel. He had rather commanding eyebrows, she thought, and looked as though he was cleaning something from his boot as he cast a casual eye over his papers.

The mood in the makeshift court seemed to swirl and pulse, with the crowd chattering among themselves as they occasionally pointed at both the parties. At last a court recorder made the call for the court to rise. Manning appeared, looking confident in his robes and taking his seat with obvious pleasure as the jury processed into their box.

And so we begin, Kinchela thought to himself, as he contemplated the rather ramshackle stage upon which this next act of his life was about to play. Although winter had made its presence felt outside the courtroom, the crush of all the people inside had already created considerable warmth and the air around him felt hot and heavy. Kinchela wondered how long it would be before the reporters tired of it all. And the girl, he wondered, how would she cope with all this? She had seemed such a lively thing during their encounters but there was no telling what had happened to her over the past weeks. He thought with some discomfort about her father and what she had said about him. The look in the man's eyes that morning at the racecourse. Those damn pistols and, most offensive of all, the way he had spat at his boot outside the court. No doubt he would have raised hell for Mary Ann, Kinchela realised, and was no doubt intent upon doing the same to him now.

Manning reminded the jurors that Kinchela was facing two charges of abduction according to the ancient legislation of 1557, which had been revised in 1828. One charge was concerned with the fact that the defendant had allegedly taken the girl from her parents without their consent, and the other that he had done this to a girl under the age of sixteen. No sooner had Manning finished than he gestured for Lowe to commence his opening address.

It was an extraordinary piece of work with more than a touch of melodrama to it. A number of jurors—among them several soap and candle merchants—nodded vigorously as Gill's lawyer described the cruel injury that had been inflicted upon familial fondness. Lowe roved and roamed, recounting the duties of fathers and the delights of daughters, his voice sometimes a whisper and other times lifting to a feverish pitch before Manning signalled for him to tone it down. All the while Sydney's wily Weathercock outlined the events associated with the case, how 'an intimacy had sprung up' between Mr Gill's daughter and the defendant while the latter had been staying in their hotel for several months. Clearly, several months too long, he added drolly, provoking a titter from the upstairs gallery. Calmly Lowe explained to the court what he assumed many already understood: that 'a woman's consent could not be proffered as defence' within the existing statutes. 'This did not have to be a situation in which any fraud or force was used,' Lowe explained, striving not to sound condescending. On the contrary. According to the law, it was 'enough for the man in question to have used no more than the ordinary blandishments of love to entice the girl away'. The point was 'not what the woman wanted,' he continued, 'and certainly not what motivated the man in question, but rather,' he said, taking several steps towards Martin and Margaret Gill, 'the *rights* of the parents. Like the good men of the jury,' Lowe continued, making a grandiose gesture towards his clients, 'these poor parents have responsibilities to their family and the colony. They also have valuable property—in the form of a daughter—and it is only reasonable for them to expect that the law should protect this.'

Martin Gill nodded energetically. Lowe then walked to the jury box and leant with one elbow against it as he cast a glance at the defendant. 'If such rights are not protected,' he continued, 'the colony might be caught forever where it is now, or even worse—go backwards,' he suggested. 'There are too many who show too little respect for honest men and decent laws,' the prosecutor insisted, before adding with a shrug, 'but, it is for the jury to decide and to do that they must listen carefully to the evidence and assess their decision according to the law. They *must* put aside all out-of-court rumours that have circulated about this case,' Lowe continued, 'and also strive to set aside their own sensibilities as fathers. Indeed, it is vital that they do so,' Lowe explained in a kindly tone, 'for only then can the court declare that they have honoured the great principle of British justice, the principle so dear to us all—the right to a fair trial.' There was a round of applause as Lowe returned to his seat dabbing the sweat from his brow and nodding modestly.

One by one the witnesses were called. The heavy-set Henry Webb said what needed to be said with both hands clasped upon the brim of his hat, every now and again casting a cautious eye at his wife who was vigilantly observing proceedings from the second row of seats. 'Yes sir,' Webb told Lowe. 'Kinchela did come back to my establishment that night,' he said earnestly. 'I told him straight up I didn't think it right, bringing the girl to my abode that way,' he gestured to where Mary Ann sat, with her bonnet lowered to shield herself. 'Go on,' Lowe gestured. 'Kinchela said I was not to fear, and that he intended to marry the girl in the morning at Parramatta.'

Holroyd stood up and asked Henry Webb to confirm that he was the manager of the Sportsman's Arms. 'A most appropriate location for this sporting affair, wouldn't you say, Mr Webb?' the counsel asked, clearly pleased with his wit, although the joke fell flat when the witness squinted and gave him a confused look. Holroyd coughed and turned to the jury referring to them as 'learned' men but in such a tone that several less-educated men shifted uncomfortably and wondered if they were being mocked for only signing the jury roll with an 'x'.

Eventually Holroyd began in earnest. 'Mr Webb,' he asked, 'did you actually *see* Mr Kinchela with Miss Gill?' Webb turned to his wife for guidance. 'I am not sure I understand you, sir,' he followed. 'Well,' Holroyd continued, 'Kinchela came to you after Miss Gill had left with her father, correct?' Webb nodded slowly. 'But was Kinchela there when Miss Gill came a-looking for him?' Webb blinked several times. 'I believe,' he paused, looking a little uncertain, 'that our servant girl mentioned a conversation in one of the private rooms upstairs between him and the girl, at least that is what my wife told me.' 'That may be, Mr Webb,' Holroyd quickly intervened, 'but you cannot refer to conversations with your wife in this matter. I am asking you and you alone—what did *you* see?' Holroyd waved an index finger at the witness. 'Mr Webb, you say you saw Miss Gill arrive and then leave with her father and that you also saw Mr Kinchela arrive, much later. So please, will you be kind enough to clarify for the court—did you yourself actually ever see the defendant with Miss Gill?' The court hushed as Henry Webb cast about for an answer. 'My wife . . .' he started but then trailed off as Holroyd shook his head, 'Well then,' he said as he looked about in desperation, 'I don't know how to go on.' Several jury members looked sympathetically at the witness and one man even tutted at Holroyd's condescending manner.

'Yes, Mr Webb,' Kinchela's counsel continued obliviously, 'but your wife is not in the witness box. It is your evidence we must hear, so please, tell us, did you or did you not see Kinchela with Miss Gill during the time that they were at your inn?' The man looked about the court desperately before finally shaking his head. 'No indeed, Mr Webb,' Holroyd said triumphantly. 'You also mentioned', he continued, 'that you and Kinchela shared some spirits in the early morning?'. Webb agreed more confidently. 'Is it not possible that you might not be able to recall the contents of your conversation?' Holroyd asked but allowed the question to fall unanswered, before giving a little cough and starting again. 'I feel compelled to ask, Mr Webb, what a creature of Miss Gill's age might have been doing in a place such as yours—let alone in Mrs Kelly's establishment,' he paused for effect before adding, 'something that surely makes us all shudder to imagine.' A murmur rippled through the court as Martin Gill shifted tetchily in his seat and cast a sour look at Kinchela.

'You may also recall, Mr Webb,' Holroyd continued, clearly intent upon using the witness to advance his own opinions, 'that after Miss Gill was retrieved by her father, she dared to leave her home a second time the following morning, and that she did so, she insists, at my client's request. But again,' Holroyd persisted, 'I must ask, is there *any* proof other than Miss Gill's word that the defendant intended to meet her at the place she said they were to meet?' Holroyd didn't wait for the witness to answer but walked to the jury box and locked eyes with the foreman. 'The answer, my friends, is no. No. In all likelihood there was no rendezvous, no licence, and, as this and other witnesses shall reveal, there is absolutely no evidence that this entire episode was anything but a fabrication of a young girl's fancy, which has been tortured into an abduction by a father who wishes to save her shame and who may also be intent,' Holroyd finished curtly, 'upon some other more nefarious motivation consistent with his past.'

Holroyd left the statement dangling and signalled to Webb that he was dismissed and could return to his seat. Kinchela's counsel did likewise, confused by the menacing buzz that had suddenly filled the room. The defendant nodded swiftly at his counsel and looked away. This might have been brilliant stagecraft for the London courts, but in Sydney it was horribly off-key and everyone but Holroyd knew it. The new chum lawyer had not only insulted the jury's intelligence and questioned the modesty of one of the colony's young women by making a reference to one of the less reputable local parlours, but gravest of all he had made an allusion to Gill's criminal past. Kinchela tapped at his cane. He was already longing for an interval, so he could draw succour from the liquid courage therein.

Martin Gill was next in the witness box. He fixed his collar and locked eyes with the prosecutor. 'Mr Gill,' Lowe began, 'can you tell us what happened on the night of 21 May this year?' 'Webb came to my hotel,' Gill started abruptly, 'and told us,' he said, gesturing to his wife, 'that my daughter was at his establishment. It was well past ten o'clock and we could not believe it. We went looking about the house, but when we found she wasn't there I went off with Webb, and found her at his establishment, and then I brought her back . . .' he finished, his jaw set tight.

'And did you give your daughter permission to embark upon this evening expedition?' Lowe asked innocently. 'Certainly not, sir,' Gill replied with great indignation, 'I would not,' he insisted. 'I would not want the girl out at night like that and,' he turned to the court, 'I would never give permission for her to meet with anyone at night, let alone the defendant,' his voice rose half an octave before he swallowed and made himself calm down. 'I very clearly told her before any of this had happened,' he said, tapping his index finger on the bench as he set Kinchela in his sights, 'that she was not to see him again.' Lowe thanked his client and returned to his seat.

Holroyd approached the witness with an air of mock confusion, asking in a playful tone if Kinchela had ever come to him and asked about Mary Ann. 'Had there, for example, been talk of marriage?' he asked coyly, to which Gill nodded. 'Indeed, sir, and I put an end to that quick smart.' Holroyd smiled sympathetically. 'So Kinchela did ask you for your daughter's hand, sir?' he continued, and again Gill nodded. 'Would you tell us why, sir,' Holroyd asked, stepping back to gesture at his client, 'you were so opposed to this match? Surely marriage to such a gentleman would afford certain advantages for your family and be of benefit to the girl?' The court sucked in its breath and hushed to hear the answer. All eyes were on Mary Ann's father, although one or two people turned to consider Kinchela, who was leaning forward, hoping to finally discover the source of Gill's fierce loathing. Martin Gill looked about the gallery and then with some energy pointed his finger at Kinchela ready to release a great spume of pent-up vitriol.

But before he could speak, Lowe objected. 'The answer to such a question, my lord, is of no relevance. We all know that not only do the statutes in these cases reject a woman's consent as a mitigating factor in this instance, but my client is at perfect liberty to take an active role in the choice of his daughter's future husband.' Manning nodded in agreement and Holroyd conceded the point with a flurry of one hand. Undeterred, Kinchela's counsel unleashed his next question in a staccato pace clearly designed to unnerve the witness, 'Mr Gill, did you or did you not throw two chairs and a table at your daughter when you visited her at her grandparents' farm a week before she left your home?'

Mary Ann heard her mother gasp. Up in the gallery the bumptious boy stood up and yelled out, 'He did, he would, he flogged me, too, that Gill, damn his eyes.' Manning quickly intervened, cautioning the court that 'Martin Gill has been judged by his peers and found to be a man of character. It is the defendant, Mr Kinchela, who is on trial here today.' He instructed primly, 'Mr Holroyd, you must contain yourself to the matters in this case.' Holroyd nodded but he was not done. 'My Lord,' he addressed the judge, 'we have heard various rumours outside this court, which we believe are relevant to this matter because they bestow upon the delicate creature at the heart of this unfortunate affair compelling reasons to quit her home. Reasons,' he flourished, 'which appealed to the protective spirit of my unfortunate client and compelled him to assist her escape physical peril.' Gill stared fiercely at Holroyd and Lowe stood to object until Manning waved him down and gestured at Kinchela's lawyer to proceed with due caution. 'I must ask you directly, sir,' Holroyd said looking squarely at Martin Gill, 'did you or did you not show your daughter your guns before threatening to murder her?'

The court exploded in an uproar and Lowe rose again, this time greatly peeved. 'I must insist that the court disallow this question and dismiss these insinuations as salacious gossip.' Manning did not need anyone telling him how to nip matters in the bud. He pointed for Lowe to sit and gave Holroyd a look. 'You may return to your seat now, Mr Gill, Mr Holroyd has quite exceeded his case here I am afraid. And may I extend my apologies for any offence experienced during this unusual line of questioning.' Gill sneered at Kinchela's counsel and fixed the back of his collar again before stepping from the witness box.

Next, Lowe sought the mother's story. By nature Margaret was ill-equipped to perform publicly but in her modest, almost monosyllabic, answers the court became perfectly apprised of her situation. She had 'detected an intimacy between the pair,' Margaret Gill explained, and had taken it upon herself to ask the gentleman to leave. 'And then, I saw him hanging about the hotel from time to time, and once he even passed by the front door. I wondered if something might be about,' she finished.

Kinchela had not mentioned this exchange and Holroyd felt wrong-footed. Normally he would have cast doubt upon this woman's morality as well as her maternal instinct, but he was getting a sense of the mood in the court and had a feeling it might be best to leave certain rocks unturned. He asked one or two questions of the witness and then quite abruptly signalled for her to return to her seat. He would need to put his finger on the pulse of whatever was going on before it was too late.

At last it was Mary Ann's turn to be called into the box, but it was now early afternoon and the court decided upon an adjournment for luncheon. Members of the public filed out to stretch their legs and the Gills followed Nichols so that they might take their luncheon with Lowe in his rooms. Wishing to enjoy what might be his last moments of freedom, Kinchela stepped out into the winter afternoon and strolled over to where his driver was resting with his horse and gig. The day had a good chill to it and despite the disappointments of the morning, Kinchela enjoyed the feeling of the frost pouring from his nostrils as well as the crunch of his boots over the last of the autumn leaves. He leant against the side of his mother's vehicle and unfastened the gold lion's head of his father's cane, taking a quick swig and then another as he surveyed the view from the top of the Woolloomooloo Hill.

CHAPTER NINE

The Gloves Come Off

While Robert Lowe regaled Martin Gill and his wife with stories in which his achievements featured prominently, Mary Ann sat in silence dreading all that was to follow. Although she was permitted to join the party for a simple luncheon, Margaret signalled to Lowe's servant that she was not to be given any of the treats introduced at the conclusion of their meal. When the time came for them to return to the courtroom, Martin and Margaret trailed off after Lowe, who sprang from the chair the moment the announcement came that proceedings were to resume. Bob Nichols lingered behind, and when the room was empty but for the serving girl he turned to Mary Ann. 'You must be hungry, child?' he asked gently. 'A shame not to eat when you will need your strength.' He placed a small tart inside the girl's gloved hand and Mary Ann gulped it down. It tasted like apricot jam and the sweetness of the thing was so stunning that she blinked several times before giving Nichols a grateful look. He returned a kind but brief smile and motioned that they must press forward.

Mary Ann stepped inside the courtroom, stealthily wiping any suggestion of crumbs from her dress as she tried to compose herself. Having watched all those clever men during the morning session she was now gripped with dread for all she was to face. They were going to delight in her shame, she realised, and feed her to a crowd hungry for her ruin.

No sooner did the court recorder announce that proceedings had resumed than her name was called. Margaret nudged her daughter, and next thing Mary Ann was walking down the aisle and up into the witness box. She closed the door to the box behind her and turned to face the court. Immediately she saw James Butler. Her heart lifted at the sight of him but then plunged suddenly as she considered all that was to unfold.

From the box she could see her father's lawyer watching her with detached amusement, like a cat, paw poised above its prey. That strange-looking man with darkened spectacles and a twitching gaze— he was hardly human, she thought, and certainly not at all manly like her James. She quickly became conscious of her parents, who were intently following her every move. Her father was sitting forward, eyes fixed on her, two fingers tapping his lips. Her mother, however, appeared distant as if she was somehow looking through her. Mary Ann looked over to James' lawyer, whose penetrating blue eyes were also sizing her up. Behind her parents she saw her grandparents, who seemed so humble and small against the elevated ceiling of the courtroom, she could not quite believe they were the same people she had known all her life. Mary Ann allowed her eyes to shift back to James and for no more than a few split seconds, if even that, the pair looked at one another and as they did so she realised—they were both done for.

Mary Ann moaned, to herself at first, but as the noise escaped out into the courtroom it was heard by some of the audience. A gaggle of rough-looking women in expensive dress seated near Mrs Kelly leant over the gallery barrier to get a closer look and some began to whisper excitedly to one another. A collective hush descended across the entire court and Mary Ann's breathing sharpened as her head began to spin. She held a gloved hand to a shaft of late afternoon sunlight and noticed she was shaking. She placed the same hand onto the ledge of the witness box and swallowed hard.

And then, the young witness began to weep. It was hardly audible at first, but the more Mary Ann tried to bury it the more violent her crying became. So she stood helplessly before the court, face obscured by her bonnet, slight body wracked with sobs. Kinchela shifted uncomfortably in his seat, as did Margaret Gill. For several moments the courtroom was held in the thrall of Mary Ann's heart-wrenching sounds until finally Manning coughed dryly and insisted that the witness compose herself. 'You must command your feelings in the court, Miss Gill,' he said, 'and perform the solemn duty required of you.' The witness sniffed and nodded. After wiping at her face with her gloved knuckles she took several deep breaths and finally lifted her face to the court.

Lowe approached the witness box and gently asked Mary Ann to recall the events leading up to her 'little elopement', taking pains to ask questions that required her to dwell upon the occasions when the lodger, James Butler Kinchela, had been most assertive in demonstrating his affections. He made Mary Ann recall the finer details of their exchange at the window; her meeting with Kinchela at Somerville's; the moment when Kinchela had burst into her bedroom at the Sportsman's Arms; the note Kinchela had written for her the following morning.

Lowe insisted that the note contained proof of the promise Kinchela had made three times earlier that he intended to wed her. 'Although, perhaps,' the wily lawyer paused, 'we need to consider if the defendant was using this promise to conceal a more vile purpose? The evidence suggests that it is entirely possible,' he continued brusquely, 'that Mr Kinchela sought to trick Miss Gill into thinking he wanted to wed her, when he had no intention of so doing. You see,' Lowe said, as Mary Ann shook her head, 'once the defendant had been removed from the family's hotel by the mother, he took matters into his own hands because, like many of his sort, he considered himself above the law and had little regard for my client's paternal authority.'

Mary Ann stood frozen by the horror of it. Lowe stepped back from the witness and stifled a smug smile. Then he turned to the jury and with great solemnity reminded them that as both fathers and men of the colony it was their responsibility to determine if the evidence was sufficient to secure a conviction. 'Without a marriage licence, we can only conclude that the defendant had lured Miss Gill from her home with the sole objective of seducing her.' This roused yet another ripple of titillation and several newspaper reporters wrote furiously in their notebooks. 'If that is the case,' Lowe continued with a grave expression, 'the girl is indeed most fortunate that her father's energetic devotion has protected her from such an eternal shame.'

No sooner had Lowe returned to his seat than Kinchela's counsel strode towards the witness box. He would need to strike hard and fast if he was to counteract the prosecutor's unpalatable suggestions. Holroyd did so by asking the witness to repeat her previous account word for word and as she did so, stopped to focus upon different episodes, beginning with Mary Ann's shocking presence in Mrs Kelly's front parlour. 'How is it,' he asked, 'that my client was not at the agreed destination when you first arrived there, Miss Gill, and why do you think he was also not at the Sportsman's Arms when you arrived there?' Mary Ann shook her head. It was a question for which she still had no answer and it still stung. 'Perhaps,' Holroyd began, 'we might entertain the possibility that you simply knew where my client would be and had the cunning to precede him to each destination so that when he arrived you would be there waiting for him?' Mary Ann shook her head vigorously. 'No, sir,' she said firmly. 'Mr Kinchela had given me clear instructions, and I followed these on each occasion. He promised to meet me, and,' she stopped, feeling breathless, 'he made me promise to meet him. Twice.'

Holroyd shrugged doubtfully and asked Mary Ann to recount her voyage to Cutt's the following morning, 'when you once more decided to quit your father's home without his permission'. Mary Ann blushed and recounted how Somerville 'knew where to take me'. 'And then, Miss Gill,' Holroyd asked, 'when Mr Kinchela was not where he said he would be again, you say Somerville came back with a letter?' Mary Ann gulped. She was still incensed by these events and wanted James to understand what he had done, but, when she looked at him, Kinchela's head was bowed.

Holroyd pushed on. 'Miss Gill, will you tell the court how you came to leave Mrs Beaton's Inn and find yourself in the hands of Police Constable John Ryan?' Mary Ann shook her head; she had no desire to recount how she had tried to escape from the young policeman. But Holroyd dragged it from her phrase by phrase and in such a way that prompted one of the Cabbagers to call out, 'Bet she could outrun you, your honour,' which provoked a flurry of hooting from the gallery.

Holroyd paced the court, tapping the side of his nose with his index finger as he waited for the court's full attention. Eventually he turned to the witness, 'Tell me, Miss Gill,' he said, 'have you not stated out of court that it was the ill-usage you received from your father that compelled you to leave his house?' Lowe leapt from his chair again, but before he could speak, Holroyd pushed on, all the while fixing the witness with his fierce blue eyes. 'In truth, girl, tell the court, was it not this, rather than my client, that made you quit your father's home?'

Mary Ann winced to think of the consequences, but in the quick seconds that ensued, she could also see there might be a chance for James in this. She stood, dead still, heart pulsing, unable to form words, wanting desperately to say something that might change everything for the better. She looked at her parents. Her father glowered at her and she bit her lip. Lowe strode to the judge's bench. 'This, your honour,' he insisted, 'is the same petty blow Mr Holroyd attempted this morning.' He turned to the jury, 'and it cannot be allowed.' Manning was peeved by Lowe's interjection. He instructed the witness to return to her seat which Mary Ann did, noticing that her skirts brushed past Kinchela as she stepped through the tables to her chair. Her mother cast a sideways glance at her, but Mary Ann lowered her head and returned her gaze to her gloves.

It was now well past eight o'clock in the evening and one or two of the jurors were checking their pocket watches and looking at the door. They were getting to the end of this, surely. Holroyd read the mood: he must deliver several rapid but lethal blows, he realised. This was his moment and there was no chance for Lowe to upstage him. 'Men of the jury,' he began, taking a sure stride towards the tired looking tanners and factory bosses in the box, 'surely you would agree that this young woman has demonstrated a determination to get married that was not entirely, or perhaps even slightly, matched by the object of her affection?' His voice was thick with syrup. 'I ask you to consider if you have at your disposal any facts that confirm that Mr Kinchela even encouraged the girl to leave her home at all? Facts, I must hurry to qualify, that are not dependent upon the word and whims of a young girl, who like many of her age is highly susceptible to all sorts of imaginings and romantic yearnings?'

He smiled sadly at Mary Ann and shook his head. 'Is it not clear,' he sighed, 'that the poor child was desperately in love with Mr Kinchela and that she had, in fact, run all over town after him. Could this unfortunate young gentleman be so deficient in gallantry that he had any choice but to be chained hand and glove to her, particularly,' he coughed and raised his eyebrows, 'once she had recounted her unfortunate domestic circumstances?' He fixed the jury with a solemn expression, 'Yes, certainly, it is natural for a woman in her situation to strain every nerve to shield herself from blame so that she might regain her position one day. We understand her need to do so. But,' he paused to consider Kinchela who was now looking quite withdrawn, 'to incriminate my unfortunate client,' he said shaking his head, 'surely a young girl's folly is too great a burden for even this good gentleman to bear?' There was a swell of murmurs about the court as Holroyd nodded politely to the jury and returned to his seat.

Manning looked as if he had been waiting all day to hear the opulent timbre of his voice resound from the Supreme Court bench. He delivered his summary recapitulating the evidence before severely rebuking Mr Kinchela and his counsel for what he considered a most 'unmanly line of defence, particularly', he added, 'their attempt to impugn the reputation of the girl and her father.'

'To secure a guilty verdict,' Manning continued, 'the jury must agree that they have received sufficient proof to convince them that the defendant had taken the girl, or encouraged her to leave her family home. It makes no difference,' he insisted rather primly, 'as to the defendant's motives—whether he wished to seduce or marry the girl or rescue her . . . the jury need only ascertain that this departure from her family home occurred without her parents' consent. If they were confident that the proceedings of the day had furnished them with compelling evidence of these points, then,' said Manning, 'they must return a guilty verdict.'

It took the good men of New South Wales less than fifteen minutes to drink from the clear waters that Manning had led them to. They shuffled back into court bleary-eyed and hungry, for it was now well past their supper time. The foreman was already dressed in his street jacket when he stood and told the court, quite matter-of-factly, that James Butler Kinchela had been found guilty of two separate charges of abduction. Bail had also been refused.

The room erupted into life. Justice had been served and it was time to go home. Martin Gill leapt up and began boisterously shaking hands with everyone in the courtroom, including Robert Lowe who found the physical contact a little coarse. But, because the great man was rather pleased with himself, he indulged his client on this occasion. Holroyd scratched his whiskers and looked about the court with an expression of displeasure. He turned to Kinchela who nodded cordially at him. He was clutching his cane and looking about with a fairly grim countenance as two wardens approached him with a set of hand irons. He would have to wait in remand until his sentence was pronounced. That could take days, even weeks, particularly if they decided to mount an appeal.

Gill watched out of the corner of his eye as the wardens cuffed Kinchela and confiscated his cane. He was crowing so loudly and patting his wife on the back with such vigour that Margaret found it necessary to step away. She turned to find her father and Mary Riley who were standing rather awkwardly at the back of the court, looking at their granddaughter, their heads together in quiet talk.

Mary Ann had not moved in her seat, except that she had pulled off one of her gloves and thrown it at her feet where it lay with those mustard-coloured fingers thrusting this way and that. She was sitting as she had been throughout the day, sullen in shame, but now in the darkened courtroom something else seemed to possess her. She had known the moment was likely to come, but to see James in cuffs, his step heavy as he moved past her. It was truly awful. She wanted to look up and catch his eye, but her gaze stuck to the floor. Nonetheless, something was stirring within.

She was incensed. No, more than that. She felt guilty, yes that was true, but she was also deeply furious. Flaming with it. She was bitter about the hold her father had over her and the cruel humiliation he had wrought upon them. She was also disgusted with her mother for allowing this, but most of all she was angry with herself. She should have been smarter, like the girl in the play at the Royal Vic she had seen as a child. She should have known how to charm everyone to her cause. But, Mary Ann thought with a steely fierceness, she would find a way to turn things around. She didn't know how, yet, but she would. She tugged at the fingers of her second glove and as she did so her thoughts turned to the boy in the gallery and Rebecca seated next to him. Perhaps, she thought, remembering the ribbon and comb the girl had left on her pillow. Perhaps Rebecca would help her. Then she yanked at the fingers of the second glove and succeeded, after some effort, in removing the second one from her hand too.

'Mind her,' Mary Riley whispered when Margaret joined the elderly couple by the door. The two women looked in Mary Ann's direction. 'You would be wrong to think your troubles are finished there.' Margaret watched her daughter and, for a moment, considered Kinchela. Yes, she had never liked him that was true. He was only a few years younger than her own husband, and not right for Mary Ann, but she had not wished this upon him. Yet again, her husband had taken it too far.

There was something bad in all of this. Margaret tried to imagine what it might be like to act as her daughter had. Was it wilfulness or something else, she wondered, as she began to feel a universe of distance unfurling between herself and her eldest child. Margaret had a feeling she had lost her daughter, but to what, or rather to whom? The very sort of man who had got her locked up in Dublin when she was about the same age. The sort she had worked for all her life until she met her husband. The mother of six paused and registered her own sinking grief. I am to blame for my part in this, Margaret admitted, looking at her daughter sitting alone in the dark of the court. What had made Mary Ann bring the world upon herself like this? she sighed. Margaret didn't know the answer, but she had a feeling, like Mary Riley, that there was more trouble to come.

CHAPTER TEN

The Thoughtless and the Giddy

Eighteen forty-eight was a honey-fall for the newspapermen of New South Wales. If 1847 had been something of a slow year and the year before that duller than flies on a wall, 1848 was a great outpouring of gore and glory for which many gentlemen of the colonial press were ill-prepared. How could they not be? A number of papers had only been around for a few years, if that, and had been put together by men on their tea breaks or in-between jobs, often with more opinion than experience. In their desire to satiate the public's growing appetite for remarkable events and astounding personalities, several editors had succumbed to rather vicious partialities and as the date of the election for the Legislative Council drew closer, the colony seemed to grind into life, like a giant print machine, chugging and wheezing, spinning and spitting with all sorts of insults and innuendoes.

Unpleasant personal attacks were fast becoming the order of the day, particularly when it came to the various candidates running for the two Sydney seats. Within town there were now approximately 4000 property owners with sufficient qualification to cast a vote, and the majority of these were self-made entrepreneurs and emancipists with little regard for the settler set. Already there was greater representation in New South Wales than England and certainly more than there had been in France until the recent winter of discontent. As May and then June wore on, it began to look more and more likely that the new 'respectable' working men of New South Wales were of sufficient number to put at least one of their people in the parliament. And if that happened, the old guard grumbled, heaven help the colony.

News of European unrest, particularly in Paris, seemed to add further fuel to the fire. In France the new regime had given 'the people' the vote but no one really knew what the Second Republic was going to do with nine million votes. The mood was uncertain. There were still well over 15,000 people out of work in Paris and the majority of these were disillusioned with the recent revolution. In June a 'vile mob' of empty-bellied men and women tore through the government defences and into the National Assembly where they demanded yet another new government. No wonder that the National Guard now marched the streets with their bayonets at the ready.

In Sydney both the conservatives and their counterparts were invoking Paris—either to educate electors about the evils of unrest, or to insist that the oppressors' yoke of iron must be broken. Tempers were fractious, and all sorts lined up to crow in the streets and squares, only to find their self-aggrandisement cut to size with the bluntest of colonial slights. Such was the wild talk and high fancy that several editors had taken it upon themselves to salt the soup by following the British style of pouring scorn upon the entire notion of political representation. The forthcoming election was entirely preposterous to Charlie Nichols, chief editor of *Bell's Sporting Life* and brother to Bob Nichols. Cheeky Charlie liked to think he was writing for the most *manly* of colonists—those with an appreciation for good play and fair sport—who also knew how to enjoy a droll aside over a bottle of something strong. He used his columns in *Bell's* to convey his firm belief that the colony was best off in the hands of men of substance, not the shopkeepers and candlestick makers who were bounding about town daring to question the governor in a most impudent manner.

Men from the good end of town were likely to lay the blame for this dangerous new mood on the insolvent soldiers and failed farmers, upstart shopkeepers and factory foremen, who had arrived *en masse* in the colony over the last ten years as 'bounty migrants'. These sort were only slightly better, in the settlers' opinion, than the convicts who had come before them. Even worse were some of the mad ideas the bounty migrants had been spreading about town like a contagious rash. From what the settlers had seen thus far, most of these new men could hardly manage their own affairs let alone care for their kith and kin. Parkes, for example, had been begging favours since he had arrived and there were rumours that his shop was so steeped in debt it would not make it over the threshold of the new year. As for those who thought they could scrape a living from the papers, they were surely lost to folly but would no doubt make a wild noise as they went down. Heaven tremble to think how such men might handle greater representation if they got it. For a long time the whole thing had been nothing more than a joke but it was rapidly becoming apparent that Parkes and his associates were growing in number and influence.

While several papers took the settlers' side, there were almost as many that went in to bat for the middling set. After all, this was where most of the newspapermen had come from and certainly where, in their opinion, the colony's future lay. There was general consensus among a number of newspapers that New South Wales would be stymied as long as the settlers kept their stranglehold. This was something even the wayward Cabbagers and sullen currency lads acknowledged, although few were prepared to get in a pickle about it. Why would they, when so few had the vote to make it worth their effort? Even though all a man now needed to have his say at the polls was £200 in property or £20 in rental—this was still beyond most of these lads. So, it was up to the new men of property—regardless of how badly their pockets were patched—to ensure that liberty was wrested from the agricultural oligarchs. Certainly, this was where the momentum lay for Parkes and his 'committee of men' who were determined to push things as far as they could, particularly now they had Robert Lowe leading the charge, splendid in his florid waistcoat and flamboyant pinstripe suit, his great legal gown flowing behind him—that famous riding crop ever at the ready.

Among Parkes' like-minded associates were the editors of three local papers who shared between them an uncertain readership that required careful courtship. There was the recent Roman Catholic convert, Edward Hawkesley, who edited a relatively new paper called *The Sydney Chronicle* that spoke to the growing body of radicalised Irish poor who had arrived in the last ten years fleeing the Great Hunger. There was also a cabinetmaker named Benjamin Sutherland who edited *The Sydney Guardian*, and the young and rather dour Angus Mackay, who had grown up in Sydney after emigrating with his family from Aberdeen when he was no more than three years old. He had recently assumed the reins of Robert Lowe's highbrow weekly, *The Atlas*, and was very keen to make his mark. Indeed, they were all men in a hurry. Men who wanted to see things done better and who considered it their right, indeed their duty, to use their papers to herald in a new and fairer world.

If the settlers' papers grew ever more cruel in their references to Robert Lowe's 'ferrety, microscopic eyes', 'splayed hips' and 'dubious gender', the other news-sheets were expending considerable energy deriding William Charles Wentworth, who they considered the ultimate colonial turncoat. Their columns railed about the way their one-time hero had championed the native-born and emancipists but only until he had planted his posterior upon a parliamentary seat. As soon as he had got comfortable, they sneered, Wentworth had hoisted up the drawbridge and left ordinary men to fend for themselves. 'Self, self, self,' they fumed. Wentworth was only for himself. He didn't know who he was. Except that he chose not to acknowledge those who were, in fact, his own.

In this vicious tug of war only the rising colossus of *The Sydney Morning Herald* claimed impartiality and 'wholesome restraint'. Within their lower George Street offices there were all sorts of commotions taking place but the two young ambitious Englishmen in charge, Charles Kemp and his mate John Fairfax, kept at it, determined to impose their professional expertise upon the colonial world. After taking the helm, they had made a slow but solid start, and within a few short years had become extraordinarily successful. While other papers flashed and fumed and quickly died away, Kemp and Fairfax navigated all manner of colonial battlegrounds, all the while taking pains to accumulate the best machinery and talent. They were now the most circulated daily among both the settlers and their adversaries and by far the most influential of the papers in the colony.

It was *The Herald* where Martin Gill preferred to place his advertisements but he also tried to keep abreast of the other local press, just in case. While Gill was still riding high from his victory against Kinchela in the Supreme Court he also knew he only had a sliver of time with which to capitalise upon his position. He needed to make the most of the coming election season. He had played close to the wind the last time and after seeing what the mobs had done to the Donnybrook when he covered it with Wentworth blue in 1843, he thought better of getting too close to the action this time round.

From what he could pick up from his various associates, there was growing concern about the market and one or two banks. He had heard certain men were in the habit of buying whole cargos of tea and sugar and keeping them in storage until they could sell them at grossly inflated prices. The shifting mood and volatile trading was creating havoc for many of the middling sort and there were also stories coming in from the Monaro and further north about how the drought was taking a toll. Even the extraordinary entrepreneur Ben Boyd was coming unstuck, Gill had heard, and if he fell he would take at least one of the banks and probably a good number of investors, too. Gill wanted to sniff things out for a bit. Elections could be lucrative but they could also run up costs. It was all about getting a sense of which way the mood was turning and to do that he needed to do as other influential colonists did: watch the papers closely.

This was how Gill came up with the idea of making his daughter read the news-sheets to him each morning. She had done this from time to time ever since she began attending the school and was capable of stringing the words into sentences that flowed calmly and cleverly together. The girl's reading was now more fluent than his own cumbersome attempts, which still had him pushing his finger along the page. Better than her mother's, too, for while Margaret could read faster than her husband, she still stumbled over certain words and would not force herself over the rest of the sentence for fear of being caught mouthing the difficult words out loud. By her fourth season at school, Mary Ann had drafted a number of family advertisements. At first she wrote down what her parents concocted, but after a while the girl would come to them with her notions and they would simply add the various stock they wanted mentioned. 'Don't forget the turtle soup, girl,' her mother had added more than once, for she was sure that was why a number of settlers favoured their establishment, that, of course, and their famous pastries.

Gill was determined that this would be part of the girl's penance. Mary Ann was to wake at dawn each morning and collect the papers from the back steps of the hotel. Then she would prepare her father's breakfast in the kitchen downstairs before the staff arrived and bring it to his private quarters. She would take her place at the fire behind her father's chair and read the election news and other important stories of the day. Mostly it was *The Sydney Morning Herald*, but on Thursdays and Saturdays there were other papers like *The Sydney Chronicle* and *The Australian Journal* and once a week she also had the moralising *Atlas* as well as *Bell's* more racy prose. It was her mother who explained what was required and instructed her daughter to avoid any columns concerning what were now described as 'recent events'. 'Keep away from the court pages and contain yourself to the election,' she advised, 'and don't speak unless you are asked a question directly.' Mary Ann nodded. She had no intention of doing otherwise and was already filled with dread at the prospect of being alone with her father. But as far as Gill was concerned he had well and truly won the war with his daughter and was now prepared to play the benevolent patriarch. Never again would he trust his daughter; never again would she be taken into his favour, but he had resumed his position in the eyes of the court and the colony. From now on he would keep her on a tight rein and all the while content himself with the knowledge that if he felt the need to reassert himself he would have no qualms about doing so.

Gill had been having doubts about his legal counsel's political partialities and had declined the opportunity to let Parkes and his men hold one of their campaign meetings at his hotel, particularly after he heard that Lowe was being described as a 'radical of the deepest dye'. He was not prepared to show himself yet. He had not yet quite decided who he liked, but had a feeling that particular campaign might be more trouble than they were worth. Some of those men were even bold enough to be talking about universal suffrage. Martin Gill had earned his vote fair and square thanks to his own hard-earned money and he didn't want to share that right with men who couldn't manage their own affairs. On top of this, Gill had also received a bill for legal costs from Lowe and almost choked on his lunch when he saw the final sum. The cost of clearing his own name and tarnishing that of his foe was more than the quarter year's rent on Pitt Street. He would need a pretty windfall over the election season to pay for that without feeling it.

As Mary Ann read to her father each morning, she was drawing her own, rather different conclusions. From what she could glean, far from weakening the so-called 'Settler's Curse', the incessant stream of vitriol launched at Robert Lowe only added further fuel to the furious zeal of her father's legal counsel. What her father didn't know, because she followed her mother's instructions and avoided reading the court pages to her father, was that Lowe was also involved in another abduction case that was running neck-to-neck with the Kinchela trial. Together the two scandals were putting Lowe right where he wanted to be—front and centre in the legal columns of the papers as well as those devoted to the election. Not only were Lowe and Holroyd still locking horns over Kinchela, a point of which her father was well aware given the hefty retainer he was paying to fight the appeal, but Sydney's so-called Whimster was also locked in combat over the abduction case involving 'the mature-looking' Mary Ann Challenger, who had succeeded in her marital ambitions where Mary Ann Gill had so sorely failed. In both instances Lowe was exaggerating the part of the wounded parents and vigorously rounding on the suitors in question. Mary Ann could not glance at the associated columns without grinding her teeth. And yet, each day after she had finished reading to her father, she would return to the papers and pore over the associated columns.

From the few occasions when Mary Ann had dared to step into the town's streets she had quickly ascertained the extent to which her so-called 'Parramatta Romance' had become common knowledge throughout Sydney. There had been sideways glances and hissed whispers in her direction. She was no longer invited to visit any of the families she had known as a child and had not seen a single school friend since the week before her failed elopement. After several weeks of cool rebuffs she gleaned how things stood beyond her own home and was actually relieved to obey her parents' strict instructions and remain indoors.

There were, however, numerous other papers that Mary Ann did not know about and which were also delighting in the details of her recent amorous activities. Among these were country news-sheets from other colonies that obtained their stories from Kemp and Fairfax and rewrote them according to their own inclinations before circulating them to the Maitland and Bathurst districts as well as Port Phillip and Adelaide. Other papers went to Hobart and Launceston and even one or two to the new towns in New Zealand—as well as up to Moreton Bay, where those who knew the Kinchela name were keeping up-to-date with legal proceedings. The fact that Mary Ann never knew when the story would crop up added to the nastiness of the whole affair. Nonetheless, the columns did furnish her with information about James Butler, who she learnt was being remanded in the relatively new goal that stood directly behind the Darlinghurst Court House.

Thirty thousand tons of sandstone had been quarried for the massive walls that now surrounded the new goal, which had been strategically positioned at one of the highest points of the town. The decision had been made to situate the gaol up there around the time that J.T. Bigge, a royal commissioner, visited the colony to inspect conditions in the second decade of the new century. Bigge had been appalled by the latitude of life under Governor Lachlan Macquarie, particularly the freedoms enjoyed by convicts in Hyde Park Barracks. He thought even less of the hulk out in the harbour where the governor had been compelled to send second offenders. Bigge wanted a statement that would remind the people they were living in a penal colony and when Governor Ralph Darling arrived in 1824 he was told to get on with building the new prison immediately.

The walls were built first—more than twenty feet high and two feet thick—stacked high with sandstone bricks, each of which had been carved with a darg by a convict intent upon keeping a tally of his work. Such was the scale of this imposing barrier that the gaol could be seen from just about anywhere in town. It was said that when an execution took place on the stage built high above the Forbes Street entrance, parents would lift their children onto their shoulders so that they could see the latest felon squirm and writhe at the end of the rope.

Such public executions were common in Sydney at that time. Indeed, in 1844, over ten thousand locals had made their way through the Hyde Park Racecourse up to the new gaol to watch the hanging of John Knatchbull, a client of Robert Lowe's who had used a tomahawk to smash in the head of a young widow he had tried to rob. After the trial Lowe adopted the widow's two children in penance, some said, for having defended such a violent wretch. But even though Knatchbull was greatly reviled, those who went to watch him swing that day received little satisfaction from his execution, for Alex Green—the town 'scourger' and hangman—made a horrendous mess of it, as usual. So hopeless was the town hangman at his trade that many said it was little surprise that he was covered in scars—including one large, rather thick white line that ran down the side of his face where a prisoner had come at him with an axe. Green had a reputation for being a simpleton who frequently miscalculated the length of the rope needed to hang a condemned man. Somehow the threat of this incompetent hangman added to the gaol's foreboding presence and this vast building presided over the town with a spirit of gloom quite at odds with the population's increasing determination to progress beyond its penal origins.

Mary Ann hoped for James' sake that the interior of Darlinghurst Gaol was less grim than its exterior. She had heard the current warden was in the habit of extending certain leniencies to those who had the money to pay for them, and she wondered if Kinchela would be reading the local news-sheets and if so, what he would make of them. From her own survey of this material she had gleaned that the public unanimously considered Mary Ann Challenger's groom more honourable than Kinchela. Indeed, several papers were not beyond suggesting that Mary Ann Gill's suitor had been bent upon her seduction from the beginning. It grieved the young woman to realise that her private life had become a platform upon which all sorts of opinionated strangers suddenly felt compelled to pontificate about the modesty of colonial women and the pressing issue of marriage.

Of these, by far the worst was Angus Mackay in *The Atlas* who insisted that the two recent abduction cases were particularly noteworthy for the way they raised important questions about the age of consent. Indeed, the errant conduct of these 'two female children', he opined, clearly confirmed that sixteen was far too young for a woman to exercise choice when it came to her marital future. The legal fraternity must give proper consideration to raising the age of consent to eighteen, the ambitious editor demanded, for 'at eighteen a woman is in possession of some common sense, while those of sixteen are clearly too thoughtless, giddy and immature to guide themselves through life without being enticed away by the most worthless individuals.'

'Thoughtless and giddy indeed,' Mary Ann fumed as she slammed shut *The Atlas*. What would James make of the insults, she wondered, and the way his name had been all but destroyed? And what of her sixteenth birthday, due to occur a month to the day of their failed elopement and just as the governor dissolved the Legislative Council in preparation for the forthcoming elections? Sure, her birthday would be forgotten and what with the great nonsense of the election Kinchela would also be left to rot in gaol. With all their electioneering, the great men of town would have no time for his appeal, she thought bitterly.

Did Mary Ann entertain secret hopes about the gifts she might receive on the occasion of her sixteenth birthday? An embroidered fan, a leather book? Perhaps some fabric flowers for her best bonnet or a new cameo brooch? Of course, she received nothing from the man Angus Mackay so energetically condemned as one of the colony's most 'needy adventurers'. Nor from her parents. Instead, on 21 June 1848 Mary Ann found herself confined to her role as family nursemaid, surrounded by her father's menacing silence as well as the hateful opinions of all those newspapers. Of the many and varied insinuations and assumptions she read, Mackay had released one arrow that dug deepest. It nagged at Mary Ann such that it was impossible for her to avoid.

They could have waited. One month later and she would have been sixteen and out of her father's hands. Legally, he would have had less say in what she did, where she went and with whom. She had not known this, but surely James had. Both his father and brother were men of the law. Why hadn't he just steadied the matter and waited a few more weeks until she was of age?

One morning while her father was enjoying a breakfast of millet cakes and hot tea, and she was scanning the columns for the latest information from Europe, it dawned on Mary Ann that in her desperation to be done with her father she may have forced Kinchela's hand. Perhaps his counsel had been correct and James was only wanting to rescue her from her father while she had tried to ensnare him 'hand in glove'. Now, however, James was in gaol and she was confined to the family home. Their fate reminded Mary Ann of one of the old *tochmarca* tales her grandfather used to recount from time to time as a warning to those who broke with the way things were meant to be. There was one in particular, which McCormick would take to explaining before Easter most years because it was at this time, he would start, particularly in the country parts, that it was an Irish custom for couples who could not get permission from their families to take it upon themselves to get married in their own way. Once there had been many violent abductions in those parts and some couples would work hard to make sure their elopement looked like one of those. During Lenten tide it was common enough for a gang to suddenly appear at a girl's house—often in the middle of the night. They would pull the girl out of her bed and then throw her across a horse that was already mounted by her future husband. But as well as those violent kidnappings there were also romances. Mary Riley had been a small girl when she had seen at least five couples, all on horseback, with the bride set at the front of the horse, galloping through the village on their way to a local priest who was known to wed such couples for a 'dacant' price.

While some in the villages loved these runaway romances, most did not, and the ancient *tochmarca* tales were told to put a stop to such nonsense. There was one such story that might have gone back to the old folk, McCormick thought, and which Mary Ann had been thinking over since she had been confined to the upper storey of the Pitt Street hotel. It concerned a woman who had by way of a dowry no more than her own personal accomplishments and a fine gold gown. Her beauty, however, was renowned and she drove one particularly ferocious warrior so mad with love that he travelled hundreds of miles just to look upon her. When he could no longer help himself, so the story went, the young warrior slipped back into the royal court belonging to the girl's father, hoping to make the beautiful girl fall in love and marry him. But the woman was a second daughter and in possession of so small a dowry that even though she did fall in love with the warrior, she had no choice but to reject his proposal. Days later the man broke into the grand house belonging to the woman's father. In a frenzy of passion he murdered the girl's brothers and then took the girl, before fleeing across the north pursued by a vast army that chased him to the Boyne River. There, at that wide river crossing, he had little choice but to turn and face his adversaries; ever since, every ford on the river had been named after a soldier who had died at his hands that day, McCormick would explain, before noting that even though the warrior had won that day he and his new bride were never happy because from that time onwards both were forever exiled. 'They were forced to travel,' Mary

Riley would add, 'never to return home and never to see their loved ones again.'

Mary Ann wondered if she and Kinchela were being punished for going their own way, too. Despite the election hubbub, her thwarted romance continued to be a subject of considerable public interest and much of it made her feel that she and Kinchela were being severely admonished—perhaps even banished. However, not all of it was grim. In stark contrast to Mackay's pompous pontifications, *Bell's Sporting Life* was refusing to take the 'Late Affair at Parramatta' seriously. In one of many columns dedicated to this 'strange eventful history', Charlie Nichols gleefully described how 'two erring children of nature' had suddenly ruptured the quiet of the town by 'taking it into their heads to become one' at 'Australia's Gretna Green'. Before the pair could 'traipse down Hymen's path towards the altar of love', however, the couple had been 'hotly pursued by the girl's papa', who tracked down 'the gay gallant' who had won 'the heart of his little Venus.' Mary Ann couldn't help but find it amusing that the first article *Bell's* published was entitled 'Gill-iver's Travels' and that they had cheekily dubbed Kinchela 'the Don Giovanni of the South' before describing the moment out at Cutt's, when the so-called 'bolter had looked white about the *Gills*' after a pistol had been levelled at his head. For weeks Mary Ann had wondered what actually happened out there, and why her father had been so celebrated. From what she gleaned, he had done nothing less than attempt to murder Kinchela. For *Bell's* the whole thing was a lark, but it wouldn't have been, Mary Ann thought, if her father had hit his mark.

One morning, in late June, the sixteen-year-old girl was reading her father the latest news from France when the germ of an idea began to develop. For three horrific days and nights, Frenchman had murdered Frenchman in a fight in which the future of France had hung in the balance. But then, Mary Ann read, the Second Republic had broken through the barricades and crushed not only the ideologue and the rebel but anyone else who dared to dream of a fairer world. From this time forth, the victorious Republic proclaimed, there would be no more revolution. Martin Gill cheered when he heard the barricades were down. He had little sympathy for rebels these days, whether they were back home in Ireland, in France or right here in Sydney. 'A lot of hot air and needless destruction,' he muttered, forking up the crisp hot bread Mary Ann had toasted in the embers of the kitchen fire. 'You can't run a business or build a town with pitchforks and clasp knives,' he said. 'You need a firm rule.'

But Mary Ann wondered. She had read the news with a heavy heart and could not help but compare the Republic's oppression to her father's, to see in the people's capitulation her own. She must do something before it was too late, she decided. For the past few weeks she had been watching from her bedroom window as the campaigners gathered around Pitt Street in greater numbers. Indeed, many of the speakers were drawing huge crowds. As winter set in over the harbour, and June turned into July, the speeches seemed to ward off the wet with fiery talk about how the time had come for the colony to bring an end to wrong rule. Mary Ann could not hear all that was being said but some carried well enough and the thick-set toyshop owner from Hunter Street was one she heard mention the recent affairs in France in a particularly strident tone.

Mary Ann had also noticed that there were occasions when the mood about the speakers could turn very quickly. Usually it was the same troublemakers—a couple of Cabbagers who began by heckling the speakers before giving someone in the crowd a bit of a push. There were now well over two thousand men with no 'visible means of liveli-hood . . . lurking about the purlieus of Sydney' and many had nothing better to do than stir up mischief. Several papers were expressing their considerable dissatisfaction with the failure of the ordinary constab-ulary to control the election crowds and one or two campaigners had organised a few big men from the docks to come and stand around the perimeter of their meetings, their work tools slung over their shoul-ders, just in case. In the past week alone there had been two occasions when Mary Ann's father had needed to step in with several of his hotel servants until the police arrived.

'All I need,' Mary Ann explained to Rebecca, a night or two before polling day, 'is another situation when my father is distracted and I can get up to Darlinghurst Gaol and be back at the hotel before anyone notices.' 'What will you do up there?' Rebecca asked uncertainly. Mary Ann didn't know herself, but she felt an urgent need to see Kinchela and decide for herself. Was James a villain who had been bent on her seduction, she wondered? Or had she, as Holroyd said, chased the reluctant settler about town because she was so 'desperately in love'? There had been so much talk—Mary Ann wanted to see Kinchela for herself and know her own mind on the matter.

'Do you think they will just let you in?' William asked in astonishment when Mary Ann shared her plan with him the following morning. His sister shook her head and reminded William about the notoriously lax prison governor. 'The gates are not even finished yet, Will, and Kinchela is only on remand,' she said trying to keep her voice to a whisper. 'A gentleman seeking an appeal,' she hurried on. 'Don't you think the governor would want to show a little latitude?' William scuffed his boot before looking away. 'This is not a good time to be out,' he said, 'and you know you are not to go beyond the house. If you got into something,' he asked a little tetchily, 'who would help you?' Mary Ann leant forward and fixed her younger brother with a look. 'You, Will,' she said, a slight dare to her voice. 'You could chaperone me.' But Will only sucked in his breath and shook his head before turning back to the stable yard where his father had him overseeing the shoeing of the hotel horses.

CHAPTER ELEVEN

A Story Without a Hero

The rumours were right. Despite the foreboding appearance of the prison walls, life at Darlinghurst Gaol was hardly horrific under the governor, Henry Keck, the bespectacled dandy from Dublin. Prisoners could earn a reasonable living by working the huge bundles of leaves that were brought in each day to be woven into wide-brimmed cabbage-tree hats, or if inmates were too thick-thumbed for this task, they could work the vegetable garden or tend to the various cows and chickens that provided a regular supply of milk and eggs. They could also do laundry for Keck's family as well as several of his acquaintances, including the Police Magistrate, Captain Joseph Long Innes, who had become something of a close personal friend of the prison's governor. One or two inmates were even dressed in livery so they could drive the coach Keck used to call upon his mistress—a young woman he had accommodated in the judge's rooms next door at the court while her house was being whitewashed. Keck had been forced to dismiss this young woman as the governess of his six children when—much to his surprise—his 'dead wife' suddenly appeared in Sydney, intent upon assuming her role as matron of the new gaol.

Some of the governor's favourite inmates were trusted with the care of Keck's beloved birds—ducks, turkeys, parrots, gulls and crows—all of which were housed in elaborate aviaries from whence exotic warbles and wails, clicks and shrieks were said to express the only sounds of real distress that ever came from the gaol under Keck's governance. Two emus wandered freely through the gardens, as did two pet monkeys. Each evening the emus, the monkeys and the inmates were all returned to their cages and locked up for the night. Otherwise, during the day, all three might roam as they wished. It was even said that several prisoners were allowed to pass in and out of the gates at the governor's pleasure as long as they returned each evening. Instead of the corn hominy that represented the prisoners' staple diet in most institutions at the time, inmates were encouraged to donate this humble fodder to Keck's livestock and use the income they had earned from their toils to purchase—at a generous mark-up—butter, bread, milk and meat from the prison store. In the evening this same place of commerce became known as the grotto, and it was possible to purchase not only hot roast dinners but also two lethal forms of 'rum' nicknamed blue- and black beard.

Keck had it made. He resided just within the walls of the gaol, in a rather splendid stone manor, which he shared with his wife and brood of children and which was generously equipped with several large rooms for entertaining. Resplendent in his fine plum-coloured waist-coats and top hat, the prison governor was said to enjoy every pleasure his position, and the profits he turned from it, could conceive.

After his day in court, James Butler Kinchela was led through the dark tunnel that ran from the courthouse to the gaol. There he was required to provide the prison clerk with his age, height, education and place of birth as well as his religion. These details, along with his conviction, were carefully noted in the columns designated for that purpose. After surrendering his possessions to the administrators, Kinchela removed his clothes and suffered the indignity of a bath at the hands of one of the wardens. He was then dressed in prison garb and taken to a tall, whitewashed building with three tiers of stairs, curved walls and high ceilings, known as A Block, where he hung his hammock and slept among the vagabonds who were likewise accommodated in Henry Keck's institution.

On his fourth day at Darlinghurst Gaol Kinchela was led to the work shed by a turnkey who wanted to see how well the new inmate might weave cabbage-tree hats. As they walked together the prison guard quickly realised that Kinchela was a gentleman and immediately informed the prisoner that there were numerous comforts a man in his position might enjoy—provided he had the funds. By the evening Kinchela was comfortably ensconced in the governor's quarters exchanging fond recollections about St Stephen's Green with Mrs Keck and her daughters, and enjoying the governor's enthusiasms for everything from birds to bassoon playing, monkeys and mazurkas.

Of those who came to visit Kinchela during his so-called incarceration, Jim Davidson was most warmly welcomed into the Keck household. He came to visit at least once, sometimes twice, a week, although Kinchela suspected that he might have grown a little sweet on Keck's second daughter. They were taking a turn around the prison garden one afternoon when Jim revealed that he had received a letter from John. 'I see,' Kinchela said, trying to subdue a pang that his brother had responded to a letter from a friend before replying to one of the many he must have received from his own flesh and blood during the same period. 'And?' Kinchela asked, pretending to be distracted by one of Keck's monkeys happily attacking a bunch of scurvygrass. 'He has been busy in the Bathurst parts it seems, and had to head up to Hawkwood for some urgent business with a potential buyer,' Davidson replied. 'He has affairs to settle, he said, and was looking to come back on one of the Moreton Bay steamers soon enough, but he doesn't know if he will be back before the appeal.' 'Well,' Kinchela eventually replied after the monkey scurried off into a nearby plot of chicory, 'if anyone can drag this appeal out until John returns and rid me of my money in the process it will be Holroyd.' 'Mmmm,' Davidson mused, looking away as he did so, for he was not sure that even the great John Junior could help James now. Let alone if he would want to.

Meanwhile Robert Lowe was having a most marvellous time. He was caught on a swell of his own brilliance and becoming ever more compelling in his argument and articulation, both in the court and public domain. Occasionally he surprised even himself, for far from being discouraged, he found the vitriol heaped upon him quite energising. These insolent colonial fools reminded him of the physical torment he had endured during his school days. Now, however, the tables had turned and he had the upper hand and the moral high ground, and it was profoundly satisfying to carefully craft the demise of the very sort of men who had once terrified him. It was, therefore, of little surprise to him that he was able to quickly convince the full bench of the Supreme Court that there was no legal merit in undertaking a retrial of the Kinchela case. He would, of course, tolerate an appeal, he informed Manning one afternoon when the young judge stopped him in the corridor, but was quite confident that this too would come to nothing. 'Nonetheless, Holroyd has every right to persist in this matter if', he finished with a confident smile, 'he feels it is in his client's best interests.'

But Holroyd wasn't so sure. Nor was his client really giving him much direction. Every time he visited Kinchela in the room next to the governor's main office with the intention of keeping the prisoner up to date with certain legal precedents he had diligently unearthed for the benefit of their case, Kinchela greeted him with resigned indifference. On one occasion when he was taken into the front parlour of Mr Keck's private residence, he found Kinchela listening to a new composition on the pianoforte and refusing, point blank, to discuss any of the legal matters with Holroyd. And later when Kinchela had walked him to the front gate, he had the front to ask Holroyd if he might have some fresh reading matter for him to peruse. 'Keck is the heart of generosity,' Kinchela explained, leaning forward to confide to his counsel, 'but for some reason he has a pronounced aversion to literature. He won't have books or news-sheets in here at all, although no one has any idea why.' Holroyd was not in the habit of supplying his clients with such materials, but he felt something of a debt to this man for the way he had handled his trial, so he had the boy in his chambers run up a parcel with a pile of issues from last year's London *Punch*. The later editions included a new story that was being published, chapter by chapter in each issue, by William Makepeace Thackeray. Holroyd thought it droll and hoped it might keep his client's spirit from dipping too low.

The truth was that Kinchela had cast an eye over one or two of the local news-sheets and decided he was better off inside ignoring the whole thing until his older brother returned. Whatever their differences, John would want the family name restored and once he was bent to the task of fixing things, everything would fall into place again. Of that James was sure. So really, what else was there to do, but wait, Kinchela thought, spying a vacant hammock hanging between two trees. He might as well pass his days tolerably well and to do that he would allow himself to enjoy the extraordinary intrigues of Thackeray's new work—*Vanity Fair: A novel without a hero*. And so, as the world beyond Darlinghurst Gaol grew colder and more engrossed in the forthcoming election, Kinchela became increasingly preoccupied with the scandalous conduct of a cunning orphan named Becky Sharp, who was intent upon hooking a handsome officer named Rawdon Crawley, who had more than a slight penchant for cards.

Several days later, Kinchela was coming in from an afternoon on the hammock and was about to head upstairs to prepare for an early evening game of Klaberjass with Mrs Keck and her daughters, when one of Keck's domestic staff informed the new guest that Mr Alex Green required his immediate presence at the Eastern Gate. The life drained from Kinchela, but he followed the servant to the gatehouse on the opposite side of the prison. It was a fair walk and all the while Kinchela puzzled over what the town 'scourger' might possibly want with him. Perhaps it was some sort of hoax, Kinchela mused, for he had heard that the governor could be something of a trickster.

When Kinchela arrived at the Eastern Gate he immediately recognised Green by the large scar that ran down the side of his face. The town hangman was shuffling back and forth in a rather excited way and rushed towards the prisoner when he saw him approach. 'Mr Green,' Kinchela said curtly. Green pointed past the gate. 'A lady,' he said with a leer before looking again to make sure she hadn't disappeared. 'A lady, come to see you, and a young one, too,' he grinned. Kinchela nodded with some relief and thanked the hangman before stepping beyond the gaol gate to greet his mysterious visitor.

Mary Ann was standing with her back to the gaol, studying the trunk of a nearby tree with great interest. There was a moment of rather awkward silence as Kinchela walked towards her. Mary Ann self-consciously tended to her bonnet. 'It is polling day today,' she began as Kinchela drew closer, 'and the crowds in town are considerable.' Kinchela listened but also quickly looked about him. He was pleased to see the girl but held some fear that her father and those infernal pistols might suddenly disrupt the fragile equanimity of his current circumstances. He cast another glance around as Mary Ann rushed on. 'They have put troopers in front of the banks and there are police stationed everywhere,' she said before stopping and waiting for him to speak. As the silence grew Mary Ann began to wonder for a terrifying moment if she had ventured all this way for someone who was not, in fact, entirely pleased to see her.

Kinchela sensed her discomfort and frowned a little at his own rudeness. 'Well,' he began awkwardly, 'you have given me a surprise, I must say,' he thrust his hands in his pockets as he gave a sort of involuntary shrug. 'You are the last person I ever expected to see. How on earth did you get up here?' Mary Ann gave the slightest smile. 'The town is full of campaign speakers,' she explained. 'And my father is much distracted by the crowds about the hotel.' Kinchela whistled. The girl had pluck—that was for sure—and she was also looking much more alluring than the last time he had seen her during the trial when she had been wearing that dreadful dark garb. 'I don't suppose it was hard to get the gateman to do your bidding,' he said, tossing a quick glance towards Green. Mary Ann shared a look of amused repulsion for the scourger and then focused her attention on the prisoner. Kinchela shook his head in amusement. He felt curiously nervous around her and was also acutely aware of the compromising position that she had yet again placed herself in—for him.

'Well,' she continued, when the silence became a little more comfortable, 'I have come to tell you off.' And then in response to Kinchela's perplexed look, she added, 'for missing my sixteenth birthday,' pouting so prettily that Kinchela could not help but smile. He pulled two empty hands from his pockets to signal his penury but then as a quick afterthought added, 'You know, I've the beginning of a new book you might like. Cracking read, in fact.' He rushed on, keen to amuse her with the winding tale of Becky Sharp and her not-so-gallant Captain. How their secret marriage so aggrieved his rich aunt that she disinherited the newlyweds and forced them to make their own way without any good society. 'But you see,' he added, 'I've only got up to the Christmas issue of last year's *Punch* and I've a mind the story will go on another six months or so,' he said, 'so we will have to wait until the next boat comes with the latest issues.'

'We could make it up,' Mary Ann suggested, keen to keep the mood lively and capture some of the frisson that had infused their first conversations at the hotel. She was also more than a little intrigued by the story. 'What would you like to happen to the newlyweds?' she asked. 'Well,' Kinchela said uncertainly, as he cast about for an idea. 'It is a shame Becky Sharp has all those ways about her, when she is so smart and pretty and also . . .' he added as he watched Mary Ann blush, 'that her husband is such a bounder.' Kinchela thought another moment before adding more quietly, 'Perhaps she would be better off if they had never met or,' he said, dropping his gaze to his boots, 'if she forgot him altogether.'

Mary Ann focused on her gloves so he wouldn't see her face. Sensing her disappointment, and not sure what else to do, Kinchela took a step forward and, much to her surprise, reached out and lightly touched the young woman's arm. 'Mary,' he said with the sort of gentleness he usually reserved for a new prize stepper, 'I don't know how I might speak with you on this,' he said, with such seriousness that Mary Ann looked up in surprise. She had never heard him sound so solemn. 'I have had much time to think on it all,' he said, searching her face, 'and honestly I don't know why you would ever want to look upon me again. I certainly didn't think I would ever see you again.'

Mary Ann darted a quick glance at him and then returned to her gloves. 'I see,' she replied quietly, taking pains not to meet his gaze. 'And do you think Mr Crawley would be better without the troublesome Becky Sharp?' she asked tartly. Kinchela jerked his head at the impertinence of the question and realised he had yet again been charmed by her direct way. He grinned and rubbed both hands together before putting both to his lips.

'Well,' he began, a little more playfully, 'she does have a lot of spirit, that one,' he replied, 'as well as a certain way of finding trouble wherever she goes. And I can't help thinking that she must be his equal, or perhaps even a little cleverer . . .' he mused as he watched the young girl take in his words. 'So now you make me think of it,' he finished with a grin, 'yes, I have no doubt that Becky Sharp will draw Crawley into all sorts of mischief.' He watched Mary Ann's brow grow heavy and full of frown before he hurried on. 'But, you know,' he said taking another step towards her, 'I suspect some people fit together—so they might as well work out how to make do.' He smiled as Mary Ann's expression began to lift and lighten. 'After all,' he finished, 'a man like Rawdon should be honoured Becky thinks him worthy of her . . .' he trailed off, not sure what else to say. Mary Ann looked intently at Kinchela and then spoke with such solemnity that the older man was yet again taken aback. 'I am quite sure, sir,' she said in a steady voice, 'that Rawdon Crawley is entirely worthy of such an honour.'

Kinchela felt hopelessly humbled. After all the awkward disappointments of their thwarted romance this young girl was still prepared to look upon him. No one had ever thought so much of him, he realised, nor stood by him, and for that moment he felt unable to do anything but stand before Mary Ann and take in the great force of her conviction.

Eventually he swallowed and spoke, his voice almost a whisper. 'I will never let you down again, Mary,' he said simply. 'That is, if such an opportunity to prove that to you should ever come my way.'

Mary Ann gave an almost imperceptible nod and then reached out to place a gloved hand upon Kinchela's shoulder. Only for a moment though, for within a second she was tossing her head and giving him a mischievous look. 'But, I suppose, James,' she teased, 'you know that book better than I, so I will have to take your instruction about the characters and their fate.' Kinchela grinned and the pair stood, smiling at one another until, after the smallest time, Kinchela swallowed and said, 'I shall be delighted to recount to you all that happens with this story the next time we see one another, Mary, and I hope by then,' he added slowly, 'we will be somewhere more fitting for husband and wife.'

Mary Ann nodded again and the two figures stood beneath the bows of one of the few trees that still remained on the windblown rise of Woolloomooloo Hill. Suddenly, Mary Ann became aware of the encroaching darkness. 'I must go,' she hurried, 'heaven knows what my father will do if he discovers I've disappeared again.' And with one quick look she was gone, hurrying down the pathway along the side of the prison wall. Kinchela stood watching Mary Ann's small figure move towards town until she disappeared into the falling dusk.

As Mary Ann made her way from the gaol a smile played upon her lips. James was still her own, she thought. She had been right to make her way up to the gaol. And she had held her own. She had not stepped inside the compound, nor stooped to the depths of her early sojourn via Mrs Kelly's during their failed elopement. She could hold her head high and know that her bold adventure had merited sure rewards. All the shame and suffering of the past months had suddenly dissolved. She had the answers she was seeking and one way or another she was now assured that she would also have the future she wanted. With James.

As she descended into town, however, Mary Ann became increasingly aware of the menace that polling day had brought to the streets.

Sydney Cove, after 1845 by Harriot Anley. Government House (right) was the home of Governor FitzRoy at this time. Mary Ann would have been familiar with this view. (State Library of NSW)

Dr John Kinchela, Attorney General of New South Wales, 1831–1836, painted c. 1810. (Private collection of Annette Miller)

Portrait, c. 1810, of Anne Bourne, John Kinchela's pretty second wife. (Private collection of Alicen Miller)

King Street Looking East, ca. 1843 by Frederick Garling. The man on his chestnut mare is dressed in a style similar to the way our gentleman settler, James Butler Kinchela, probably dressed. (State Library of NSW)

New Post Office, George Street, Sydney by F.G. Lewis, 1845. This image evokes a sense of 1840s Sydney as a sort of London in miniature. Gill's Family Hotel was probably behind the post office on the other side of the Tank Stream. (State Library of NSW)

Court House, Darlinghurst by Frederick Garling, c. 1840. The fields in front of the courthouse were used for festivities such as the St Patrick's Day Ball in 1840. *Regina v. Kinchela* was heard here in 1848. (State Library of NSW)

Prisoners next to the wall of Darlinghurst Gaol, c. 1880. The uniform, including the cabbage-tree hat, is similar to that which Kinchela would have worn during his time there. Note the 'dargs' etched into each brick by the convicts who built the wall.

Detail of a map of Sydney drawn up in the mid-1840s by Francis W. Sheilds.

Eloping to Gretna Green was not only the stuff of Jane Austen novels, but also surprisingly commonplace in Regency England. (© The Trustees of the British Museum)

By the 1840s the Parramatta racetrack appears to have become the colonial counterpart to Gretna Green. *Parramatta Races, Boxing Day 1861* shows a summer's day at the races. (State Library of NSW)

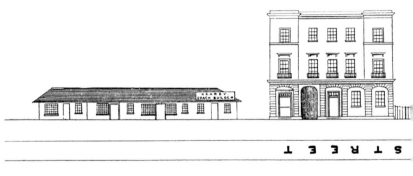

Gill's Family Hotel was the only three-storey hotel in town in the 1840s, and is the building shown second from left (top) in this illustration from Joseph Fowles' book, *Sydney in 1848*. It was considered 'without exception the best family residence in Sydney'.

GILL'S FAMILY HOTEL,
LATE THE RESIDENCE OF SAUL LYONS,
ESQ., PITT-STREET.

MARTIN GILL hastens to return his sincere thanks to his numerous kind friends and patrons in all parts of the country, and takes the earliest opportunity of apprising them of his removal from George-street, to the Hotel in Pitt-street (as above), where neither pains nor expense has been spared to render his new establishment comfortable and convenient for families or single gentlemen arriving from the interior.

M. Gill has the pleasure to inform his patrons, that he has laid in an entirely new stock of the best Spirits, and superior Wines, with London Ale and Porter, &c. &c.

Families and gentlemen will find this establishment superior to any other in the city of Sydney, being in a central situation—private hall entrance,—and totally unconnected with the bar trade; also, possessing that great luxury in the summer, a beautiful Bath.

Families and single gentlemen can be accommodated with suits of rooms exclusively.

Luncheons daily at one o'clock.

N.B.—Excellent stabling and coach-houses.

Sydney, October 14.   6187

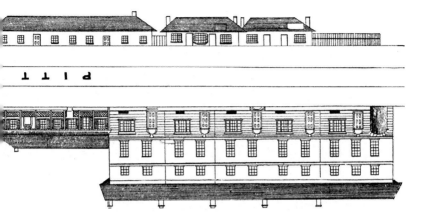

Opposite (left): Advertisement in *The Sydney Morning Herald*, 16 October 1846. Note the mention of the beautiful bath.

Opposite (right): Contemporaries of Margaret and Martin Gill, shown here in a daguerreotype from the 1840s. No images of the Gill family survive from this period. (Missouri History Museum)

Left: A contemporary of Mary Ann Gill. This girl is probably the same age as Mary Ann at the time of her elopement.

Henry Parkes around the time of Mary Ann's scandalous elopement.

Arthur Todd Holroyd, Kinchela's legal counsel and later MP. (State Library of NSW)

TRIAL OF FRANK GARDINER, THE BUSHRANGER, at the Supreme Court, Sydney.—SEE PAGE 11.

This illustration of the Supreme Court in session is later than *Regina v. Kinchela* (1848) but captures the austere atmosphere, which was no doubt intimidating for Mary Ann. (State Library of Victoria)

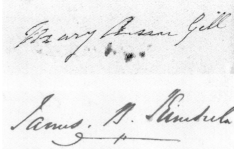

Left: The deposition of James Butler Kinchela, 1848. (State Records NSW)

Above: The signatures on the depositions of Mary Ann Gill and James Butler Kinchela. Note the tear blotches that punctuate Mary Ann's signature and the contrast between her uneven signature and Kinchela's confident hand. (State Records NSW)

Mary Anne Gill sworn (The witness was too agitated to be sworn for several minutes) Was the daughter of Martin and Margaret Gill; they kept a hotel in Pitt-street; remembered Saturday, the 20th May; drank tea with her mother that night; after ten witness went out; had sent some clothes out before, by a servant named Rebecca; she went out to meet Mr. Kinchela; she walked out; had seen Mr. Kinchela that day, but not to speak to him; he was passing by the door; she met him in the street, at the corner of York street; when she went out on the Saturday evening, he had not appointed to meet her there; had had a conversation with him the previous evening, Friday; that conversation took place at the window of her father's house, looking into the street; he asked witness to go away with him to get married; witness said she would; he said she was to meet him the next night at the corner of York-street; she saw him there, and he told her to go to Mr. Webb's public-house, in Parramatta-street; she went there in a cab; he said he would be there directly; when she got to Webb's she waited for Kinchela; she went to bed, and when Kinchela came up again; Kinchela did not stop long; after that her father came and took her home; while

'Shooting with Intent', the original newspaper clipping from 5 June 1848 that my mother gave me and which inspired this book. (Author's photograph)

A sketch of Viscount Robert Lowe, aged 58, for *Vanity Fair*, 1869. (National Portrait Gallery, Canberra)

Ormond House, the Kinchela family residence from 1831 to 1838. This fine two-storey house was built on New South Road by emancipist Robert Cooper in 1824 and named Juniper Hall. It was considered the finest house in Sydney for over a decade. (Mitchell Library, State Library of NSW)

Durundur Station, shown in this 1843 sketch by Charles Archer, is an example of an early colonial station in Queensland similar to the property owned by the Kinchela brothers. (State Library of Queensland)

The hanging of Whittaker and McKenzie, two Sydney Ducks, by the San Francisco Vigilance Committee in mid-1851. It is likely that Kinchela and perhaps even Mary Ann witnessed the lynching.

View of Sutter's Fort, near Sacramento City, California by Frederick Gleason. The fort was built in 1839 and deserted by the mid-1850s. Kinchela's ranch was located a mile east of the fort.

A photograph of Sanger Street, the main street of Corowa, taken around the time of Mary Ann's death. (J.T. Keating presentation album, Wagga Wagga City Library's Photograph Collection)

The gravestone of Margaret Gill and Mary Beatty, as Mary Ann was then known, in the Roman Catholic section of the Corowa Pioneer Cemetery. Both women died at 69 years of age. (Author's photograph)

She would need to be on her wits, she realised, as she eased herself into a party of five or six domestic women heading in the direction of Hyde Park. Just in front of her was a group of rough and ready men shoving and jostling one another in a loud and fractious way. The mood was most unpredictable, she thought.

When she reached the edge of the park Mary Ann suddenly stopped in shock. Through the darkness she could just see men in uniform, some carrying buckets and others chasing Cabbagers, who were scattering—this way and that—as fast as they could. The mood was chaos and she had only taken a few steps before a heavy lad who was trying to escape from two policemen pushed roughly past her and knocked her to the ground. Mary Ann crouched in the dark where she had fallen for several minutes as she tried to make sense of her surrounds. In the far corner of the park she could just make out a squadron of mounted troopers, who looked to be organising themselves into formation. Somewhere in the centre, a giant structure was ablaze, its bright orange plumes and sparks spuming high into the night sky. 'The polling booth,' she whispered to herself, as the smoke swirled about her. 'It's been set alight.' How long, she wondered desperately, before the park itself was engulfed in flame?

It had been one thing to get up to the Darlinghurst Gaol, but she hadn't considered getting home. Nor had she thought it would get dark so soon. Her plan had been to use the election commotion to her advantage. And to a large extent this had been successful. Her father had been entirely distracted by the crowds around Pitt Street, many of which were making frequent sojourns to the Gills' establishment in between the various campaign speeches. Mary Ann had chosen to slip away the moment she had seen her father's favourite—the shabbily attired statesman, William Charles Wentworth—standing astride the omnibus waiting to begin what she suspected would be a long-winded oration. She had given herself a couple of hours to get to the prison and back and figured the crowds would cause enough commotion during that particular speech to keep her father busy. It had been an excellent plan, but now she could see the mood about town had changed and conditions had become treacherous. She had been foolish, she thought, regretting how she had dismissed her brother's disapproval for its lack of courage.

But Mary Ann shook her head and refused to give in to the fears that were rising in her belly. Quickly, she got to her feet and was soon hurrying along King Street. The town reeked of stale ale and rum and the soles of her boots were sticky with it. It made her feel heady and sick, but she kept pushing away from the glowering chaos of the park, towards home.

So far so good, Mary Ann said to herself as she turned into Pitt Street. But then she was brought short again. All the way down the street, were hundreds, perhaps even a thousand electioneers crammed up against one another. She could hear their screaming and calling, pushing and shoving. They were Cabbagers mostly, but among them were a few desperate women. All were swept up in a mob that was thrashing about like a furious snake—lashing out first in one direction and then the other. Mary Ann flattened herself against a wall as she tried to work out what to do. She was standing like that, clammy with perspiration, when out of nowhere, forty or more mounted troopers suddenly thrust their heavy horses into the wild turmoil. Thwack, thwack, the uniformed men went with their bludgeons, smacking them down sharp and fast as they pushed their way through the screaming mass. Mary Ann had never seen anything like it. Nor heard, either, for all about her was shrieking and cursing.

She had to get home. She could not stop here. She must keep on. Her mother would be starting to think about her and Mary Ann knew that if he was asked, William would tell. He would have to. She began running, as well as her skirts would let her, up King Street until she found George Street. This was a safer passage and she got all the way down to Hunter Street before she came upon yet another large crowd. This one had a hundred or so men in it but they were no mob, Mary Ann thought with relief as she spotted in their midst several prominent townsfolk. Four of them had rolled up their shirt sleeves and were heaving a brightly painted carriage up George Street. They looked so jubilant that they were oblivious to the great bulk they were hauling. Behind them trailed a great band of men, many of whom were carrying torches and lanterns as they sung and clapped and cheered together, some with their arms tossed across each other's shoulders. Mary Ann wondered who or even what might be in the carriage at the front of this triumphant procession but when it rolled past her and she looked inside she saw nothing. The men pushed further up George Street, and this time when she looked again Mary Ann was astonished to behold— up on the carriage roof—the People's Idol standing aloft, like a grand colossus, resplendent in a pinstripe suit and spectacles, waving to the great throng and occasionally cracking and snapping a stock whip into the smoke-thick night. Mary Ann grimaced. 'The very man', she muttered while she waited for the great procession to pass by.

Once the last of the revellers had passed she continued onto Hunter Street which felt curiously empty and then turned quickly into Pitt Street. She was close to home, she thought with growing relief. She was going to be fine. She could feel how satisfying it would be to slip into her bed and muse over all that had taken place at the prison gate. 'Becky Sharp indeed,' Mary Ann smiled to herself as she slipped into the hotel's coach yard.

Great piles of thick blue election ribbon had been torn from the walls of her father's hotel and everywhere she looked there were smashed crates. One of the stable doors was hanging from a single hinge while both the coal cart and wood box, which usually stood by the kitchen door, were smashed to splinters. The mob had passed through, she realised, as she picked her way across the yard and care-fully slipped inside the servants' entrance. The kitchen staff were busy with the organised chaos of serving time and Mary Ann made her way upstairs unnoticed. Once inside her bedroom she removed her bonnet and gloves and checked her reflection in her looking glass. Her pupils were quite wide and she was still struggling to settle the fast pace of her breathing as she stepped into the nursery.

Despite the great madness about town it was eerily quiet upstairs. Mary Ann lit a candle and gradually the glow of the single flame revealed the sleeping forms of Isabella, Harriet, little Thomas and baby Martin. There was a peace to their steady breathing that was a world away from the commotion of the day. She stood there a moment, savouring the relief of all that had transpired. She had been successful. She had returned home unscathed and undetected. And more than that—she had also seen Kinchela and secured his heart. But slowly, as her breath finally steadied, she felt the presence of someone sitting in the high-backed chair that occupied the middle of the room. It was someone, she suspected with a sinking feeling, who had been awaiting her return.

CHAPTER TWELVE

The Manly and the Unmanly

No sooner had the smoke cleared from the election hullabaloo, than Holroyd headed back to the prison governor's quarters on Woolloomooloo Hill to have a word with his client. Kinchela appeared in the side office looking, Holroyd thought, considerably more sober and settled than usual. The lawyer still harboured a sense that his client had been hard done by and he was prepared to do all he could. But he needed his client to play his part, too, Holroyd advised, 'particularly now' that the appeal had been set for the end of the week. Kinchela gave a convincing nod and proceeded to listen to his counsel with a respect that came as a pleasant surprise to Holroyd. He had expected the same indifference he had been subjected to over the past month, but as he began to furnish his client with various details he learnt that Kinchela not only had a renewed interest in his appeal, but was also greatly relieved that his old family friend, Roger Therry, would be on the appeal bench.

Less welcome was the news that Therry would be joined by Dickenson, and, of course, William Montagu Manning, with whom both Holroyd and Kinchela were already well acquainted. Both men were still seething about the astounding rebuke they had received from Manning regarding their defence. Unmanly indeed. Both men felt that Manning had been less concerned with exercising sound legal

135

judgment than establishing his position on the bench, and Kinchela could not help recalling that it was not so long ago that men would have duelled over such an insult, in Ireland at any rate.

Holroyd brought Kinchela up to pace with all the newly elected representatives on the Legislative Council. 'Lowe got himself a Sydney seat, of course, as did Wentworth, although,' Holroyd offered with a cough, 'although most reckon the two squeaky cartwheels will cancel each other out with all their bluster. Bob Nichols won one of the country seats,' Holroyd continued, 'a very easy win.' Then he added, with something of a raised eyebrow, 'Lowe only won by a cat's whisker, you know, but you wouldn't think it by all the fuss he and the mechanics have been making about town.'

As he prepared his papers for their day in court, Holroyd reminded his client of the potential sentence he must expect if things went against them. 'As much as two years with hard labour I am afraid, James,' he swallowed before adding, 'but at least they can't hang you for abduction anymore.' Kinchela nodded, watching Holroyd slide one set of papers into his leather case and remove still others for his client's attention. No indeed, thought Kinchela, it had been six years since they had executed a man in Ireland for such a crime. Nonetheless, two years was a long time to be imprisoned. He had been wrong to rest upon his brother's laurels, he realised miserably. He had probably left his run too late.

Martin Gill was overseeing the repairs about the hotel and already wondering if his sweet moment of vindication in the Supreme Court in June was beginning to rot like the peaches McCormick sold to the hotel, which always looked better than they tasted. Many of the 'Up Country Gentlemen' who had been crucial to his trade were less frequent customers at the hotel than before the trial. He wondered if winter was to answer for that, or the sudden plummet in the price of wool. He couldn't fight off the feeling that by setting himself against Kinchela he may have warned off others of that set. Good riddance to them then, Martin Gill scowled to himself as he set to sharpening the kitchen knives. But the truth of it was that their absence was not good. He had built his business on the back of the settlers. Their money had fed his family and given his establishment the right air. He might not like them and certainly didn't want any such man in his family, particularly not an Irishman, but these men had been his bread and butter. If they were struggling it stood to reason that it wouldn't be long before he did too.

Still, the election had brought in some solid cash—even if a good deal of it would have to be spent on repairs. Gill hoped that the windfall might signal the beginning of a new season. The past two months had been a tight squeeze, that was for sure, and he would need to get set right in terms of pounds and pennies for the coming season. Sooner rather than later, too, for he knew as well as any businessman that things could turn on a coat pin in this colony. You could not afford to be caught out. You rarely got a second chance and there was always someone ready to take your place. People would cross the street to avoid a man on the downward spiral. Hypocrites, he muttered to himself, the lot of them. Nonetheless, it was time to get his nose out and find what was about.

From the way things were looking, though, the girl would have to make amends for all the damage she had done and find a way to bring in some proper money. If she wasn't fit for work now that her name had been in the papers, he would have to get her set up with a rich husband and make her bring in some money that way. Simple. She owed it to her brothers and sisters as well as her parents. They could not be brought low and forced to live in the shadow of her recklessness. It would work, too, Gill thought, feeling more certain about the matter the more he mused it over. It would also put a stop to the various whispers he had been hearing around and about, which had made him feel violent with shame. He was pretty sure that Mary Ann was still clean. Had not been touched. But he also knew that rumours could be as bad as the truth when it came to shifting dubious product. If he got Mary Ann with a man who had good tin, that would shut them all up and also help to sop up the various debts rapidly accumulating about the hotel. Who knows, the right match might even help to cover Robert Lowe's costs. And so, Gill began to consider his wealthy associates and identify those who might be in need of a young wife and also willing to overlook what he would describe, if pressed, as his daughter's youthful indiscretion.

~

Two days after Holroyd's visit, Kinchela was escorted through the gaol tunnel and into the Supreme Court where he took his place before his father's old friend as well as two other high dignitaries of the legal profession. Holroyd was there, but not the Great Gyrator, who had loftily informed his irritable-looking client that he was now fully absorbed 'with the responsibilities of his new political office'. Bob Nichols would attend in his absence, Robert Lowe explained as he hastened from his chamber, expressing utmost confidence that 'things are set to go our way'. And Lowe was right. And yet, the three judges were so intent upon extracting as much pleasure as possible from the grand event of a full bench hearing that each man took more than an onerous hour to recall the various cases and clauses, precedents and principles upon which they had determined their final decision.

On and on it went with *The Herald* doing its best to cover the specificities in great detail. Only Therry gave Kinchela the slightest benefit of the doubt. Despite Manning's decision, Therry was convinced that there was merit in hearing the girl's reason for quitting her family home, particularly if her 'domestic discomfort was such that she had been compelled to forsake her filial duty' and accept an offer that 'only furthered the unfortunate breach that had already opened between parent and child in this matter'. But, no, the other men of the law shook their heads in disagreement. Such evidence was inadmissible, they insisted. The original verdict must be upheld.

Worse still, after much consideration, the bench determined that the defendant's motivations were such that they must be publicly condemned 'in the most unequivocal terms'. Therry could do nothing. The other judges were convinced the defendant had never intended to marry Miss Gill. Indeed, their examination of 'each element and incident associated with this case' led them to the grave conclusion that the prisoner had been 'deeply dishonourable—luring the young girl from her home with the sole purpose of seducing her'. And he had not stopped there, the bench railed, for when he had 'failed once, he had been bold enough to try yet again,' Dickenson growled as Manning sternly shook his head. 'Such a man,' they gravely concluded, 'must be kept thoroughly in check.'

Burdened as they were with the heavy duty of protecting the colony, the two judges were obliged to act in a manner that would reassure other parents that 'their affections were not for naught', and that property and dignity must be respected. The gravity of Kinchela's actions had warranted a most particular statement from the court. In the final column published on the topic for some time, *The Herald* agreed: It was necessary that men like Kinchela were punished as firmly as possible. In so doing, the authorities sent a clear message to those who might also wish to threaten 'the greatest blessing of the new society: namely the peace of the family and the happiness of the humble home'.

And so, the 'vile seducer', James Butler Kinchela, was off to the much less salubrious confines of Parramatta Gaol, where he was to serve nine calendar months, *The Herald* reported. If he was lucky, the shamed esquire might once more walk the streets of Sydney in March the following year, for, in an act of mercy, Therry had somehow managed to have the sentence backdated to the day of his conviction in early June. Kinchela stood in the court with his head hung low as the iron cuffs were clapped onto his wrists. The prisoner gave Holroyd an odd shrug and Nichols mumbled that he thought the whole affair a sorry business, before Kinchela stepped away with the two guards.

Moments later the old Black Maria prison cart trundled from the court, down Oxford Street. It was morning, and as the cart rolled past Hyde Park, Kinchela noticed that several trees had been scorched by fire—their bare and blackened limbs stretched out into the bleak winter sky with an expression of futility that seemed to match his mood. Mary Ann had no doubt crossed this way on her journey home.

What had she seen?, he wondered with some concern. Was she safe? He had no way of knowing now. The cart crossed over George Street where a handful of government men were cleaning up the last of the election debris and a scattering of domestic servants were heading towards the markets. An ordinary day, Kinchela thought as his cart trundled towards the Parramatta road, and probably the last he would see in a while.

It was a road he knew all too well, although he had hardly imagined travelling it under such circumstances. Most often he had been heading out to the races, or to check out stock in those parts. Now he was a convicted felon and all the rules had changed. As the cart pushed past the rough timber homes and makeshift inns along the outskirts of town, Kinchela realised that from this time on he would probably be considered more of a blackguard than those who had *come* to the colony in chains.

Upon his arrival at Parramatta Gaol, a mean-looking warden took possession of Kinchela's gold-plated cane and ebony-finished snuffbox as well as the pile of last year's *Punch*. 'You will find us less accommodating than Mr Keck's private Elysium,' the warden said snidely before recording the details of 'Prisoner 486' in his thick ledger book. 'Arrived in the colony?' he asked with a sniff. 'Eighteen thirty-one,' Kinchela replied. 'Height?' he barked, pointing to his underling to put the prisoner against a measuring rod on the wall. 'Five feet five, with a slight build and a ruddy complexion, sir,' the younger warden noted as the chief administrator penned down the details, occasionally looking up to check his offsider's work before returning to jot them down in the appropriate column. 'Black hair and brown eyes,' the trainee continued. 'Any distinguishing features?' the scribe asked. 'None that I can see,' the assistant replied with a snigger. It was noted that the incumbent could read and write and was also a gentleman by calling. Then Kinchela was subjected to another public bathing and kitted up in prison garb before being taken to a grim looking cell. The guard slammed the gate on the prisoner and locked him in for the day, 'and so the real penitence begins,' Kinchela sighed glumly.

Martin Gill had been making discreet enquiries. He had been spending more time out and about the town than usual. The news was grim. Indeed, even grimmer than he had first thought. The drought had got its teeth into much of the country and in the past few weeks alone two of the most established men of the land had come in with the dust of a rainless season on their boots and not much else to show for their efforts. The farmers were just walking away—he had heard—leaving their stock to starve because they couldn't afford the shot or the poison or because they had lost the spirit to kill them even for the melted-down tallow that might bring in a few pence. It didn't bode well, particularly since there was also a lot of talk about uncertain money conditions in England and this would no doubt make local exports and the price of sugar even more exorbitant. He would need to act smart and fast, Gill decided, if he was to get things back on track.

It was to his advantage that there were still too few women and far too many men in the colony. Although, he would just need to play his cards carefully and keep a close hand. He wanted a fellow with money as well as decent connections. He wouldn't throw his daughter away for nothing. It had to be a match that would advance the standing of his family. He didn't care if the fellow was tubby or poorly groomed or long-in-the-tooth. In fact, a part of him relished the idea of his daughter having to suffer such a match after the trouble she had caused.

He liked old Alexander Moore, the unfortunate older brother of the handsome auctioneer, W.G. Moore. Old Alexander was a recent widower. He would want a wife to keep him and his five young children sooner rather than later. Gill suspected he could handle Moore. Better still, with half of his teeth knocked out from a horse-riding accident that had also left him with an awkward right leg, he was also confident that Mary Ann would not have to compete with many other colonial girls for the widower's attention.

There was also Lewis Samuel, the man who took the hotel rent from him each quarter. Gill found the mercantile brother of the better-known magistrate Saul Samuel hard to stomach with his exaggerated sense of importance, but he was the nephew of the powerful auctioneer and emancipist Samuel Lyons and also had a number of different business interests in the southern interior. Never married, Gill thought, and would no doubt make a generous settlement. And who knows, with Mary Ann as his wife the brothers might even decide to give Gill the hotel, or at least waive the outstanding rental for the last quarter.

He didn't know why, but Martin Gill was quite certain he didn't want another Irishman in the family. 'Plenty of other sorts with money for the taking,' he reasoned, looking about his own dining room and observing that with winter over, the hotel was still emptier than he liked. He was keeping all of this to himself, hoping that Margaret hadn't picked up on it yet. No use bothering her with money concerns nor with his plans for Mary Ann until they were firmed up.

It didn't take long for Mary Ann to learn of Kinchela's failed appeal. It was a blow but hardly a surprising one, and after their interview at the prison gate, Mary Ann decided to focus on their future rather than dwell upon the frustrations of the present. For the time it also suited her to oblige her parents. She did feel guilty for the trouble she had caused her family and was also aware that her mother appeared to be under some sort of strain, but she associated this with the new baby, Martin, who was now a little over six months old. Most of that winter Mary Ann had been content to stay on the upper floor of the hotel in the family's private quarters, tending to her brothers and sisters and when possible, retreating to her bedroom where she could muse upon all that was to come.

By early September, however, spring began to spread across the harbour and surrounding hills, teasing those who had been awaiting its arrival, with light green buds as well as sea breezes full of sun-warmed eucalyptus. From her bedroom window, Mary Ann had taken to following the gradual flowering of a rather pretty line of fruit trees that were sprinkled through a swathe of gums that curved around

Circular Quay. And as those early blooms began to unfurl into light bright sprays of whites and pinks, they came to feel, to the young woman patiently awaiting her lover's release, like the promise of a fresh beginning.

CHAPTER THIRTEEN

A More Exalted Position

The Colonial Secretary, Earl Grey, had broken his promise. Things had got so tight at home that the current climate compelled him to give first consideration to the immediate interests of his country. Despite a solemn commitment he had made to the Legislative Council of New South Wales, he had little choice but to send out a fresh boatload of convicts. No one in the colony could believe it. Almost ten years had passed since there had been such reviled vessels in their harbour. The colony had been purged of this shame. How, they fumed, could Earl Grey dare to insult the respectable people of this land by once more imposing upon them the great ignominy of men in chains?

For the better part of a decade the colony had been able to hold its head high, the papers huffed. Indeed, in recent years, all sorts had arrived, specifically because they had received reassurance from Earl Grey that there would be no more convicts. Men had made plans, nurtured visions, invested family fortunes and even dreamed of a new Britannia in the southern seas. Free from the old taint, business confidence had risen and the colony had prospered to the extent that many were convinced that New South Wales now occupied an exalted position among the dominions. Their efforts had brought them to the brink of self-governance. Even universal suffrage, the toyshop owner told anyone who would listen, although the men he accosted on the topic cautioned him that the latter might be too much, for now anyway. Even so, a good number of men now knew what it was like to be treated like an Englishman, many, for the first time in their lives. This had been their moment. The wind had been in their sails. Surely Grey would not rob them of their future?

The news of Grey's broken promise stirred fear and loathing throughout New South Wales. Colonists were fiery with the insult, particularly shop men and paper tigers like Parkes and his associates who were now busy manoeuvring around town. They were also peeved that Lowe had shown little thanks for the work they had undertaken on his behalf. Worse than that, Sydney's Weathercock had also taken to avoiding them, and on several occasions had even flagrantly contradicted them in public. When, for example, Parkes had gone to the hustings after the votes were finished on polling day and declared Lowe's victory 'the birth day of democracy in Australia'—the new member for Sydney had visibly recoiled. Lowe wanted no such thing and he quickly disabused Parkes and his friends of this point as well as any assumption on their part that he might owe them any favours.

It was also apparent to the toyshop owner and his friends that far from wielding greater influence, their election success had earned them the dubious dishonour of being snubbed by a number of important men who had decided that Parkes and his associates had got ahead of themselves. Rather than feel deterred by such a slight, this 'committee of unknown men' decided it was time to go it alone and in such a way that would show others just how much influence they could wield. So now Parkes and his associates were out and about, hustling the middle and lower orders as they organised meetings in each city ward—determined to send a most unequivocal message to the Colonial Secretary, the governor and all their friends about the price they would pay if they tried to sail any such boats into their harbour.

～

In October, a less controversial vessel docked at Circular Quay—carrying among its passengers a man who harboured his own colonial ambitions. It took the barrel-chested John Kinchela Junior less than a week to realise that Sydney was in quite a different mood than when he had left it for Hawkwood at the end of autumn. At first the doctor's eldest son couldn't put his finger on what it was about Sydney that felt different. He wondered if it was perhaps the drought. But it wasn't just that. There was something else. The papers were a lot riper than he remembered them—that was certainly clear to him after skimming a couple in the Club while enjoying a very pleasant beef and pheasant pie.

It wasn't until he finally went out to Parramatta Gaol to see his brother that John Kinchela got a clear whiff of what it was. He had been utterly appalled the first time he saw his own brother shuffling into the room in that uniform. And also deeply incensed—a felon in the family, he fumed. But as James talked him through the damaging events of the past few months, it occurred to John that this entire episode could never have happened even a few years ago. An emancipist pointing his pistols at a free settler's son and being acquitted of attempted murder? He snorted incredulously. Even more outrageous was the fact that this hotelier had actually been successful in his prosecution of a gentleman when the courts knew full well who had the better social standing. And all for a convict's daughter, he sniffed in disgust.

He would have to turn things around and to do that he would need to leave Hawkwood on the market and hope for a sale while he stayed closer to home, at least for a time. So John took to calling upon many of his old associates, including a number of family friends. Roger Therry was first. After all, he had been 'the true hero of the Mudie affair,' John flattered the little man as they sat down together to a glass of sherry and caught up on news. But Therry was being far too philosophical for John's liking. 'Moods changed, John, simple as that,' he told his old friend's favourite son with an apologetic expression. 'It's like that everywhere around the colony these days. You would be a fool to try and push things the other way, hold back the tide, so to speak, especially,' he added, much to John's horror, 'when it might be for the better in the long run,' Therry finished, turning the fine etched glass between his thumb and middle finger. John had no idea what he meant but couldn't believe that his one-time champion was ready to roll over like a dog. He left the meeting with a most uncomfortable feeling.

John had a long lunch with Davidson up at the Club, where he had acquired yet another perspective on the whole matter. He was at a loss as to why his brother had played his hand so badly, and over such a creature. That was clearly the most shocking point of all to him, but even Davidson didn't seem to want to pick it up. Instead, he cautioned his friend about the way certain words were being used these days. After all, the girl was hardly a criminal for having convict parents and both her parents had got their ticket-of-leave more than twenty years past. 'Emancipist be damned,' John exploded. 'In the books of John Kinchela Junior,' he reminded Davidson then and there in no uncertain terms, 'a felon is a felon through and through and for the rest of his life, come what may. Unless, of course,' he softened a little, 'the crime is something honourable in the name of the King or Queen, for example, or for the greater cause of justice.' As far as John could see, James' actions had hardly been honourable, let alone for the greater good. The longer he spent with Davidson the more he began to suspect that his old friend also had some role in the absurd adventure.

Nonetheless, John needed to do what he could for his younger brother and the family name and to do that he would need a different sort of position, closer to home, that could also wield influence. He picked one up at the end of his second week after meeting directly with the governor, Sir Charles FitzRoy, although he decided not to bring up the issue of James at the time. He would, soon enough, but it wouldn't do to start on it right away. FitzRoy had been most affable, and made it clear that sporting squires with knowledge of the land—like John— were exactly what the colony needed. Particularly, he added, a little cryptically, 'in the current climate'. John nodded. Something was clearly brewing right under his nose and he would need to be on the right side of it when the storm finally broke.

The best appointment the governor could offer the doctor's son was Superintendent of Schools. John thought it a good role—one that would get him out and about but still allow him to visit town regularly.

Perhaps even set him up for a country seat in a year or two, FitzRoy added generously, if that was what he wanted. He would be very pleased to see one of his own on the council. But if that was going to happen, John mused to himself after he had left the governor, he would need to clean up his brother's mess quick smart and also set a few other affairs in order. Anne Bourne's eldest son bent himself to the tasks before him with characteristic energy and by the end of September the new Superintendent of Schools was dividing his time between rural tours to Blackman's Swamp near Orange, where he was setting up a new National School, his mother's home in Liverpool and Parramatta Gaol, where he had already organised a writing desk and chair for his brother as well as a weekly delivery of local newspapers.

During one visit John also brought his brother news from London. 'The Battle of Ballingarry is all over the papers,' John noted, explaining how certain parliamentarians had been describing it as 'the most monstrous sedition that has ever taken place in misery-ridden Ireland.' 'Then they don't know their history, too well,' James snorted before reminding his brother of the things they had seen as boys when the Rockites had taken the south to the brink of insurrection just before the family left Ireland for the sugar colony. He also reminded John of what their father had told them about the blood that had run through the family millstream during the United Irishmen's Uprising of '98, and how—years after that—no God-fearing Protestant would ever ride alone after dusk.

'Twenty fires at least,' John continued, for both men shared an interest in the country of their childhood, even though neither held any particular desire to return there, 'all through the countryside stretching from Kilkenny to Limerick,' John trailed off. For a moment the two brothers imagined the bonfires blazing through the close wet countryside of their childhoods. 'I heard,' John started again after a while, 'that when the police came after them, the rebels chased the troops about a mile or so into an old farmhouse belonging to a widow. Mind,' he paused, 'you won't be surprised to learn that the police didn't help themselves much, either—they took the widow's children hostage and then barricaded themselves inside her house.' Both boys were familiar with the sort of butter-coloured stone farmhouse where the uprising had taken place, the sort that lay nestled within the rolling hills like a yellow button pressed into a green velvet cushion. A manor house, no doubt, much like their own home in Kilkenny.

'Around forty dead all up they say,' John added before opening another paper and pointing to a column. 'Blood spilt on both sides, and it looks as though they have given the ringleaders a platform for what will no doubt be the most written about sedition trial in Ireland for years.' Yes, James thought, sharing with John an instinct for how it would all play out, and aware that the men his brother was speaking of, lads like Willie O'Brien and Thomas Meagher, were close to their own age. Men both the Kinchela boys might have gone to college with if they hadn't been in that wretched sugar colony. 'No doubt they will all hang now,' James mused out loud. 'Aye,' John followed, 'or if not that, they'll find themselves in Van Diemen's Land, I would wager, which might be the worse option of the two.'

Martin Gill had also heard the story about the skirmish in the widow's cabbage patch. Once those boys—the Young Irelanders—had parted with Daniel O'Connell and his Repeal Association, Gill had no time for the lot of them, quite frankly. Despite O'Connell's recent death, the Great Emancipator remained Gill's hero as well as the only hope that there would ever be peace let alone prosperity in Ireland as far as he was concerned. He hated the thought of Dublin being held in the hands of a bunch of hot heads who had gone off to Paris and come back with a whole lot of foolish ideas as well as a national flag that was bound to cause as much trouble as the French tricolor. This was a mad, bad year as far as Gill was concerned. Not one where a businessman could afford to take his eyes off his investments for even one minute.

After several weeks of looking about, Gill made up his mind. He would have his daughter wed by the middle of the new year. Earlier, if possible. He wanted the hotel looking good before he began inviting certain gentlemen to join their family for the luncheon Margaret insisted that the family enjoy after mass each Sunday. This would give them time to get the repairs right, and hopefully by then the crowds would be supping on their turtle soup and knocking back their fine pale Indian ales again.

A month or so before Christmas, Martin Gill gave his wife a good wad of notes with which to purchase his daughter two new dresses, in the latest fashion of course. They had the dressmaker call to the house for the fittings rather than have the girl travel around town while the mood was set against her. Mary Ann was heartened by the dresses and assumed they were a gesture of forgiveness from her father. When she learnt of the gift she had rushed to her father and kissed him warmly on both cheeks only to recoil a little from his coolness.

But Margaret had her suspicions. She had a feeling that there was something else about all this and it had something to do with money. One Friday evening she came down to the early dinner seating and found the dining room almost empty other than for an unkempt sea captain drinking cheap bitter, and three men, from the haberdashery trade by the look of their cases, who were drinking at the bar. She checked the books and noticed that there had only been a few families among their residential guests over the past weeks, and that none of the usual sorts from Wellington Valley or Moreton Bay had stopped in for months.

Tricky. The situation was tricky, and Margaret spent several days thinking through how to raise the matter with her husband. First, however, she went and spoke with her father about it. Old McCormick's reply quite stunned her. 'Best start thinking about putting a bit away for yourself,' he said quietly as he went about packing the garden rakes into the makeshift shed at the side of his vegetable patch. He wasn't surprised at all. In fact, ever since the trouble had started with Mary Ann and news had been spreading about the cost of the local drought and wool prices and the like, he had got to thinking along the same lines. If the hotel went under and Martin Gill went up in another bout of hot and bluster, those children would need something. Four little ones, all under ten and the youngest one not yet a year. You couldn't afford to wait and see. Not with that one ruling the roost.

~

Once upon a time, James had been convinced that his brother's return to Sydney would be worth every fatted calf in the colony. All too often he had felt lost without John out the front, leading the way. John liked to solve things, and over the years James had grown accustomed to letting his brother step into the breach. John clearly preferred it that way and James was sufficiently at ease or perhaps lacking the confidence to make it otherwise. Recently, however, James had become less sure. He couldn't put his finger on what it was that was unsettling him about John until a few weeks before Christmas when his brother arrived for his weekly visit.

No sooner had John sat down than he began to tell James—in some detail—about a dinner the gentlemen from the Bathurst region had held in his honour. John had not quite finished repeating the content of the various speeches made to welcome the new Superintendent of Schools when he suddenly launched into a robust interrogation about the foolish enterprise James had recently embarked upon—and with a girl from that station. Kinchela had been waiting for it, indeed he was surprised John had not asked earlier. After all, John had been coming to the gaol for over two months now. As his younger brother fumbled about for an explanation, John crossed his arms across his chest and looked at him with a sour expression. 'The thing is,' John interrupted, 'I have been attracting a good deal of admiration among the right sort of colonists recently and was finally being asked to wield some influence, only now . . .', he trailed off before shrugging his shoulders in irritation. There were several minutes of awkward silence and then John demanded that James explain what he had ever seen in a convict's daughter worth ruining the family's fame and fortune.

That had made James smart. The two men had had their differences—particularly after the last of the Adelaide overland expeditions—but even though there had been a cooling off between them, he never thought his brother would so deftly sink the boot in. His comments brought James up straight. He hadn't given the matter of family reputation much thought. Nor had he considered certain financial concerns relating to his mother's pension and the fact that their brother-in-law, Thomas Gore, was on the brink of insolvency since his warehouse business had been hit by the slump. James began to feel sick, particularly when he remembered his recent conversation with Mary Ann. It was suddenly blatantly clear that his older brother would never approve of such a match, and if he pursued the matter further he would end up like the other men who married beneath themselves in the colony. Never invited anywhere because, well, no one would share a table with such a woman. Just as bad was the fact that James might have brought down the entire family. Kinchela swallowed. He had only been thinking of himself, John reprimanded him curtly, and not very well either.

The entire conversation was utterly unpleasant and that particular meeting finished with John departing in righteous indignation as James slouched sullenly in his chair. But even as James digested the gravity of his actions, he could not avoid the fact that his brother had recently acquired a spirit of rather brash high-mindedness. Nor had John mentioned the £4000 he had borrowed from their brother-in-law, which played no small part in bringing down their sister Mary and her husband Thomas. What with these deflections and denials and John's mocking of his 'bit of native skirt', James was beginning to wonder if he had placed too much faith in his brother. Perhaps the great John Kinchela was not the salvation he had hoped for, James mused as he returned to his cell.

Still, old habits die hard, and James deeply admired his brother, which was just as well for that was entirely how John expected it, particularly when, after several weeks of absence, the doctor's eldest son suddenly appeared one afternoon just a day before Christmas, his arms laden with jolly treats from their mother's larder, as well as other exciting news. 'There's been a crew of South Sea Islanders docked in the quay for less than a week,' John began after the two brothers had settled down to a feast of their mother's scotch eggs. James detected excitement in his brother's voice and discerned that John must have decided to push past their recent difference. 'Their schooner has just come in from the Sandwich Islands,' John began, 'via New Zealand, and since it arrived there have been all sorts of rumours as well as strange activities around the docks.' James looked at his brother expectantly.

'Well that was until yesterday,' John went on, clearly enjoying keeping his younger brother in suspense, 'when *The Herald* and then *The Maitland Mercury* both confirmed it.' He produced the daily newspaper from his satchel and pointed to a column, which bore a slim bold title—in capital letters. John only gave his brother a moment to glance at it before he snatched it back and began to read the column out loud, skipping over the boring details and rushing on to the key facts.

'We this day copy the details of one of the most extraordinary discoveries of almost any age or time,' John started, 'a discovery that eclipses all the fabled legends of Cortess and Pisarro.' Kinchela listened, leaning forward with his hands on his chin as he tried to make sense of what he was hearing. 'It outstrips the wildest vision that lured a Drake or a Raleigh on an El Dorado hunt.' John drew in his breath and looked at his brother, raising his eyebrows before he continued to read in a slow and steady tone: 'Gold, glittering, glorious gold,' he said, looking up to gauge his brother's surprise. 'Gold has been discovered in amazing quantities and utmost purity . . . in California.' 'Gold,' Kinchela whistled and rocked back on his chair, trying to make sense of what he had just heard. John chuckled a little and then began to furnish him with other tidbits and conjectures he had heard for Sydney was fairly buzzing with 'the dazzling discovery', he declared.

For John, however, the excitement of the whole thing was that he had been the first to share it with his brother. Once he had relished that moment he hastened to share his opinion of the entire matter. The doctor's son had more than a few suspicions about the so-called 'yellow fever'. 'This sort of madness can afflict a country in all sorts of ways,' he cautioned, 'let alone what it might do to our colony. Labour for a start,' he hastened to explain. 'What would happen if all the bounty boys hightail it to California when we need them watching our stock and tanning hides? The papers are saying other things, too,' John followed, pointing to the section where it warned of neglected harvests as well as the 'utter absence of law and order' that had already consumed the fort town of Sacramento. 'The whole thing will turn everything upside down and inside out if we don't keep an eye out,' he nodded shrewdly to his brother. 'Put an end to industry and sobriety as well as good morals,' he finished, closing the paper and handing it to his brother as if the matter was now settled for both of them. But James was not so sure. It would be tempting for anyone who didn't like where they were to just get up and go, and he wondered if there was still any gold left, given how long it took the papers to get to Sydney.

But John would not be distracted. He had even better news, he said, producing two tin cups from his bag into which he poured sweet, syrupy madeira. It was the first drop of alcohol Kinchela had smelt since his incarceration at Parramatta. Thanks to John's strenuous petitioning, as well as a recent conversation 'directly with the governor', John announced, handing one tin cup to his brother, FitzRoy had decided to exercise the mercy of his personal prerogative. James looked at him uncertainly. He would not have to serve the entire nine months of his sentence, his elder brother declared with satisfaction. He was going to be released early. Kinchela jumped from his seat and clapped his brother on the back with such exuberance that John bade him stop so they could both raise a toast to the governor's good health.

John had come good after all, Kinchela thought, ashamed of his recent grumblings and thrilled to think that freedom was now only a few weeks away. From now on he would work hard to keep on a good footing with John and not let things go astray again. James raised his tin cup and grinned as the two men tapped them together and both took a generous swig. 'On the first day of the new year,' John declared with obvious pleasure as he filled their cups again, 'James Butler Kinchela shall be reunited with his cane and his snuffbox and free once more to walk upon the world.'

CHAPTER FOURTEEN

In the Soup

No one was quite sure why the wily old auctioneer was coming to lunch, particularly just a day or two after Christmas, but Martin Gill seemed to be making quite a thing of it. He wanted William and Mary Ann looking their best and Margaret to make the excellent turtle soup to which Alexander Moore was so partial. Their father had certainly been acting in a peculiar manner over the past few weeks, the two eldest children concurred. Brooding one moment, disappearing from the business unexpectedly the next and returning much later and often in an even greater state of agitation.

Margaret was watching all this but minding herself just the same. Her father's caution had put her on her front foot. She had a feeling that he might be right, but she was at a bit of a loss as to what to do. Martin was her husband. For right or wrong, she had made a sacred vow. He could be difficult at times, no doubt about it, but she was still certain—well, most of the time she was—that her husband had their best interests at heart. Margaret wanted to do the right thing by him. Their lives were bound tight to one another and with four young children as well as William and Mary Ann there was no other sensible path forward but the one they took together as husband and wife.

She had seen other women, her own sort, who had married just weeks after arriving in the colony but had, within a few years, set off on their own. Some had needed to salvage what remained of their lives after their husbands had given them a thrashing that had taken them too close to the end of themselves. Other women had just pushed off when they got tired of the sight or smell of the man they had hooked up with. Still others had run because that was what they had always done. None of those women had prospered, Margaret knew, for she sometimes recognised a familiar face down at the market. Mostly, these sort of women were forced to live among the broken people of the streets and some were hardly what you would call female anymore. Sydney was a mean town for a single woman, and worse still for a deserted wife and mother. She would have to make do and the best way to do that was to be her husband's helpmate.

Margaret determined that they would get to fixing whatever was going on, together. Only, try as she might, Margaret could not find the entry point into her husband's secret. He was closed to her in a way that was not only perplexing but also, as the days went by, increasingly infuriating. Had she not carried twelve of his children and raised six of them to good standing thus far? Had she not also brought good sense to his various enterprises and taught him certain tricks that had made their confectionery business the finest in town? Had she not also drawn upon her father's modest earnings to pay her husband's bail when he had lost his mind out at the Homebush racecourse? All this time she had stood by him and accepted his rule, even after he'd made some particularly foolish decisions. Margaret was on edge with the way her husband was keeping to himself and now she had to serve that soup at her own table to that shuffling ox of a man. And then it occurred to her—Mary Ann. Her husband was going to try to get rid of their problems by fixing their daughter up with some monied old gull. It was one thing for parents to choose their children's match—that was right and proper as far as she was concerned—but to sell their own daughter to a man like that—just to save your hide? With no word of it to his own wife. It was too much.

On Sunday old Moore called at the hotel for his long-awaited luncheon with the Gill family, looking scrubbed and washed and quite chuffed as he made his way upstairs to the family dining room. He was surprised to receive quite a cool reception from his friend's wife. He had met Mrs Gill on several occasions and considered her a modest, well-conducted matron equipped with obvious talents in the kitchen. But now Margaret was barely cordial.

William, who had no idea as to why his mother was behaving in such a manner, felt the need to extend greater interest to their guest than he may have otherwise. Mary Ann felt the matter even more acutely than William. Looking quite fetching in her new red dress, she made a particular effort with her father's guest. She asked considered questions about his work and smiled attentively as Alexander Moore pontificated about the various trades he had worked in and what he thought of the colony's future fortunes. Seeing that this was pleasing her father, Mary Ann showered Moore with her attention and yet the more she basked in her father's appreciation, the more she roused her mother's ire.

But Moore was oblivious to these subterranean currents and clearly felt encouraged by the young woman's interest. 'Everyone is talking about gold these days,' he opined rubbing his hands together when the splendid soup finally arrived. 'Quite a few of the old hands have already slipped away to San Francisco, desperate to try their chances in the west,' he continued, nodding knowingly at Gill. The auctioneer was aware of the terms upon which Gill had come to the colony and assumed his host must know some of the men concerned. Margaret sniffed and looked away. The children recognised this as an expression of utmost disgust. But still, Mary Ann and William bore on, encouraged by their father and keen to hear more of California. So Moore continued, entertaining his hosts with stories about the Chinese, who were said to be flooding into San Francisco and how small children had been picking up giant nuggets that they had found right in front of their feet.

Mary Ann wished to know if their guest knew anyone who had gone to the goldfields in search of such a fortune? But Moore was not of that persuasion. He had heard of people 'going mad', he cautioned the young creature, 'from silver and diamond mines and the like'. There was no doubt that gold would be even worse, he warned, 'particularly as the crops are drying up here. Fool's dust,' he said, wagging his spoon at the girl before wiping a lick of Margaret's soup from his chin. 'The best money,' he said, noisily spooning more of the green creamy liquid into his uneven mouth, 'is the money you make with your own wits, the money you can feel in your pocket. Isn't that right, Mr Gill?' he finished, looking up at the family patriarch, who shifted uncomfortably under his wife's glare.

She would not have her daughter married to that pelican, Margaret told her husband that night when the pair were finally alone in their bedroom. She rarely spoke directly like that to her husband, but this time, he had gone too far, she said. She was expecting a fight and was ready for one. But instead Gill said nothing. He simply looked at his wife, or rather, sort of through her, then raised his eyebrows and whistled something sharp through his teeth before pushing off to sleep in one of the empty guestrooms.

Martin Gill had also reached the end of his tether. He was just about done with trying to repair every disastrous situation his foolish family got themselves into. If every time he put something forward he was second-guessed, or even worse, undermined by his wife in front of his children and his guest, then he would be done with it all. He had never expected Margaret to show him up like that, particularly not in front of a guest. Some men would thrash their wives for such disrespect. She had already shown him, in more ways than she realised, that she would not back him when it came to the girl. As if that was his fault, too, he grimaced, curling into one of the hotel beds and thinking how pleasant it was to get away from her infernal breathing. She was onto him, too, he reckoned, and knew the business well enough to see when something was not right.

But Gill hadn't given up yet. He was still looking about, patching bits and pieces together, working out how they would get the hotel back into the swing of things again. He had approached a private shipping agent and got him to set up his offices in the dining room, so now there was a steady stream of hopefuls coming in to book their passage to California. Hundreds of colonists now had an eye for the goldfields, Gill knew, and he was going to make a profit from them. These days the streets were full of news from California. From what he had heard from one old sea dog who hung around the shipping agent in his hotel, there was plenty of land for the taking. All a fellow needed was a few nuggets and he could buy himself a big slab of land with a river on it, like you wouldn't get in these parts anymore. But Martin Gill had heard other things too—about whores spreading disease through the streets, wild floods that destroyed everything in their wake and fires that had seen the whole tinderbox of a town go up in blazes not once or twice, but almost every couple of weeks. Still, there was real money to be had in California, and it wouldn't be there for long. Gold, Gill thought, drifting off to sleep in the splendid isolation of his new bed. If only some of that gold dust, even a few flakes, would float his way now.

~

On a crisp morning on the first day of 1849, the air was full of magpie warble as James Butler Kinchela stepped through the front gate of Parramatta Gaol and into the waiting world. He was dressed in the fine winter suit he had been wearing when he attended the trial, although it now hung loose about him thanks to months of prison slops. He had hardly adjusted to the bright morning light when he noticed Somerville's coach sitting squat and familiar on the dusty track, right in front of him. The old driver was up in the top seat, swatting flies with his crop and looking as portly as ever. Kinchela greeted him with such genuine heartiness that the old man could not stop nodding with the awkward pleasure of it. 'Come now, sir,' Somerville eventually insisted, 'or we'll never get you to the Adelphi.' And with that, Prisoner 486 opened the door of the carriage and hauled himself into the familiar cabin where he began to reacquaint himself with his snuffbox.

A few hours later he was comfortably ensconced in his old room at the Adelphi, looking out the window and getting a feeling for the mood in the town. Kinchela was keen for a bit of life. He had missed a drink, there was no doubt about it, but he also saw the sense in keeping a bit of a lid on it for a while. He knew that John was up in the Orange district and that this would allow him a few days before he had to head out to his mother's in Liverpool, where John resided when he was in town. Before then, however, Kinchela would have a few days to ease himself back into the world and see what was what.

The town was thrumming with New Year festivities and Kinchela had a feeling there was fun to be had. The races, he thought. There would be a few good horses out at Shaw's and there was no reason why he couldn't clean himself up and make a day of it. He thought of sending a note to Mary Ann informing her of the governor's benevolence and asking if there might be some way for them to meet in the next week or so, but then he recalled his conversations with John. He was, in truth, a little torn. What could he say to her?, he wondered, particularly now he could no longer ignore his brother's strident opposition. He would think on it a while longer, he decided, before dashing off a quick note to Somerville requesting that he call by his mother's Liverpool property and collect a summer jacket as well as a few clean shirts for the races.

Next Kinchela busied himself with a number of man-about-town errands. He couldn't believe a shave at the barbers could yield so much satisfaction, he told the man at the Market Street store as he flipped him an extra coin in thanks. Everyday liberties, he thought happily, as he made his way back to the hotel. Halfway back to the hotel he realised he was out of snuff, so he turned about and headed towards the George Street tobacconist.

The bell over the door of the store announced Kinchela's arrival with a vigorous clang that was quite at odds with its shrouded interior and the curious figure of Joseph Aarons sitting in the almost-dark, crouched over a small set of iron scales, carefully balancing a pile of brown snuff against a set of dull-looking weights. 'How d'you do on this fine day, good man?' Kinchela asked in excellent spirits. Aarons acknowledged his customer with a grunt and barely looked up. 'I'll have an ounce of what is in your scales,' Kinchela said casting an eye about the store. As his back was turned a young girl, perhaps fourteen years old, slipped out from behind the back curtains and began speaking loudly to the old man. 'The gentleman would like some snuff, Father,' she said as sweetly as she could, but the old man scowled at her. 'I heard,' he grumbled, 'but I can't do much when I am in the middle of something else.'

The young girl gave Kinchela an apologetic smile before returning to her father. 'Shall I help, then?' she asked, but perhaps a little too brightly. 'You will not, girl, indeed you will not,' Aarons snapped tetchily, clutching his scales to his chest before scurrying under the bench and fossicking about for something, only to emerge several minutes later with a small tin scoop, a roll of brown paper and some string. 'Now what was it that you were after?' the shopkeeper asked, craning his neck and squinting at his customer. The girl interjected, repeating Kinchela's request before standing back with her hands clasped in front of her as she struggled to resist the desire to take control of her father's shaky transference of the powdery substance onto the sheet of paper. Smatterings of the rich-smelling stuff fell this way and that onto the bench and floor, just about anywhere, in fact, but on the paper itself.

Kinchela watched and waited and remembered what it was like. His own father's infirmity and the thick lump he would get in his throat after spending time with him—watching the once fine man fumbling for words and sometimes even thoughts. James felt sorry for the poor girl stuck inside on such a pretty day with very little chance of any fun. He tried to lift the moment with a little light talk, and turned to the shopkeeper's daughter with what he hoped was an amiable disposition. 'And will you be going to the races today, lass?' he asked. The young freckled girl blushed and shook her head. 'No, sir, just another trade day for my father and I,' she replied rather wistfully, and for a moment Kinchela considered asking her to join him at Shaw's.

But before he could open his mouth, Aarons peered at Kinchela from under his spectacles and then, with an agility that surprised James, bounded from his bench towards the door. 'You are still meant to be in gaol, are you not, Mr Kinchela?' he barked at his shocked customer as he flung open the store door. 'I will not have you in my store, sir,' the small man proclaimed indignantly, and he seemed to rise miraculously in stature, 'thinking you can take my daughter as you did to that other fool of a fellow.'

Kinchela hastily put two good coins on the bench, took the not-quite-wrapped package from the bench and left the shop. He heard the door slam behind him and the sound of the clanging bell seemed to follow him halfway down George Street. The old shopkeeper had put the wind up him that was for sure. He had been foolish enough to assume that things would return to normal. He would need to keep himself to himself, he realised. If that was a taste of the way things would be now, he was best not to be too friendly, particularly towards the local girls. He would need to play a straight bat, he determined, heading back to the Adelphi and downing two good tall glasses of Indian ale while waiting for Somerville to take him out to the New Year's races.

But the moment he caught sight of all the tilburies and such lined along the road to Shaw's Racecourse, Kinchela forgot the morning's unpleasantness. No sooner did he have the smell of horses in his nostrils, than he began to think about which horses would be running and what he had to bet with. They had already run one heat by the time he paid and got through the gate. He gave Somerville a few shillings to enjoy himself for the afternoon and went off in the direction of the Gentleman's Green where he thought he might find Davidson having a crack at the bowls in between race heats.

He ambled through the crowd, pleased to be reacquainted with his cane and also enjoying the feel of the top hat Somerville had brought back from Liverpool along with his shirts. It was a fine afternoon and half of Sydney looked to be out and about delighting in the Christmas season and the sunshine. There were children running around the back hedges and a group of slightly raucous girls entertaining themselves with a game of quoits, while already one or two less fortunate sorts lay slumped against a canvas marquee, having already succumbed, he suspected, to one swizzler too many.

Kinchela saw Jim Davidson with three other men and was thinking twice about approaching the group when his friend spied him from a distance and beckoned him over. Kinchela stepped forward and shook hands with the various well-to-do fellows and then joined them, drink in hand, as they chatted about who they liked for what. It was hard to go past Old Jorrocks, everyone knew, but you didn't stand to win much on him these days. A fellow with flushed cheeks and fly-away blond hair fancied putting money on the Drapers' Purse and he liked Mr Patrick's Moustache for a place at least. Others were talking up the merits of Creeping Jane in the Union Plate, while Davidson was sure that Mr Lucas's Ratcatcher would win the day. There was a lot of talk, too, about the Timor ponies, and Kinchela was keen to see how they would run.

He felt rather grateful to Davidson for not making a fuss. He shouted his friend more than a few shandygaffs and the two were having quite a jolly time when he spied young Healy, who he hadn't seen since that night back in late May the year before when he had asked his young friend to keep an eye out for Mary Ann when she arrived at the Sportsman's Arms. Kinchela was not so keen to see Healy, who, in his opinion, had hardly lifted a finger to help him. He ducked behind a party of carousers at the back of a rather rowdy tent, but the stout little fellow had seen Kinchela and began pushing towards him. He greeted Kinchela with a slap on the back and asked how he had been getting on. He had been reading the papers and thought the whole thing a very sorry affair. Not done at all, he said, knocking back a whiskey and ordering another two. Healy was halfway through some excited talk about how the colony had gone mad for the middling men, when one of Davidson's chums looked Kinchela up and down and tapped himself on the forehead, 'Of course, that is who you are, isn't it, old boy?' the young gent said with a mixture of amusement and admiration. 'You are that fellow who took that girl from the hotel,' he chuckled to himself as he knocked back his Jenny Lind. 'What a lark, eh,' he said sizing up Kinchela. 'Well I hope you got some pleasure for your suffering,' he snorted with a lecherous grin.

Davidson looked away. Kinchela said nothing but carefully studied his race guide for a moment before stepping away to place a bet. Such talk. Try as he might he could think of no suitable reply. It was best to bow out as quickly as he could. Still he was sorry not to bid Davidson farewell. Kinchela wove his way through the crowd until he finally got to the railing. He was keen to lose himself in the thunder of the ponies, so he found a prime position near the bookies and spent the rest of the afternoon moving back and forth between his spot close to the track and the betting circle. When, several hours later, he found Somerville it was quite late in the day and both men were worse for wear. The day had had its pleasures but it had not been entirely pleasant, Kinchela realised as the coach trundled back to the Adelphi. Still he was glad to have seen Davidson and also greatly relieved that he had not come across any luncheon booths proudly displaying 'Mr Gill's Best Produce from Home'.

When, however, he stepped inside the Adelphi Hotel, the manager informed Kinchela that Captain Joseph Long Innes was waiting for him in the back parlour. The impatient-looking magistrate gave James an imperious stare as the convicted felon sat down. Before he could so much as order a drink, Innes asked if he had seen the girl. 'Eh?' Kinchela replied, as he looked at the Captain with an expression of confusion, 'Which girl?' He had seen a lot of girls that day. Fetching ones and plump ones as well as a few rather coarse and overdressed creatures, too. Which girl was Innes on about, Kinchela wondered, and what was it to him? He stumbled through his slightly inebriated thoughts and then realised who the man must be talking about. 'I've no intention of causing any trouble down that end of Pitt Street, if that is what you mean,' Kinchela asserted indignantly.

But that was not what the Captain meant. 'The Aarons girl,' he interrupted. 'Mr Kinchela, do you know where she is?' James was vexed. 'I don't even know who she is,' he blurted out. The Captain opened his notebook and began recounting Kinchela's morning activities with such a degree of detail that the gentleman settler was rather taken aback. 'You went to a tobacconist on George Street this morning,' the

Police Magistrate started, 'and you asked the young girl there to accompany you to the races.' He scrutinised Kinchela's response as the man in question rubbed the back of his neck, trying to make sense of it all. 'The girl has not been seen at the store since,' Innes continued, 'and her father is now determined to have you.' Kinchela slumped into a chair. He had not seen the girl, had not thought of her since that morning and had certainly not stepped out with her anywhere, he insisted. 'I was friendly and that was all,' he told the Captain and explained how old Aarons had sent him packing with a flea in his ear.

The Police Magistrate began to suspect that there was probably not much to the whole thing. Indeed, it was entirely possible that the episode had been orchestrated by a well-known hotelier from the harbour end of Pitt Street. Nonetheless, 'Given the circumstances of the past year,' he explained, 'and the gravity with which the public considers such matters, I must give this matter its due, Mr Kinchela. I trust you understand my obligation,' he said, 'especially since you are out early, on the governor's mercy and all that.' James Butler shook his head in disbelief. It had been a long day and he had been looking forward to his first good night's sleep in months.

The Captain stood up and asked Kinchela to walk with him to the police station. Old Aarons had been insistent, Innes explained, and when he visited him that afternoon, he had thumped the police desk and demanded that someone find his daughter. Kinchela nodded. He felt a little sorry for Innes, having to respond to every bark and shadow that happened in the colony. However, as he stood before the town magistrate and listened to the now familiar charges relating to the crime of abduction—for the second time in less than a year—Kinchela realised that he was feeling a good deal sorrier for himself.

CHAPTER FIFTEEN

A Gross Breach

The Colonial Secretary was persisting with his madness. He had decided to ignore the stream of assertive, private correspondence and public epistles that continued to arrive from New South Wales, all of which were clearly aimed at discouraging the resumption of transportation. And, for the first time in almost a decade, Earl Grey, second Baronet and only son of Sir George Grey, had dispatched a boat with over two hundred British felons on board, bound for New South Wales. Only, cholera was delaying the ship's departure and all through January the *Hashemy* lay idle in the cold winter docks as each day yet another young corpse was dragged from the vessel.

But Grey had no intention of stepping back. He had many concerns that were much more pressing than a group of pushy radicals and working men from that far-flung colony in the south. Trying to find food for the survivors of the Irish famine was one thing; keeping a handle on the treason-felony trial of the Ballingarry boys was another. All last year he had to look on as France toppled this way and that, and then a bunch of mad Chartists and other unstable sorts had organised a rally right under his nose, in the heart of London. 1848 had been horrendous. But the New Year had finally come and Grey was intent upon fixing his position and staying the course. He would not be put in his place by anyone.

Meanwhile, rumours of an epidemic on board that loathsome convict ship had reached Sydney and the papers were frothing at the mouth about how Grey was daring to infect the good people of Sydney with the vile contagions of the old world. Hadn't the colonists of New South Wales resolutely striven to purge themselves of all those foul diseases?, Mackay and Hawkesley asked in the numerous columns they devoted to what they were now referring to as Grey's 'Gross Breach of Faith'. It was time to say no, Parkes and others insisted, as they went about the Sydney taverns, preparing the working men of the colony to take a stand against the greatest insult they had yet experienced from the Colonial Office. They would stop the authorities in their tracks, Parkes promised, playing up to the men in the docklands, and the government would learn they best not take the loyalty of their so-called underlings for granted.

John Kinchela had never read such ripe stuff. He preferred to read the better press, but had been advised by some of his friends, in particular two conservative magistrates from the Bathurst district, that he should apprise himself of the inflammatory tracts coming out of the town papers so he could make up his own mind. Some of these papers were sounding decidedly American, John thought, as if they might tip the convicts into the harbour, as had been done in Boston during that tea and taxes affair. But while these men were going about it in the wrong way, John could not entirely disagree with their sentiments. The colony would be better without convicts, he had decided. He had done his time as a magistrate out in those parts of the valley when he was a good deal younger and other men had refused to share the bench with him because of his youth. He had seen, first hand, how wily government men could be. Many were little better than pustular lesions that required lancing, and he had never regretted the reputation he earned for licking the worst of them with his lash. It was what had earned him the loyalty of the landowners as well as other magistrates. Some might quibble, he had told his father when the old man had raised the matter, but he had no qualms in treating a man like a dog if he behaved as one. So yes, John would be happy to see an end to convicts in the colony, particularly when they were capable of producing children like the creature who had recently caused his family so much trouble.

John was pushing through the January papers on the verandah of a rather pretty widow's property near Blackman's Swamp, where he boarded while in the Orange district, when a story in *The Maitland* caught his eye. It was impossible. No, he thought, turning the page back and scanning the sheet until he found what he thought he had seen. John read it again and again. It could not be. But after the fourth reading, he saw that it was and once he had digested the extremely unpalatable facts the Superintendent of Schools stood up, and, in a state of considerable irritation, went to pack his bags.

❧

But nothing matched the shock Mary Ann experienced a few days later when she stumbled across the same story. With the election gone, she was no longer required to read the papers to her father. Nonetheless, Mary Ann maintained an interest in the local news-sheets. She and William would often spend a few hours each week reading the key stories to one another while her parents were distracted with hotel business. Will was particularly interested in anything to do with gold, while Mary Ann looked for news of Europe, specifically France.

They had been scanning over the weekly copy of *Bell's Sporting Life* when William suddenly fell silent. Mary Ann could see from his expression that something had floored him, so she snatched the sheets out of his hands before he could stop her. Looking over the page for the source of his expression, Mary Ann thought she saw Kinchela's name and when she found it again she read the title of the article in puzzlement: 'The Love Chase'. Mary Ann could not understand what would compel the papers to return to the events of last year, but as she read on she discovered that the report concerned a more recent 'melodrama', which, *Bell's* teased, 'had opened on George Street in the new year with the principal parts being played by none other than James

Kinchela, Esquire, of high extraction, and the young Louisa Aarons, in a role, they hoped, 'that would be her first and last appearance in this character.'

William watched Mary Ann in dread. He had not had time to read the entire piece but had gleaned enough to see that the story was as bad as it could be. 'The curtain rose,' Mary Ann read, 'to the monotonous tones of the deposition clerk, who recounted how "the lordly James" had asked "the gentle Louisa" to decorate his arm at the Drapers' Races and afterwards deposited her in a most notorious house of ill-fame from whence her desperate father had eventually fetched her.' Mary Ann gasped. James had been released from gaol and made no effort to contact her, she realised with a sinking heart. After all that had been he had preferred the races to her own company. She put an involuntary hand to her stomach where she suddenly felt that she had been whacked hard. The parallels with this absurd event and their own thwarted elopement were too similar to be ignored, even if the girl was a little younger.

As horrific as it was, Mary Ann read on. 'Here, however, the curtain was compelled to fall,' Bell's lightly trilled, 'for no actors had come forward to provide testimony in support of Joseph Aarons, so the presiding judge had dropped the charges. Nonetheless,' Bell's drolly noted, 'they were quite sure that Captain Innes had made every effort to soothe the injured sire, assuring him that the case could be reopened any time fresh evidence became available.' 'The charges have been dropped,' Mary Ann said dully as she pushed the paper to Will. She walked to the window and leant her cheek against the cool glass. Her mind was racing. She could make no sense of it. She watched Will's appalled expression as he took up the paper and finished the last sentence in which Bell's hastened to add that they hoped they might declare 'this sordid performance finally done'.

Brother and sister looked at one another and William noticed that the colour had drained from Mary Ann's face. She was pale, he thought, as pale as she had been on election night when he had been waiting for her in the nursery. He hadn't meant to shock her, but he had needed to let her know that while he had helped her this time—feeding the children and putting them to bed—he would not be party to such deceit again. She would be on her own, he had told her quite firmly, if she tried such nonsense in the future. Mary Ann had bowed her head as her brother had admonished her. She had been careless in her thoughts and actions, she said quietly and carefully, and, he was correct, she had thought only of herself. She promised she would never embark upon such an undertaking again.

When, however, she could see that she had appeased him with this promise, Mary Ann had rushed on to explain why she would not need to. 'I have his promise, Will,' she had said, triumphantly. 'He wants nothing more, he said, than for us to marry when he is free.' Will was not entirely convinced by what he heard, and also doubted that such a union had any hope of improving their family's circumstances, but he noticed how the glow stole back into his sister's cheeks as she recounted her adventure and felt such a wave of admiration for her courage that he eventually conceded. 'Well,' he said, a little uncertainly, 'if there can be a happy ending to this, it would be the best for all of us. But,' he finished, leaning forward in the nursery chair to fix his sister with a stern look, 'mind yourself, Mary Ann.'

And now? Will watched his sister struggle with the shock of it. Her face was quite pale. Just once she made a little noise—something between a choke and a whimper. Will could not think of what to do or say, so he simply walked to Mary Ann and squeezed her hand.

John Kinchela arrived in Sydney and stopped at the Club for a refreshment before heading out to see his mother. He was aghast to see that the tables were strewn with news-sheets no doubt carrying similar reports to the ones he had read in *The Maitland*. He ordered a double whiskey and asked a waiter to collect all the papers and bring them to him. Then he slid just a little deeper into his sofa so that he was obscured by the large open pages as he scoured them for more of the same dreadful stuff.

And there it was. In the Hobart *Courier*. 'The man had not even finished his first sentence,' the editor fumed, 'so how was it that Kinchela could be at large again? Surely the case was much too serious to be discharged by Captain Innes, particularly since Mr Kinchela had been tried and convicted of a similar offence less than a year before-hand. Indeed, wasn't the man in question still meant to be serving his sentence?' they asked. 'With a case this serious, the magistrate should have subpoenaed witnesses,' another paper fumed. John could imagine that Captain Innes was going to have some difficult questions to answer. But then, as he read on, it also occurred to him that the matter might have consequences even higher up. 'Some serious breach had clearly been made,' the *Moreton Bay Courier* raged, 'and none but the governor could be expected to explain why this double abductor was worthy of his Excellency's mercy.' Well that was that, John thought, taking a very large swig of his drink. The Kinchelas had done their dash with the governor and this time he doubted even he could turn things right.

James Butler Kinchela was done with Sydney. He had had just about enough of the clever talk he experienced every time he went out. He expected as much in the hotels, but he had hoped there might be a code of gentlemanly conduct elsewhere that would make life tolerable. But no. With the exception of Davidson, the few friends who had maintained their association with him after the first episode had now washed their hands of James Butler Kinchela and he was now also well and truly *persona non grata* at all the clubs. If not condemned as an outright cad and bounder, the doctor's youngest son had been dismissed as nothing more than a fool.

In contrast to his blustery brother, James Butler Kinchela had more of his father's temperament when it came to matters of reputation. He would not fight for his name in some hot-headed way that, to him, seemed more likely to further incriminate him. Nor was he in a mood to take another serve from his brother. John had completely failed to give James even the slightest benefit of the doubt. Indeed, the moment the doctor's eldest son had returned to the Liverpool house from his afternoon in the Club, he marched into the parlour and up to his younger brother. Right there, in front of the servants, John had given his younger brother a large and unsolicited piece of his mind. Anne Bourne had put her head down and tended to her stitching in silence but James could see that she was grieved by the force with which John conducted himself in this matter.

Things were against him, Kinchela knew. It would be best to head up north for a bit, clear his head and see if he could organise the sale of Hawkwood. Once that run was gone his brother would no longer be burdened by their financial partnership and they would be free of each other, once and for all. James was feeling hard-done-by and nursing more than a little ill-will for all the times his brother had assumed the worst of him. He was probably best out of the way, he decided, for he had clearly damaged his brother's standing and also placed his family upon precarious financial footing.

Kinchela took Pitt Street towards Circular Quay and the Moreton Bay steamer. It was the most direct route and he was entirely fed up with having to avoid that particular hotel. He had nothing to hide. After all, he had not really done anything of which he should be ashamed. Indeed, the whole business had been a succession of confusions and he should not be held to blame for all of them. He would leave this damn town on his own terms, he decided, and with his head held high. Some part of him was hopeful that he might somehow bump into Mary Ann and be able to find a way of explaining the whole dreadful mess to her.

It was now the middle of summer and the season was in full force, with the hills and gardens about the harbour pulsing with the heat. It looked superb, he had to admit, the deep blue of the harbour and the white and honey sandstone of the finer buildings about town. All under the vast, humming summer sky. And there was Gill's hotel, standing squat and confident, the third-storey window reflecting the morning light, catching his attention as he walked by, almost as if it was winking at him. The entire episode had been a poor business, Kinchela sighed, and he had made a mess of it, all round. On top of that he had also broken his promise to Mary Ann—but there it was. He had tried to fix things and he had been stopped at every turn by the cruellest and most peculiar incidents imaginable. He could see no way of fixing it. She could not be expected to believe him after all that had been. Best to be off, Kinchela decided. Leave the poor thing to make do as best she could. He was heavy with the shame of it and wanted nothing more than to be away, out on the land. Free of it all.

Several weeks later Martin Gill had another of his friends join the family luncheon. This time they served roast beef and it was Mr Lewis Samuel who came to call. Martin Gill had decided to host the meal downstairs in the formal dining room. There were no guests booked for the hotel's luncheon and Mr Samuel had often expressed his appreciation of that particular room. It had been his uncle's favourite, he had said, more than once. In such a public environment, Margaret would have to conduct herself with composure and Gill was pleased with the way he had outsmarted his wife in this matter.

Mr Samuel arrived in his Sunday best and Gill ushered him into the formal room, sitting the well-connected bachelor opposite his eldest daughter. Margaret was present but clearly seething. So great was her indignation that she had planned to be too unwell to attend but at the last moment decided she best be on hand to watch over proceedings and, in particular, Mary Ann. She was, however, finding it exceedingly difficult to be civil to Mr Samuel, who much to her disdain, was insisting on engaging her about the fittings in the room and the care she had taken with the choice of drapery and the like. Margaret nodded primly and kept her head bowed to discourage further conversation, but Mr Samuel was agonisingly impervious to her discouragement. Again, Mary Ann felt compelled to shield their guest from her mother's stiff demeanour which she did by asking her father's guest to describe his own home.

'It suffers from the lack of a good woman, I am afraid my dear,' Mr Samuel replied to Mary Ann with a solemn sigh. 'It is a fine home—that is true. One might even say, the very finest in the Macquarie River region, with a sweeping vista and a generous staircase, and yet,' he continued, gesturing with both hands, one of which held a fork skewered with a generous portion of red meat that flapped about as he gestured, 'there is none of the finer spirit a woman brings to a house,' he finished, fixing Mary Ann with a particularly melancholy expression.

Martin Gill looked down at his meal and ignored Mary Ann's look of bewilderment. But Margaret who had been eating her meal in silent fury had had enough. She put down her knife and fork and stood up from her meal as the entire room turned at her sudden gesture. 'I will not have it,' she said, laying her palms square on the table as she prepared for a fight. 'I will not have you marry my daughter off to such a man, and for no reason but that you like the look of his money, and all because you have lost all your own.' Margaret was quivering with rage as she stared down her husband at the other end of the table.

The next minute all hell broke loose. Mr Samuel coughed to sputtering point, choking on some of the beef he had swallowed whole in shock. William jumped up and tried to help by patting the unfortunate gentleman on the back as he called for one of the kitchen staff to help. Meanwhile, at the other end of the dining table, Martin Gill had picked up the carving knife and was waving it in the air in the direction of his wife. But Margaret was not in the least perturbed; she glared back at her husband with an expression that was thick with contempt.

Mary Ann went and stood beside her mother. She had no idea, really, what to do, but it seemed right to take her mother's part as she tried to make sense of all that was unfolding. So Mr Samuel had been brought here as a suitor and she was meant to marry him? What about old Alexander Moore? Was he another of her father's plans, she speculated, her mind racing as she took in the horror of it; her father had these men in mind as her husband, and all because of their money? Then she recalled her father's curious conduct over the past two months as well as the considerable number of deliverymen who had taken to leaning insolently by the kitchen door, refusing to leave until they had received cash payment for their goods. Two birds with one stone, she thought bitterly. Get rid of a ruined daughter as well as all the hotel debts. How long had her father been planning all this?, she wondered. Then her mind strayed to the dresses. They were not a gift, she realised. Her father had been fattening her up for sale day.

No sooner had Lewis Samuel managed to reclaim his breath than he wiped his wet brow and retrained his shirt and collar, which had come undone in his choking frenzy. Gill had taken him for a fool, he saw. He had wanted him to marry his daughter so he would quit his debts. The family must be in even deeper trouble than he had assumed by the delay in the last rental quarter. Why hadn't he thought of that before, Samuel seethed, annoyed with himself for being so gullible. Why would he want a girl like that—reputation spoilt and no substance to bring to the match, he sniffed as he fixed his tie. He was better off as a bachelor than as the husband of a sullied girl with a cunning rat for a father.

Mr Samuel stood up from the table and brushed William away before straightening his waistcoat and reclaiming his hat from the hall-stand. 'Mr Gill,' he said, wagging his index finger at the patriarch who was now fixed upon his wife, as he shifted back and forward on the balls of his feet, the carving knife in his grip, 'you have made a grave mistake here, you will see,' Mr Samuel threatened, puffing out his chest as his voice rose an octave. 'And you will need to prepare for consequences that will no doubt prove most inconvenient to you.' With that the portly gentleman put his hat on his head and stomped out of the hotel.

Mr Samuel's departure broke the trance in the dining room. Martin Gill suddenly threw the knife onto the dining room rug and slunk off. Next minute horse hooves clattered across the yard and up along Pitt Street. Martin Gill was gone. At least for now. A moment later Rebecca hurried into the room; several of the children had woken during the commotion and little Martin needed help. Margaret was still standing, legs set a distance apart, knees slightly bent, arms up in front of her when she woke from her curious stance. She wiped her hands on a napkin and made her way upstairs to the nursery. And then, there was only Mary Ann and William looking at one another across the dining-room table in a state of utter bewilderment.

CHAPTER SIXTEEN
The Thwarted Plot

No sooner had the Moreton Bay steamer made its way out through the Heads than the disgraced gentleman settler began to breathe more easily. He found a decent seat up on the deck and settled in with the various papers he had purchased for his journey north. As always he started with Charlie Nichols' paper as it most suited his interests and humour. There was the regular exchange between Betsy Pumpkin and Kitty Cucumber as well as an interesting piece concerning plans to commence building railroads in the interior. In among the racing pages there was a more serious article concerned with Earl Grey's 'absurd scheme' to resume transportation. Even *Bell's*, who typically sided with the governor, could not brook the arrival of such a boat.

Next, Kinchela was drawn to a long piece dedicated to the 'talented and enterprising Mr Kennedy', who had sailed to Cape York with the hope of finding an interior route back to Sydney. Kennedy had been in the company of eight or so men including his trusted Aboriginal companion, Jackey Jackey, who he had to thank for surviving previous expeditions. From the beginning of this particular voyage, however, 'the nature of the country' had presented the exploration party 'startling presage of the dangers' that lay ahead. Kinchela nodded to himself. He had not been to the Cape himself but he had pushed north far enough to have a sense of things. Few would know the heavy humidity in those districts or the dense green that closed in before the rains. No doubt there were all sorts of vile swamps and lurid snakes as well as insects as big as your fist. *Bell's* account of the tragic expedition concluded by recognising how Mr Kennedy had set an 'unrivalled' example of 'determination, perseverance and self-sacrifice'. 'Mmmm,' Kinchela mused, 'the northern districts would make heroes or corpses of us all.' Still he was glad to be heading back. After the froth and folly of the past year, the Upper Darling seemed more straightforward. At least you knew who your enemies were, or where their fires were, at any rate.

Kinchela was musing over this when he came upon a lively piece of prosody in *Bell's* entitled 'A Chapter of Whens'. It was full of cryptic allusions and seemed to be a satirical challenge from *Bell's* to *The Atlas*, which was now struggling under Mackay's moralising editorials. Kinchela was pleased to see *The Atlas* getting a serve, so he read on. 'When battered puddings grow on trees and civil counsels learn to please,' the poem began before making a sly aside about that Justice Stephens, who had invited Manning to preside over his abduction trial last year. There was also a reference to Bob Nichols, the new member for Northumberland. The poem was all wit and sly fun and Kinchela was greatly enjoying himself identifying all the well-known personalities being subjected to satirical scrutiny, until he came to the final stanza. 'When bushmen shall come bouncing in,' he read, 'without a hair on lip or chin, or cease to kick up any ruction, with sires about their girl's abduction'. He read the lines again. There could be no doubt, he thought, particularly incensed by the reference to the shaven appearance he maintained while residing in town. They had made him sound a foolish boy, he fumed. But it was also clear—after the Louisa Aarons affair he was damned in Sydney, innocent or not.

Kinchela stood up and walked about the deck until he found a wastebasket in which he energetically stuffed the offending newssheet. Clearly he was a laughing stock, something to finish a stanza. Sydney smugness, he thought grimly, it left a nasty taste in his mouth. In this foul mood he made his way to the salon within the steamer, nudging in among two heavily tattooed Maori sawyers already 'liquoring' themselves. He signalled for a rum and knocked it back quickly before pushing his glass forward for another.

A day or so later the *Raven* took Kinchela up river and into the small township of Moreton Bay. An air of menace seemed to hang over the northern settlement. There were a few new architectural statements of civility—that was true—the site for a customs house had been pegged out and what looked to be the foundations of a church, but even so a sullen rage pulsed within the thick wet January heat. Kinchela decided to give himself a week in town to get provisions and catch up on the local news before starting out for Hawkwood.

He picked his way over the deep ruts that cut into the town streets and entered one of the better hotels, keen to have a quick ale before taking a turn around the stock yards. No sooner had he put his lips to his glass when a leathery-looking barfly sidled up to him and took it upon himself to tell him how things had been. Kinchela knew better than to leave a man like this one thirsty so he ordered a round for both of them and asked his drinking companion about the immigrant ship that had arrived just before Christmas with Dr Lang's new labour market on board. 'Well you know,' the man said after he had knocked the top off his new ale, 'the more immigrants we have, the more land we are going to need and the more we had better all watch out.'

The man recounted a few more stories to Kinchela to prove that the hostilities were as bad as ever. Kinchela listened grimly and eventually mentioned he was keen to know, given the mood, which route would be best up to the Boyne River. The leathery old man darted him a quick look before taking a swig of his drink. 'You know young Blaxland headed thereabouts a year or so ago, with about 30,000 sheep as well as the Pegg woman and her boys.' Kinchela nodded. Since they had left in '47 just about everyone in town had kept an interest in the long slow journey they had taken, pushing slowly through the scrub and rugged parts, sometimes stopping a few weeks here and there to shear the sheep and send the wool back to town. It had taken Blaxland and his team a year or so but eventually they had got as far north as just about anyone before them.

'Well they are set up now,' Kinchela's drinking companion said, 'near a creek of sorts, at a place they've called Tirroan. I've heard they've built themselves a set of blockhouses with plenty of loopholes,' he wiped the sweat from the back of his neck, 'so you could take some of their route, I would say, but I'd speak to Petrie first,' the old man added, 'word is they're living in a hornet's nest and needing to keep their wits about them—day and night.' The man jiggled his empty glass at Kinchela who shifted uneasily on his heels as he realised he was going to be stuck on the grog with this man for the afternoon. It stood to reason, Kinchela thought as he ordered another pair of ales, that there would be unrest on most of the roads. He might be better off making his own way, he thought, off the beaten track, so to speak.

～

Mr Lewis Samuel had not exaggerated the many and varied inconveniences he wished to bring upon Martin Gill. Nor had he overestimated his ability to have these delivered through a host of overt and covert mechanisms. To say Mr Samuel wished to bring pressure upon the life of Martin Gill was putting it lightly. But then again, to say he wanted to destroy the man might have been placing too much weight upon the grave insult he believed he had suffered that particular Sunday afternoon when he had been invited to the Gill household as an honoured guest, only to be subjected to contempt, insult and physical peril. He might have died right there in their uncle's old dining room, he explained to his brother, Saul, in a state of excitement. It was thanks only to his fine constitution that he did not choke, given the little help he had received from those about him.

As well as his brother Saul, Lewis Samuel had a host of well-connected friends throughout the colony and those friends had friends, too. It was quite within his remit, indeed the successful businessman considered it his duty, to inform those associates with whom he was most intimate, that there was something rotten in the hotel that nestled down the northern end of Pitt Street. Those, like himself, who had 'connections' with that particular establishment best be on their guard, he warned, taking pains to caution a goodly number of his brother's magisterial colleagues. And every time Mr Samuel recounted this episode to anyone who was prepared to listen, the story became a little more exaggerated. Indeed, it was now going around town that Mrs Gill had tried to poison old Lewis with a rotten leg of beef and Martin Gill had come at his guest with a carving knife—all because the wealthy bachelor had graciously declined their unappetising invitation to engage in matrimonial union with their now infamous daughter, Miss Mary Ann Gill.

Some part of these rumours had made their way to the auction rooms up on George Street and Alexander Moore was feeling quite unsettled. Mr Samuel's near-death experience was being recounted from coffee house to shop counter in a certain tone of voice and soon everyone was pretty sure that Martin Gill had set old Samuel up with the hope of addressing two pressing domestic distresses: his disobedient daughter and rapidly mounting debts. Only the deed had come undone when his wife had refused to have a bar of it, one gossip sniggered. Alexander Moore listened to the story and did a good job feigning disinterest, although later he could be found looking about his brother's stores of luxury and everyday goods with a forlorn expression on his face. He had liked the young Gill girl but could not shake a sinking feeling that Gill had been cooking him up for the same meal. Had he intended to play the two men off against each other, Moore wondered—to auction the girl to the highest bidder, so to speak? The whole thing made him decidedly uncomfortable. The news was also making a number of other men about town scratch their mutton-chops and consider what to do. Deliverymen were now refusing to leave their goods at the hotel kitchen door without direct payment. They had been told they had to have cash in hand, one snivelling fellow explained to a red-faced Mrs Gill, who was clearly running the show while her husband came and went from the hotel as he wished.

Husband and wife were hardly on speaking terms and Martin Gill had assumed permanent occupation in the second-storey guestroom. While her husband was trying to work out what to do next, Margaret was having unpleasant conversations with the men who came looking for her husband. Margaret had been carefully paring back the family expenses so the hotel could continue, although the number of customers frequenting their establishment these days rarely made up for the running costs. Still, Margaret was determined to keep at it, and was hoping for a few good weeks so they could get on top of the most pressing debts.

These days Margaret increasingly relied upon her father, who had been doing what he could to put things in place, even as he was fast realising that he was going to get his fingers burnt if he ran about town trying to put out all the fires that his son-in-law had set alight with all his hot and bluster. The fool had rung up considerable debts, and in the current climate it would be impossible to pay them. From what McCormick could glean, just about everyone was having a hard time these days. The country was stuck up with drought and there were fewer boats around the quay—a clear sign that trade was coming to a standstill. No one was in a position to help, even if they wanted to. After a few weeks of careful enquiries, Thomas McCormick suggested to his wife that it might be best for them to move closer in to town, where they could keep an eye on things, at least for a while.

It didn't seem possible to get on top of what Margaret considered a great mountain of financial shame, something they could have avoided with a bit of common sense. No wonder then that she looked at her father somewhat askance when he told her they would work it out, one way or the other. 'There are things that can be done,' he said, sleeves rolled up and trowel in his hand when she came to visit at the farm and found him down on his knees in the gooseberry patch. Margaret was glad to be somewhere other than the hotel. After all the ill-will there, she found her father's ambling form an even greater comfort than usual, although she was not entirely sure she wanted to know what solutions he might have in mind for her husband's debts.

Their desperate situation took her back to being no more than a girl in Dublin. The things they had had to do then. It made her wince. McCormick sensed her worry for as he fossicked with some string he called out, 'It will be fine, Margaret, you've done naught wrong and we are not in Dublin anymore.' Margaret gave a half-hearted nod and began weaving the other end of the string amongst the prickly bushes. She wanted to know there would be a way through all of this, but there was a tight dread about her chest she hadn't known for years. Sure, it was not the same as then. Now she was a mother of six, with Isabella, Harriet, little Thomas and baby Martin all under ten. How she would have kept things going without her father she had no idea, and she thanked Mary Riley in her prayers for keeping an eye on the youngest one since she let Rebecca go.

'What other choice do we have?' she had exclaimed when Mary Ann came to her with an appalled expression on her face. Rebecca had offered to stay on until they got straight again, but Margaret said no, it wasn't right. Honestly, she did not know how, let alone when or even if, they would get back on top again, and she didn't like the thought of owing anyone anything, especially not a servant girl such as she had once been. She knew how they thought and how they might choose to hold it over you if things didn't work out. Rebecca had been with them some time, true enough, but she was not family, Margaret reminded her eldest children when they spoke to her again about the matter. 'It is not right for the girl to think she is.' So the young girl packed her worldly goods into the second-hand carpetbag Margaret gifted her and then Mary Ann and Will accompanied the defeated-looking creature to the Quay. There was a barque ready to sail for Port Phillip where a family had agreed to take her on, thanks in no part to the excellent reference Mary Ann had written on her mother's behalf.

But if Rebecca was longing for the comfortable familiarity of the Gills' domestic arrangement, Martin Gill was not. Nor was he prepared to entertain another moment of doubt. Having inured himself to his wife's cautions it was now full steam ahead as far as he was concerned. He was feeling decidedly cocksure and chin up about the future.

So much so that he was even taking particular delight in walking down George Street, greeting the storeowners who had once been his friends and who now preferred to turn inside when they saw him approaching. All these snubs only added to his defiance. He had absolutely no intention of giving in or going on as he had before. He had a plan, several plans, in fact. Not all the pieces were in place yet, but they would come together, of that he was quite certain.

After all the months of subterfuge and shadow work, trying to stop the flood of hotel debts and hide them from his wife and the rest of the colony, Martin Gill was strangely relieved that everything was out in the open. As he travelled about town depositing certain items into auction rooms with the hope of making a few extra pounds, he felt curiously light as if he had been released from the burden of trying to be someone other than who and what he really was. 'Respectability—*pah*. Family—*bah*,' he grumbled contentedly. After the last several months, Martin Gill suddenly didn't give a tuppenny damn about any of it anymore. It was all other people's huff and puff, he decided, and, quite frankly, he no longer cared who knew what. Plenty of good men had gone down in the past year. Indeed, he was in the company of some exceedingly prominent colonists.

Whatever it took Martin Gill was going to come out on top, of that he was sure. It was just a matter of when, he muttered to himself as he made his way back to the hotel, and how. As he walked into the old dining room he nodded to the shipping agent, who was busy selling a couple of middle-aged artisans their berths to San Francisco. And then with surprising clarity it dawned on Gill—of course. He whistled under his breath, marvelling at what had been right under his nose all along. It wouldn't be too hard to get enough money to buy a passage to California, he chuckled to himself with satisfaction. That would put everything right, he reckoned; well, at least for himself, anyway.

～

Rather than follow the more trammelled northern road, Kinchela decided to take the western route and head up through the guts of the country. He had a feeling there would be less trouble that way and he would also be able to break up his journey at some of the stations along the way. He knew he would be safer travelling with others, and had considered getting a few immigrant boys from Dr Lang's boat to help him fix up the run but the truth of it was Kinchela had a hankering for his own company.

A while back John had passed one of the Hawkwood leases over to John Walker, a neighbour with a run nearby and one of the few men in the district who wasn't Irish. Walker's cows had got fat on the brother's block and ever since, Walker had been talking about taking on the rest of Hawkwood, when they were ready, of course. Just before their recent spat, James and John had agreed it might be best to make Walker an offer. After their recent falling out, James had decided it was time to get on with things. He had sent John a perfunctory note explaining his intentions and the day before he got on the Moreton Bay steamer he had received a curt reply from his eldest brother: 'Go ahead with Walker, yrs, John'. So that was that. Once he had sold the last link between himself and his brother, Kinchela could start to think about what to do next.

He crossed over the spindly bridge that led westward out of town. A few men would have been useful when it came to fixing fences and the like, Kinchela knew, but he couldn't put aside his desire to see how the country had changed since last autumn and to do so on his own without too much talk. Since the rush of '45 the northern Downs had been parcelled out so quickly that each time Kinchela travelled back up to Hawkwood there seemed to be a couple of new stations. Mind you, in that short time, just about the same number had disappeared, many of them overnight. That was how it was among the Goonneeburra blacks, Kinchela thought. They had a clever way with fire, and when they didn't kill your stock or scorch the grass so you had nothing to feed them, the smoke alone could taunt you—whipping up out of nowhere until you could hardly see in front of yourself. You had to have the capital and the stomach, as well as someone watching your back, to make it work in these parts. No doubt that was why most of the northern Downs had been taken by brothers; the Hawkins boys at Boonara, the Archers up at Eidsvold, the Herbert brothers over at Ban Ban and of course, the two Irish lads, Paul and Clement Lawless. All those boys had been determined to stick it out. He and John had been part of that set, indeed, they had been among the first up there and many of the others had come to Hawkwood for advice or a bit of company. But now the Kinchelas were calling it quits. It was hard to see what else could be done really, when the two brothers were hardly on speaking terms and there was so little money. Still it stuck in Kinchela's gut. All that time and money and not much to show for it, even if he managed to strike a good deal with Walker.

A day or so out of town, Kinchela stopped at Bull's Head Inn in Drayton. He filled his pack with salt junk, leatherjacket, a couple of mallets and a box of nails as well as plenty of powder for the muzzle-loader. Next morning he was up at dawn, guiding his mare through the swamplands that lay between him and the northern interior. By late afternoon he was making his way over the ranges, counting the tree stumps that had been chopped a foot or so from the ground so the drays could be dragged over the mountain. He kept going for a day or so, stopping a night at Taabinga and then Ban Ban and from there he took the river systems eastward.

For him the last stretch to Hawkwood was always the best part of the journey. Giant granite boulders dissolved into sudden deep gorges and gave a pink hue to the country while turning the waters that rushed over these ancient forms a curiously creamy white. There was a sound to the land too, Kinchela thought, as he and Surus picked their way up over the cliff tops, something made from the motion of the rapids and the heat of the place. As he came upon the perimeter of Hawkwood, he recognised the hundreds of thin black-trunked trees punctuating the grass lands; their silver leaves glistening in the heat and giving off a sharp familiar smell. Kinchela rode on, looking about for signs of his stock. But for cattle tracks here and there, the land was curiously empty. He nudged his horse forward, nerves a little on edge. 'Come on, Surus,' Kinchela said, perhaps a little more loudly than necessary, 'let's find the hut then and see what's left for us to live on.'

CHAPTER SEVENTEEN

Defiance

Robert Lowe had heard that the *Hashemy* was due to arrive any week now. He had told Mr Parkes in no uncertain terms that he did not approve of the sort of political campaigning he and his men had been up to. 'It is one thing during election time,' he instructed his previous ally curtly, as he stood by his chamber window wondering how to get rid of his unwelcome visitor. 'It is, however, quite unacceptable to go about campaigning at other times. It sets a bad example,' Lowe continued, avoiding eye contact with the nuggetty-looking fellow, who was insisting on maintaining an association despite the obvious discouragement he received from his newly elected representative. 'Such behaviour invites others to think their opinions are more important than their work and if everyone went about behaving in this manner, Mr Parkes,' Lowe finished in a querulous tone, 'where *would* the colony be?'

However, Parkes was no longer particularly concerned about Mr Lowe's condescending airs. In fact, he had decided that such attitudes were evidence that he and his associates were growing in influence. 'Lowe can like it or lump it,' he told the large crowd who had come to listen to the Committee Meeting at the Royal Hotel, 'we are going ahead,' he finished with a firm nod. Sydney's former mayor James Wilshire stood up and looked about the room. 'Thanks to the strenuous efforts of those here today, we can confidently say that all of Sydney is now primed, like a cat before a mouse hole,' he said with obvious satisfaction. 'And now, the moment we see that boat come through the Heads,' he continued, adding a touch of fire to his words, 'the governor can expect a scene to rival London's Monster Rally.' 'Hear, hear,' the working men in the crowd cheered. This was exactly the sort of stoush they had been waiting for.

~

Kinchela had been on his own at Hawkwood for about four months when the visitor came. During that time there had been one or two scares, but on the whole, he had been able to get on with it. He had had a devil of a time finding the stock. It must have been a difficult season for most of the sheep had gone down to the water and got stuck there. At least that was what he assumed from the sun-dried carcasses he found scattered among the rocks. Half of the cattle were gone too, but he had expected that, although not the sight of them, with their guts ripped open. That was something of a shock. And a warning, he realised.

It would be best to include what remained of the cattle into the deal for Walker, Kinchela decided, he certainly didn't fancy trying to run them back to Moreton Bay at any rate. Over the last few months he had been steadily sorting out the property. Fixing the fences as well as the hut roof that had caved in after the rains. He had spent a week or so clearing out the thick roots that had clogged up the closest creek. All that time he had been thinking. Well, actually, to start off he deliberately avoided certain topics. His future, John and, of course, Mary Ann. But one evening he allowed himself more rum than usual and by the end of the night he was wracked with shame and anger. The next morning he went down the creek and washed himself. He was leaning against a red gum trying to get his boots on when he realised he was talking out loud. 'I am man enough to make my own decisions,' he heard himself mutter, 'Damn John, Damn them all.' Kinchela finally shoved his feet into his boots and looked about him, perplexed at his own temper. Was the girl unsettling him, he wondered, or had he just been on his own too long?

Kinchela was in his hut one afternoon in early June, outlining the details of the Hawkwood sale in a letter he planned to pass on to Walker when he thought he heard a whistle. He stopped and listened and then slowly reached for his muzzle-loader. Another whistle and then nothing. Quietly, Kinchela began to load the weapon. Next minute, he was sure he heard horse hooves so he put down the gun and went to the hut door. It was the younger Bouverie brother, looking red in the face from a fast ride, no doubt. Kinchela had seen him six weeks past when he had paid a visit to Mundubbera, keen for a little company and needing to swap some meat for palings. 'We have to get to Tirroan by tomorrow,' the young man said when he pulled up in front of the hut, still struggling to catch his breath. Kinchela noticed the thick sweat about the shoulders of his mount. 'There's been trouble,' Bouverie swallowed, 'and two of the Pegg boys are dead.' Kinchela shook his head before asking how. 'With spears,' the rider finished, licking his cracked lips before taking the water Kinchela offered him. Just as well Surus was rested and his rifle loaded, the older settler thought, as he went inside to prepare his pack.

On the day that news got about that the *Hashemy* had entered Sydney Harbour, the rain was bucketing down so hard you could barely see two yards in front of your own face let alone out on the grey water of the harbour, where the offending boat was bobbing up and down against the fitful winds. Rather than dampen spirits, however, the great downpour seemed to sharpen the resolve of the committee and their followers. By eight o'clock in the morning large groups of men were marching through the east and west wards of town as hundreds more made their way through The Rocks and onto the quay. Many had put on their Sunday best to prove they were the same sort of respectable Britons as those who had rallied at Kennington Park in London the year before. They were, after all, loyal and law-abiding British subjects.

Their mission was to hold the empire to its highest purpose and keep their colony clean.

By ten o'clock there were as many as 4000 people, possibly more, assembled around the harbour, some holding canvas shelters to protect themselves from the rain and others standing under umbrellas, while still more braved the elements with only their top hats or working caps to shield them from the wet. There were men from the factories, as well as shop owners and industry men, a number of bookish looking characters and even one or two of the clerical set, clearly visible in their collars. All walks of colonial life—pouring into Circular Quay. An hour before lunch the town gave up any appearance of an ordinary day and one by one the shops down George Street closed their doors. Twenty minutes later the factories followed suit and shortly after that, another great slough of men and several daring women also joined the crowd about the quay.

Half the city, Captain Innes thought, assessing the rally from the sodden slopes of the Government House lawn on the other side of the harbour. FitzRoy had asked him to keep an eye on things and had also stationed twenty soldiers with bayonets along the old picket fence of his vice-regal boundary. News of last year's European mobs may have excited the Sydney mechanics but they also provided the governor with a salutary warning about how quickly things could turn. Innes was intent upon being firm, and knew the governor would expect a show of strength. He was the man to do it, up on his fine mount, trotting back and forth along the soggy lawn. At least Innes hoped so, for he needed to bring the right sort of answer to the questions that had been raised after news about his friendship with the corrupt governor at Darlinghurst Gaol made their way into the press.

Just before noon, the committeemen arrived in an omnibus. By now the rain was even heavier, but the horses pushed through the crowd until the large coach came to a stop in the middle of the wharf. The thought of that ship battling in the harbour winds held the committee and the sodden crowd to their purpose and there were fierce looks and set jaws among those who had heard that the governor had trained a number of Fort Macquarie cannons upon the quay.

From the third storey of the hotel, where Mary Ann had been reading to her siblings, the steady clap, clap, clap of the crowd seemed to grow louder and firmer with every minute. It was impossible to avoid the fierce energy swirling about the town and harbour and, after a time, Mary Ann could bear it no more. She left the children with a set of wooden blocks and hurried to her bedroom. Even at this distance, she could see the great throng stretched around the quay. They were different from the unpredictable mob she had encountered on election night the year before, Mary Ann realised. There was something fierce and stubborn to them. She felt a presence behind her and turned to see William standing at the door, his face bright with excitement. 'You've got the best seat in the house,' he said rushing to join her at the window.

Brother and sister crouched forward and if they squinted, they could just see the omnibus driver taking the reins of the two black mares at the front of his vehicle. Next minute, one of the passengers— both sleeves rolled to his elbows—began climbing onto the vehicle. The crowd clapped louder as the stocky man scrambled up onto the vehicle roof and found his feet. Next moment, Henry Parkes was leaning down and with arms thick from years of bone turning and breaking rock, hauled James Wilshire onto the deck beside him.

Even with thick sheets of rain slanting across the quay it was possible to see the two men astride the improvised platform. They were drenched to the bone but nonetheless the two men began to unfurl a giant canvas banner. It took a minute or two for the heavy fabric to stop flapping in the wind and twisting around their legs, but when they finally pulled the canvas tight enough for the crowd to read, the quay erupted in a frenzy of excitement. Both men responded by turning to the crowd and thrusting a clenched fist into the air.

Brother and sister crammed closer to the window, peering through the glass even as it grew foggy with their breath. They could just see Parkes and Wilshire fasten the canvas sign against the side of the omnibus. It was difficult to see everything from this angle of the hotel and both Will and Mary Ann craned their necks, trying to make out what was scrawled across the large banner. It looked like a single word,

Mary Ann thought, and had been written with bold curvaceous letter-ing. 'It starts with a "D",' she said, squinting to make out the next letter. She stood back for a moment and wiped the window with her sleeve before leaning in again. Then she inhaled sharply. The audacity of it, she thought. It felt too thrilling to speak, but even so, Mary Ann turned to her brother, eyes shining. 'Well?' he asked impatiently. 'What does it say?' Mary Ann swallowed, and then in a rushed tone, she half-whispered, '"Defiance", Will, it says "Defiance".'

More than fifty men rode out to Tirroan when they learnt the two Pegg boys had been out at early dusk watching sheep when one got a spear in the gut and the other, a fatal blow to the head. Riding from Hawkwood with the Bouverie boy, Kinchela stopped to collect the Lawless brothers, then the two Herbert men and the station manager at Degilbo. When they arrived at Gregory Blaxland's property, both of the Thompsons were already there as well as a number of other men Kinchela hadn't met before. The widow Pegg was in a state but even so her only surviving son was determined to join the party and though he couldn't have been more than fourteen, no one tried to stop him.

So that was how young Abraham Pegg came to be among the party that rode out behind 'the friendly trackers' the Thompson brothers brought with them from Walla. It took Blaxland's party several hard days pushing through the west scrublands before they finally came to a large stretch of river that was at least half a mile wide. 'Here,' the two trackers gestured at the marshy flatlands around them, 'hiding all about.' At least two hundred of them, the Pegg boy reckoned, when he told the story later. It had been a filthy, wretched battle and it had gone on all day and well into the night. Spear against clumsy muzzle-loader. Shooting through the smoke of the powder and the fires and trying to keep shy of the shower of spears that came from every direction. When it was done there were bodies strewn all through the bush, most with their flesh ruptured open from shot, some still breathing. The rest had fled, Pegg said later, swimming against the currents of that giant river, as the settlers stood on the bank, firing the last of their ammunition, which some did as a warning so they could see the matter finished, while others set their loaders down low into the water out of spite or for the sheer sport of it.

Out on Sydney Harbour, the thickset Captain John Ross watched and waited as the rain continued to sleet down. It had been a wretched sail. Nothing good to it from the beginning. Six boys dead to cholera before they left and another sixteen men and boys surrendered to the sea on the way over. After less than hospitable anchors at the Cape and Port Phillip they had finally arrived at their destination—only now no one would take the blasted cargo. Two days ago a government boat had rowed out to the *Hashemy* and told Ross to hold fast and that was what he had been doing ever since. But every day meant more meals and less money. So Ross had been toying with the prospect of breaking the line and dumping his human cargo on that wretched wharf. Let them fight it out themselves, he scowled, only he knew he would get nothing for his troubles if he did. So instead, Ross scratched his beard and squinted through the rain where he could see a great crowd gathering on the quay.

Since Parkes and Wilshire had set the mood with their banner, several other committeemen had taken to the roof of the omnibus, and although the rain had drowned out much of what they said the wind still carried the crowd's cheers to the third storey of Gill's Family Hotel. 'This is a free town and a clean colony,' Captain John Lamb declared as he strutted about the wet and dangerous deck. 'We are all loyal British men who have the courage and the conviction to stand our ground and say "no", he railed. 'We will not allow our proud town to be degraded and polluted once more as a penal settlement.' Factory men and insolent Cabbagers were among the thousands who felt the sting of Earl Grey's insult. So too, the clergyman and even the humble clerk and shopkeeper. They held themselves against the grim wind, certain that the time had come to hold fast. They would not have it. Their families and their fortunes depended upon it.

And then Mary Ann saw the man himself. He was pushing through the crowd in his trademark pinstripe suit and bright vermillion waistcoat, his curious white hair a stark contrast to the blackness of his damp top hat. He clambered indelicately on to the vehicle, almost losing his footing on the way. The crowd held their breath as he regained balance, then cheered as he hauled himself onto the upper deck. Coming to full height, the People's Idol then fixed his spectacles and planted both feet firmly on the deck before finally raising both arms to summon the mass to hush.

And then, at last Robert Lowe began. Slowly at first, so that his clipped consonants carried further across the crowd than the previous speakers. 'The threat of degradation has been fulfilled,' the Great Gyrator called out fiercely. 'The stately presence of our city,' he said, gesturing towards the Botanic Gardens and the swell of winter sea behind him, 'as well as the beautiful waters of our harbour, are this day polluted with the presence of a floating hell—that convict ship,' he hissed, thrusting a finger at the boat on the distant horizon.

William stood up impatiently and put his hand to the latch. 'Let the rain come in,' Mary Ann agreed with a nod as they pushed open the window and the achingly cold air rushed into the room. Sure the winds would snatch away many of his words, but brother and sister were determined to hear what they could of their father's lawyer.

'This is a struggle for liberty,' Lowe called out. 'We have lived again to behold the cargo of crime, borne across the waters to us.' He swallowed, shaking his head with disgust. 'In our port, right now,' he continued, 'is a ship freighted not with the comforts of life.' A smattering of jeers rippled from the wharfies standing with their arms crossed across their chests, stoic in the rain. 'Not with the luxuries of civilised nations,' Lowe continued, before stopping to look upon the thousands before him, 'but with the picked and selected criminals of Great Britain.' The crowd roared against the great injury that had been inflicted upon them and their town but after a moment or two Lowe gestured for them to hush. 'Let us exercise the right that every English subject has,' he began again when the crowd stilled. 'The right,' he repeated, 'to assert our freedom.'

The crowd thundered in furious agreement. But then the wind began to whip around to the west, and for several minutes Robert Lowe's words were swept away from the quay and the Pitt Street hotel. Without the power of his voice, people could only look upon the agile form of their great demagogue as he strutted this way and that, his arms rising and falling in hypnotic rhythm. Few could hear him, but still he carried the mood of the masses. Indeed, to many Lowe appeared curiously luminescent, as if his physical form—those thin, spindly legs and that wild shock of white hair—somehow added to his potency.

And then Sydney's great Weathercock appeared to take command of the heavens for the winds lulled and the rain stopped. Lowe looked about him, feigning modesty as the crowd hooted in delirium. Lowe smiled and then stopped, before crouching down on the roof, as if to make a solemn pledge. Fathers and sons, tallowmakers and tanners all pushed forward, squinting into the rain as the great demagogue stretched out his arm and opened the palm of his hand. His voice rang forth. 'As sure as the weed will grow into a plant,' Lowe called, 'and the plant into a tree,' he continued, 'in all times and in all nations of the world,' he bellowed with such emotion that several men thought they heard him sob, 'so will injustice and tyranny ripen into rebellion'. Then he rose to standing and thrust out both arms as the wharf shook with outrage.

What chance did the *Hashemy* have? Mary Ann thought shifting her gaze from the omnibus to the small vessel thrashing about in the capricious weather. What chance did any of them have against such a force? For a moment Mary Ann considered Kinchela and how he had been fed to this lion of a man. We have all been caught up in this storm, she thought heavily, but then the repulsive memory of the Aarons girl came rushing into her mind and she shook her head. 'No,' she said, as much to William as to herself, 'no more,' and with that, Mary Ann pulled down the window and turned away, shielding herself from the gusts of rain-wet wind that were still pulsing within the room.

CHAPTER EIGHTEEN

Lions After Slumber

After the Pegg business, Kinchela decided he would go and see John Walker himself. It would be quicker to settle everything in person on the ride back. After some solid work Kinchela knew he had the run in as good a condition as he was likely to get it, and the recent episode at Tirroan made it impossible to avoid the unpalatable truth of his current circumstances. He was not safe, particularly out there on his own. There would be further reprisals, he reckoned, on both sides.

Kinchela was riding towards Walker's property with Edward Hawkins from Boonara. Hawkins had been spending time with Thomas Archer and the pair had been getting excited about California. 'The last time we were down in Moreton Bay at a settlers' meeting,' Hawkins told him as they picked their way across a portion of stony ground, 'we couldn't go anywhere for all the talk of gold.' Sure it was speculation, the young man said, brushing away a great swarm of flies that had settled on his horse's rump, but it couldn't be more risky than trying to make a go of it up north.

His comments got Kinchela thinking. He had been out at Hawkwood for over four months and all that time he hadn't been able to see a way forward. He knew that once the run was sold he would have a little money from his part of it, but he was also dreading the fact that he still had no idea where to go next. He wouldn't be welcome back home, he reckoned, and his brother had well and truly washed his hands of him. Thanks to John he never really had to go it alone before, and he didn't like the rootless feeling he got each time he tried to think about what he might do next. He didn't really have enough capital to buy stock for a fresh start and he knew he was best to keep out of the towns for he could easily end up blowing the little money he had coming to him.

That night, as they sat before the few dry branches they could find for a fire, Hawkins drew a map of the Sacramento region in the dirt and pointed to where he reckoned the two large goldfields had started up. Kinchela remembered the report his brother had shown him when he was in gaol, the year before. At the time it had occurred to him that there was real money to be made in California but not grubbing about for gold. Cattle, meat, leather goods, he had thought then and said as much to Hawkins. 'That might be,' the younger man replied confidently, 'but if Archer and I get lucky we can pay someone to do all that, eh.'

The following morning the two men continued their ride east and Kinchela mused further over the idea. He would be hard put to bring further shame upon the family name in America and who knows he might even make good out there, perhaps even well enough to put his mother on firm footing again. His head was full of the stories Hawkins had recounted the night before, about the size of the nuggets men were scooping from the rivers and the great crowds that were flooding in from all over the world. The place sounded even more treacherous than the colonies and Kinchela couldn't help but wonder how much of it was true. Probably a lot of wild talk, he thought. It would pay to ask around and see what the newspapers had to say before he did anything, but still, the idea of a fresh start far from Sydney held a certain appeal.

That afternoon Kinchela farewelled Hawkins and took the path out to the Walkers'. The man had come up in the world, he noted as he followed the perimeter of Walker's property, and noticed how it was now fixed with solid wooden fences and that the stock on the other side looked as plump and safe as any in those parts. Wonder how many men he has out at dusk keeping an eye on his future, Kinchela mused. Instead of the modest hut that Walker had been living in the first time he and John visited in 1847 there was now a fine looking cottage with a commanding view over an expanse of lawn and some distant paddocks. It was all his land, Kinchela thought with a twinge of envy. This had been what he and John had worked for. As he was tying up Surus, Walker came out of the house, followed by a woman with her sleeves rolled up, as if she had been cooking. He's got himself a wife too, Kinchela thought, as he greeted the wealthy landowner.

The two men talked for several hours and just before dark Mrs Walker came out and insisted Kinchela stay. She wouldn't see anyone on the roads at night, she said firmly. Walker was pleased with the terms Kinchela outlined for the rest of the run and the two men quickly reached an agreement. That settled, the older man wanted to know what the two Kinchela boys were going to do next. After all, they had been among the first in these parts. 'Isn't it time you got yourself a wife?', Walker asked as he poured a drink for his wife and guest. Kinchela smarted and wondered if Walker had been reading the papers. He looked away and reddened but when he caught his host's gaze he found no irony or contempt in his expression. 'Now then, John,' the hostess said, having noticed Kinchela's discomfort, 'you will embarrass our guest.'

The last time anyone made such a suggestion to Kinchela it had been Jim Davidson, more than a year ago, and it had got him into a world of trouble. And yet the idea still held some appeal. A wife, Kinchela thought for the second time in a year. He would have to sort himself out and if he did decide to go to California there were few who would be prepared to come on such a journey. And then it occurred to him. He knew one person who needed a fresh start as much as he did. The only woman in fact who he had given any thought to since he had been up north. His brother would have few chances of stopping that match in America, and he wouldn't need to, for he could hardly shame the family from such a distance. Kinchela quickly put the idea away and picked up the drink Walker had poured for him. He smiled graciously at his hosts before taking a swig and turning to admire the splendid view of the Walkers' expansive estate.

Governor FitzRoy was popular throughout the colony. Some liked his fast four-in-one carriages and tight-fitting uniforms, while others appreciated the athletic way he held himself. He was often slightly aloof but always in the most stylish fashion, and in a way that could also appear avuncular, if required. In short, the Governor of New South Wales was what most colonists considered the very embodiment of manliness. The death of his pretty wife less than two years ago in a tragic carriage accident, where he had held the reins in his own hand, had given him a tragic air. There were a number of colonists, particularly among the womenfolk, devoted to their well-connected and rather handsome governor. But recently, FitzRoy had disappointed a host of influential people, and several more sympathetic papers were finding it hard to resist making certain observations. In particular, the events that had taken place at Government House after the winter rally at Circular Quay had put a great number of people off side.

Robert Lowe was not helping matters either. After the rally the wily Weathercock had marched up to Government House in the company of ten or so committeemen. They had been appointed by the crowd and more than three thousand people had kept close behind their representatives, following them all the way from the harbour up to the gates, intent upon knowing that their petition was going to be hand-delivered to the governor himself. But FitzRoy had manned the outer perimeter of his property with troops and had been extremely reluctant to even open his doors to the party, forcing the great mob to wait in the rain for several hours before he deigned to acknowledge their existence.

To talk with Lowe was one thing, in the governor's opinion. Although he could not stand the strange-looking man, he recognised that the elected member of the Legislative Council was educated and erudite. Lowe was one of them, but among the contingent intent upon giving him their so-called petition, were a number of men FitzRoy considered beneath his station. How could he, the Queen's representative, possibly hold audience with a group of shopkeepers and pamphleteers? Captain Innes had also informed him that several of these men held convictions for crimes they had committed upon these very shores.

But FitzRoy had a sense that it wouldn't do to let them rot out there in the rain. He looked out to where hundreds were crouched under their infernal cabbage-tree hats, some trying to smoke their pipes beneath the incessant downpour, while others slouched about looking too idle for their own good. He would have to do something, he thought, peering across the lawn at the vast body of working men standing before the troopers and their bayonets. It had to be something that would sound well enough in his next report to the Home Secretary but would also quell the mood. After some consideration, FitzRoy sent his senior officer to inform those awaiting his company that he would meet with six appointed delegates the following afternoon at two o'clock.

It did the job, Innes reported back. The tension dispelled and the mob dispersed. But something felt off, and next afternoon when Robert Lowe returned in the company of Parkes and Lamb and three other men, the mood in the governor's residence was decidedly tense. FitzRoy was in a difficult situation, for he had already reassured the people of Port Phillip that the *Hashemy* would not infect their colony. What could he now, in all honesty, say to those over whom he most closely presided, with whom he daily resided, when Earl Grey insisted that the boat be processed in Sydney? He would need to stand firm, the governor knew, for there was nowhere to give, no way to buckle. Just to make sure he had stationed a few guards in his kitchen and ordered a squadron of mounted troops in his stables.

FitzRoy stood aloof, regarding the party with cool disdain. It was Robert Campbell, the popular young merchant with an honest face, who presented the governor with their petition. 'There are close to seven thousand signatures to this petition, your Excellency,' the native-born freemason said placing the large roll of yellow paper in the hands of the slightly perturbed governor. 'We would ask that you forward these resolutions from the people of this colony directly to the foot of the throne.' The committeemen made murmurs of solid agreement, as FitzRoy sucked in his breath and puffed out his chest, running one finger along his eyebrow before nodding curtly.

Lowe, who had been watching the exchange carefully, felt the matter too mannered and interjected. 'There is one particular resolution, your Excellency, upon which you may desire to give some answer now,' he began in what FitzRoy felt was an unnecessarily high-minded tone. The governor looked Lowe up and down, and imagined, for a moment, what it might be like to take the sword hanging on the wall of his study and slice the bookish worm from crown-to-navel. He coughed rather abruptly and replied. 'You will inform those by whom you were deputed, that this is obviously impossible.'

Several other men in the party rushed to speak but the governor raised his hand. 'I am not prepared to enter into any further discussion,' he finished, turning his back upon the party and looking out the window to a day that was thankfully a little brighter than the last. There was a long silence, which became increasingly awkward as FitzRoy stood unwavering in his disdain. The party looked about at one another and Lowe signalled they should depart—leaving their impertinent petition lying untouched upon the governor's desk.

As they walked towards the gates Parkes thought he saw steam pouring from the stables. He asked the party to stop a moment and listen. None were sure at first, but after a moment Campbell was certain he heard the sound of hooves inside the darkness of the governor's stables, as men tried to manage their mounts. 'He's got troops in there,' Lamb said, shocked. Lowe nodded gravely, 'And no doubt they are ready to fire on all of us if the mood turns.' Lamb shook his head in disgust as the men proceeded past the sentries at the governor's gates, towards the Royal Hotel, where the remaining committee members were waiting for them with a large party of hangers-on.

The mood was thick with drink when the delegation finally arrived at the hotel. All sorts of rumours had been flying about, none of which put FitzRoy in a complimentary light. 'The governor had a police guard in the pantry,' one fellow told Parkes, who raised his eyebrows and asked if FitzRoy thought they might steal the silver. He had been right, though, Lamb told the group—there had been troops in the stables. The committee also received confirmation that guns had been trained on Circular Quay the day before. 'It is just like Peterloo,' Lamb muttered darkly. 'Imagine if they had been given the order to fire? They would kill us for folded arms and steady eyes,' he scowled, recalling the Peterloo Massacre in 1819 when the British cavalry had charged upon peaceful demonstrators and stunned the nation by murdering so many innocent civilians. The poet Shelley had shared such disgust and mourned the moment in a poem that had quickly become famous. Hawkesley shook his head and stood up, gesturing to the room. 'And if then the tyrants dare,' he growled loud enough for those in the back bar to hear, 'let them ride among you there, slash and stab and maim and hew, what they like, that let them do.'

Lowe nodded. On this point he did, in fact, consider the committeeman correct. Rather than reason with them as gentlemen, the governor had been willing to cut them down in the street. He had seen them as nothing better than a wild mob. They really had no choice, Lowe thought, but to rise like Shelley's 'lions after slumber'. He stood to join Hawkesley. 'The time has come,' the white-haired lawyer declared, 'to shake our chains to the earth like dew'. But, he thought as he considered the great gathering of men now staring back at him with steely expressions, he had better assume command, and steer the mood in the right direction, otherwise he might end up with blood on his hands.

Lowe turned to Hawkesley, 'A long column in tomorrow's paper should start us off on the right foot, don't you think, Mr Hawkesley? If the governor fails to consider us proper British subjects and gentlemen, perhaps we might point out a few of his own shortcomings. The governor's rudeness, and all that,' he finished with a shrewd smile. The men looked at one other and Hawkesley scratched his chest. 'I will be talking of "The Battle of New South Wales" in the *Advocate*, Mr Lowe,' he said, knocking back his stout and sounding firm.

But Angus Mackay picked up the scent and saw the sense of it. The committee would play straight into the hands of the settlers if things turned violent. 'Perhaps it might be best to say something about the repulsive chill we received from the governor,' Mackay suggested, 'and how he gave us a reception that was aimed at disgusting not only the delegation but all of those in New South Wales who share a loathing for the boat and its vile cargo.' 'Mmmm,' Lamb nodded, catching the mood. 'If only the governor had shown us even a little warmth of temper.' Henry Parkes chimed in with a mischievous glint in his eyes, 'Surely such warlike preparations were entirely unnecessary. All those pickles in the pantry,' he mused, 'and nothing more than a small party of respectable men who only intended to present the governor with the feelings of *his* people?'

CHAPTER NINETEEN

The Camel's Back

It was 18 June 1849, just three days from Mary Ann's seventeenth birthday and thousands were returning to Circular Quay for a second Monster Meeting. This time, however, the sun was shining and Sydney-siders were keen to celebrate the anniversary of that famous victory of Waterloo while also sending a firm message to the governor. Mary Ann had promised her brother she would not leave the hotel alone but after the excitement of last week's rally and all that had been in the papers, it had been easy for Mary Ann to persuade Will to join her. Brother and sister made their way through The Rocks and onto the quay where they were quickly caught up in the hustle and bustle of the rally. There were men selling 'cigars and a light for a penny a piece' and young boys carrying trays of ginger pops. The 'Triumphant Car of Defiance' had returned to the quay and the usual suspects—Robert Campbell, Henry Parkes, Dr Aarons and Robert Lowe were milling about the vehicle preparing to make their speeches.

There were already thousands more about the quay than the first Monster Rally, and while the heavens had wept over the great insult of the convict boat and its shameful human cargo, then, 'the Australian heavens' were now 'smiling and rejoicing' as even more 'British freemen' rallied to the quay determined to demand their rights. At least this is what Mr Parkes declared as he strutted about the roof of the omnibus—delighted that so many shared his aspirations for the colony. The mood was lively but also tense for the governor's cavalry were present and had been told to wear their sabres unsheathed. As they rode among the families and well-dressed workers, the swords of the governor's men glinted in the sun.

Not that this was enough to deter Dr Isaac Aarons, the eccentric apothecary from Pitt Street. He had just scrambled onto the deck of the omnibus—keen to put the accused, the Right Honourable Earl Grey, the Colonial Secretary, on mock trial. 'Is the defendant guilty of tyranny and faithlessness, or not guilty?' the wily old man called out as hundreds respond with jeers of 'Guilty! Guilty!' 'Yes indeed,' the doctor enthused, 'and in this matter the governor's discourtesy is comparable to the single feather in that famous Persian tale . . . you remember the one?' he asked the vast audience with an amused expression, 'It appears ever so delicate as it floats this way and that—but when it finally alights upon a burden already stacked high,' the doctor gestured dramatically, 'it is enough to cause the over-laden camel to completely collapse.'

Mary Ann and Will found a small patch of lawn just across from the docks where they could see and hear the speakers. It was exhilarating to be part of such an occasion, Mary Ann thought although it was true to say that she was also enjoying the women's dresses and her first public outing in some time. It was a blessed relief to be out of the cloistered confines of their Pitt Street hotel, where both her parents were on edge, to say the least. Will was standing close by, with both hands thrust into his pockets, chewing his lip as he listened to the speakers. He was keen to hear Robert Lowe who had just taken to the omnibus roof, announcing that after his meeting with the governor last week he had returned to the people determined to 'bell the cat'.

'The shame of it,' he called out to the thousands before him. 'How *could* an old Waterloo hero like FitzRoy so fear a delegation of twenty-three gentlemen that he was prepared to incite the colony to a scene like that of the bloody field of Peterloo?' The people *ooh*'ed and *ahh*'ed as Lowe daringly reduced the governor's dignity to a plaything. After a few moments of such banter, the People's Idol collected himself and declared more solemnly that the time had come to talk of America. Not in the sort of whispers that were most often done around these parts, he insisted as he raised both hands, 'but in a passionate and forthright manner. I am not asking you to be rash,' he explained, 'but you must know that we are at the beginning of a great struggle, and in order to go through that successfully we must have the example of America clearly in our minds.' Many in the crowd nodded and a good number also cheered. 'The injustice that was forced upon the Americans was not so great,' Lowe continued, 'as that which has been forced upon us. And I feel it is my duty,' he finished, 'to tell you that if we are to succeed at all we must have the example of America before us.' There was much furious agreement among the assembly, although Mary Ann also noticed several timid sorts looking over to the far end of the quay where the cavalry had organised themselves into a single formation.

Mary Ann looked about at the great sprawl of people, as Will listened intently to Robert Lowe and tried to imagine what it would be like to be American. Native-born, cornstalk, currency lad, he mused. Those terms sounded good, but more often than not they were used to remind him of his station as someone who was not entitled to the land grants of a sterling settler or the righteous indignation of an emancipist. What about *his* birthright, the fifteen year old mused, surely, those who had been born in the colonies deserved as much, if not more than those who had come here? As Lowe continued to enthral the crowd, Will began to wonder if he might have more of a chance in America. True, he had heard that San Francisco was a mess and there was trouble in the new town, but there was something about that chaos that excited him. At least they had a little passion over there, he thought, trying to imagine those around him rising up to cast the *Hashemy* convicts into the sea, as the Americans had done with all that tea. Little chance. Men like his father were more interested in turning a profit from such a cargo, he thought, when, suddenly, he heard his sister gasp. He turned and saw Mary Ann searching—frantically—for somewhere to hide.

Will looked about, keen to ascertain the cause of his sister's curious conduct. After a minute or two he found it. There, just a little way along the quay, leading a large, elegantly squared chestnut mare, was James Butler Kinchela. He must have just come off a steamer, the boy thought, for after a yard or so, the settler stopped and steadied his mount, casually organising his bags before hitching himself up into the saddle and weaving steadily through the rally crowd.

When Kinchela first caught sight of them both Will was standing stock-still with Mary Ann crouched awkwardly behind him. He looked startled for a moment but then shifted in his saddle and grinned, before nudging his mount with his heel. 'Miss Gill,' Kinchela said with a nod as he brought Surus to a stop in front of Mary Ann. Brother and sister watched the older settler dismount and then gather his reins before looking them both up and down. 'I am in Sydney to seek you out,' he began when it became apparent that no one was prepared or perhaps able to reply. The young woman quickly bowed her head making it impossible for Kinchela to catch her eye. She appeared extremely composed, he thought, although he noticed the muscle along her jaw was working back and forth with tremendous energy. And this must be her younger brother, he thought, which would explain why he was fixing him with such a glare and clenching his fists.

He would need to explain himself, Kinchela realised, and quickly. 'Mary Ann,' Kinchela began with a sigh, 'there has been a world of confusion, that is true,' he said shrugging his shoulders, 'and much of the blame lies with me, although,' he continued lightly wagging his finger, 'not all of it, and perhaps not quite as you might assume.' Will thought of taking his sister's hand and leading her away, although he feared it might create a scene that would get back to their parents. 'Well then,' Kinchela continued, wondering how to proceed when he realised his affable approach was getting nowhere. He took a deep breath and looked about him awkwardly. A long silence ensued until he began again, this time a little softer. 'You know, Mary, I've a mind that there

might still be a way for you and I and,' he said, tugging at his neckerchief, 'I have been thinking it over,' he said trying to catch her eye,
'if only you might let me know that you would at least consider it?'
he looked at her hopefully. 'You see,' he continued, 'I have come to
Sydney to seek you out, and here you are, right in front of me,' he added
hopefully, but yet again Mary Ann maintained her stony silence and
kept both eyes fixed on the ground. 'Surely such a meeting is no coin-
cidence?' he tried again. He stopped and pointed up Pitt Street in the
direction of her father's hotel. 'You know this meeting is a blessing for
me,' he said a little more lightly, 'for I've been thinking I would have
to climb up the drainpipe outside your window so I could ask you to
come to California with me.'

Will felt his sister start. He turned and reached for Mary Ann's
hand but otherwise brother and sister were silent as they tried to comprehend the audacity of Kinchela's proposal. There was something
thrilling about it, Will had to admit, but Mary Ann was having none of
it. She shook her head and with her eyes still lowered, replied in a low
and furious tone that was still loud enough for both to hear. 'Not once,
nor even twice, Mr Kinchela, have you subjected me to considerable
discomfort. I was fool enough to trust you with my heart,' she said,
struggling to quell the tremor in her voice, 'but now I find that after
four humiliations,' she shook her head indignantly, 'I have nothing,
absolutely nothing,' she repeated, as she fixed Kinchela with a steely
glare, 'with which to ever trust you again.'

And with that, Mary Ann Gill was off, picking her way through
the crowd with such speed and agility that William had to run to
keep up with her. Kinchela stood on the spot of green with Surus,
watching Mary Ann push through the rally crowd with her brother
trailing behind her. He shook his head, full of admiration and remorse,
wondering how on earth he might possibly fix things now.

⁓

In the place of the solid round tables and elegant horsehair-stuffed
chairs that had previously graced the dining room of Gill's Family

Hotel, there was now a long, rough bench. On the wall above the table hung a large sign: 'Private Agent: Robert E. Ogilby for San Francisco', and behind the long table sat two or three men taking money from those who had come to buy their passage to California. When it wasn't being used by the booking agent, other activities were also taking place at Gill's Family Hotel, including several large meetings with the electors from Bourke's Ward. Whatever Gill thought of men like Parkes, Margaret Gill was happy to take their money, particularly in the current climate. Indeed, despite the actual state of things, people were still coming to Gill's Family Hotel, still using its well-known name in their advertisements and still recognising it as the grandest hotel in the colony. Even so, despite all this, the well-known Pitt Street hotel was now not much more than a façade.

Margaret had been trying to manage the hotel while also looking to her long-term interests, as her father had advised. Just a day or so ago, however, she had told her two eldest children that they must make themselves useful. She was in no position to support two adults, she told them crisply as she packed a box of silver cruets she didn't want her husband to spirit away. It would be best if William and Mary Ann found a way to earn some money, 'That is what the family needs,' she said, returning to her packing. And so, while Martin Gill busied himself loading furniture and other miscellanea onto George Page's dray cart, his estranged wife was just as energetic in her own exertions regarding their shared property. She had wished it otherwise, and had done her best to see it that way, but once her husband began removing certain items from the hotel without so much as a word to her, the gloves were off as far as she was concerned.

She had to think for herself, McCormick had recently reminded his daughter. There was word about town that Lewis Samuel was intent upon suing Gill for unpaid debts and had recently held a private meeting with several other men to whom Gill also owed money. He was determined to pursue justice and a fair return, Samuel had told those men and he encouraged them to do the same. It was then McCormick told Margaret that he was going to lease the Punchbowl farm so that he and Mary Riley could come into town, for a time at least. 'We've always kept an eye out for each other now, haven't we?' he said, brushing away his daughter's protests. 'I best be on hand now, wouldn't you say?'

～

Mary Ann was now sufficiently well acquainted with shame to suffer the indignity of their current circumstances better than William. She was, nonetheless, still taken aback when one afternoon several weeks later she stepped into the hotel and discovered the fine claret drapes, which added so much to the formal dining room's opulence, were gone, as were many of the framed sketches that had previously adorned the walls. Gone too was the fine piece of mahogany that functioned as a serving bench, which Mary Ann had helped polish during her childhood. The room seemed to reverberate with the absence of everyday objects and Mary Ann stood at the threshold, caught for a moment by the loss.

By the end of the following week, when most of the big fixtures had been moved out to the auction rooms, Martin Gill sat down with his eldest son. 'It is time to give it up,' he admitted to William, 'and it will be best to do so now.' As Mary Ann and her father had not exchanged a word since the incident with Mr Samuel and the roast beef, it was William's task to help his father compose the advertisements concerned with the sale of the hotel's lease as well as all the remaining furniture and stock-in-trade. 'There's no point begging for mercy,' Gill muttered when Will shook his head in dismay. 'It has to be done,' he said firmly, 'but in a way that puts us in front as best as possible.'

'The proprietor of this well-known establishment', the advertisement began, 'is obliged to retire from business on account of a family illness and is therefore resolved to part with his very eligible investment, which offers not only elegant furnishings but also first-rate connections. The coming season promises a return of the numerous up-country gentlemen, who have long favoured Mr Gill with their support and', the column concluded, 'the future buyer can be assured of their ongoing business'. This explanation was followed by an extensive list of sideboards and eight-day hall clocks, hall lamps and superior paintings as well as handsome bedsteads, chests of drawers and wash-stands in each of the eleven guestrooms—all of which were 'furnished in a most superior manner'.

Throughout the last seventeen or so years, Martin Gill had also kept a 'very desirable premise on George Street', where he and Margaret lived when they were first married and where Mary Ann had also been born. 'These will have to go too,' Martin Gill told his son. So the pair bent their heads together and penned another costly advertise-ment that detailed the 'commodious establishment in a central part of the metropolis' that was sure to 'prove a worthwhile investment' for an 'enterprising capitalist'. After much toing and froing regarding the glassware and dinner services in both establishments, Will showed his father the advertisements and then Gill instructed him to run both up to George Street so they could be published in the Saturday paper.

James Butler Kinchela was having a time of it. He had been reluctant to return to his mother's home in Liverpool. Nor did he fancy another run-in with his brother. He had, consequently, taken up residence in Sydney hoping it might somehow provide him with an opportunity to press his case with Mary Ann. While he was about he was also keen to pick up news about California, for after a few days back in town he had resolved that he must go. Any doubts he may have harboured on the matter were resolved when he realised he was only able to stay at any one hotel for a few days. His credit was fine, he insisted, when the first manager came to speak to him about the matter, but that wasn't the problem. As soon as those in charge of whichever establishment he was residing in put two and two together—they really had little choice, they would explain. They could not afford such notoriety under their roof, particularly in the current climate, with guests able to choose among so many fine establishments.

And so Kinchela moved on, from the Adelphi to Petty's Hotel, then the Star Hotel and finally the Union Inn before finding one or two of the better boarding houses on the outskirts of town. By late July he was bunking down at Joseph Walford's private dwelling rooms in Parramatta with the retired Major George Pitt D'Arcy from the 39th regiment of foot. The Major was no stranger to Ireland. Indeed, he liked to remind Kinchela that he had been in Cork in the 1820s when the Rockites were at their worst. Old Pitt D'Arcy was in the habit of recounting a story about how he had been attacked by a large band of Captain Rock's men in Mill Street, Cork. Single handedly, he boasted, he had beaten off a 'considerable body of insurgents' and for his troubles, been promoted from Brevet to Major. Only, he would finish with a bemused expression, sometime after that, he and his regiment had received the dubious honour of a posting to New South Wales.

But that was 1826; now the Major was feeble with gout. At least that is what Dr Stuart determined after he was woken up well past two o'clock one morning with James Butler Kinchela thumping at his door and asking him to come quickly. The settler had been reading on his bed that evening, he explained as the two of them hastened back to Walford's, when the Major began complaining of a pain in his head. Next moment there was a great thump and Kinchela saw the distinguished military man writhing on the floor. He had settled the Major as best he could before rushing off to find a medical man. But by the time Kinchela and the doctor returned, Pitt D'Arcy was dead. 'Gout in the head,' the doctor told the coroner, 'leading to apoplexy and then death.'

The Major's sudden death had been a nasty surprise for Kinchela and one that made him sufficiently wary of boarding establishments to resign himself to his mother's home as well as whatever John decided to dish out. Fortunately, however, the Superintendent of Schools was in the Orange district, devoting considerable energy to the establishment of a new school. Anne Bourne had her younger son to herself and welcomed the opportunity to pet him without her eldest son's disapproval. They were comfortable companions for neither found it necessary to inquire much into the other's comings and goings. Kinchela was still musing over his meeting with Mary Ann at Circular

Quay and drawing closer to the decision that he would have to visit Gill's Family Hotel when a letter, in a woman's hand, arrived at his mother's Liverpool home.

Mother and son had just come in from a spring stroll beside the rosemary hedges and Anne Bourne was removing her bonnet before the hall mirror when she noticed the letter on the stand. She picked up the envelope and turned it backward and forward before opening it. After reading the first two sentences, the elderly woman pushed the letter into James' hand and then steadied herself against the hall-stand. James read the opening sentences: 'John's illness had been very sudden', he stopped, feeling as if the wind had been booted out of him, 'and also tragically short'. Breathing unevenly Kinchela took his mother's arm and led her to the front parlour. He helped her to her seat and then poured two large glasses of madeira before sitting down next to her.

John had been the woman's boarder 'for over a year', James read out loud as he followed the woman's flowery script across the rough parchment, 'each time, indeed, your dear son visited the region, with the singular intention of improving the lives of the children in this district', the woman explained. 'During his most recent visit, he had been with the local magistrates, who were meeting to decide the location of a statue they wished to erect in memory of the Governor Richard Bourke, who played such an active role in this region.' Anne Bourne fixed her eyes on the opposite wall as she listened to James read: 'There had been a storm that night and on the ride home from the meeting John's horse had been caught in a muddy patch along a narrow stretch of track. He had done what he could', but after several desperate hours, 'John had been forced to leave his mount and trudge back, more than three miles, through one of the coldest gales they had suffered in years. A day or so later', the letter continued, 'John came down with a fever, and a week after that he was unable to leave his bed.'

Mrs Lynton had wanted to write earlier, she explained, but 'John had insisted she not fuss—he would be up and about again soon enough. It all happened so suddenly . . .' James stopped, momentarily unable to fix upon the page. He looked about the room, blinking back the wetness in his eyes and trying to restore his focus as he began to comprehend his mother's and then his own great grief. He felt thick in the guts for the way he and his brother had parted. The things he had said and thought over the past few months—he was sick with the shame of it. After a moment, however, he remembered his mother's presence and continued the letter. Mrs Lynton wanted the Kinchela family to know that 'their beloved John had met his passing with the courage all who knew him spoke of so often'. The funeral had been arranged in some haste a day or two after his passing but there would be a memorial within a fortnight at which their presence was greatly desired.

Enclosed with the letter from Blackman's Swamp was a separate piece of paper upon which was written a rather florid elegy concerning the death of John Kinchela Junior, Esquire. Mrs Lynton had composed this humble poem herself, she wrote, and was deeply honoured to inform the family that the very same would be read at the forthcoming memorial. There was also talk that a stanza from this might adorn John's headstone, if they were pleased for this to be so. Anne Bourne sat beside her younger son, shaking her head as James read the opening stanza of Mrs Lynton's poem:

Dear to my soul, too early lost,
Affection's arm was weak to save,
The love of justice, friendship's boast—
Has come to an untimely grave.

And then Anne Bourne placed her hand on her son's knee and signalled for him to stop. 'There will be a time for this,' she said, but now she wanted only quiet and the comfort of knowing her last male kin was by her side.

❧

'Even the very worst of our convicts', Earl Grey wrote in reply to FitzRoy's detailed account of the *Hashemy* incident at Circular Quay, 'could find

213

something to learn from the speakers at public meetings in despising truth and decency'. It was a sentiment shared by many of Sydney's well-to-do. After the Waterloo celebrations, and the second rally at Circular Quay, the governor had packaged a collection of sympathetic newspaper articles to convince the Colonial Secretary that public sentiment was on his side. The protest meeting had been attended by 'mere idlers', he told Earl Grey, 'only a few hundred at the most' and none were men of 'any real stake or influence'. Indeed, 'the great mass of intelligent, right-minded, thoughtful and wealthy, who form the REAL people of the Nation' thoroughly disapproved of such attempts to 'foment disturbance and dissension' and were also vehemently opposed to the 'few intolerant and presuming demagogues' who had rallied at Circular Quay on that day.

Perhaps the governor was correct. For despite the fact that FitzRoy had ordered that the convict boat be discreetly removed from Sydney Harbour and those on board processed at Moreton Bay, the people's victory was proving bittersweet. At least it was for Parkes and his associates. Instead of their defiant stand leading on to greater victories, the tide in the affairs of these men had stalled. And much of it was their foolish fault. The Constitutional Association had been responsible for successfully rousing the public against the *Hashemy*, but soon afterwards they had become so busy fighting among themselves that they failed to detect a change in the winds. Parkes and his men were suddenly decidedly out of favour. The people had gone back to their factories, furnaces and farms, and were irritated by any insistence from the committee that they should feel obliged to maintain an interest in the political future of the colony. Business was tough enough, they grumbled—who had the time, let alone the taste for such stirrings. And so, once more, the toyshop owner found himself not only on the outer of street politics but also subject to yet another snubbing from the Great Gyrator.

It also seemed that Robert Lowe was losing the plot. He had been riling up the Legislative Council about the considerable number of bounty migrants, who had no sooner arrived in the colony on a government-funded passage than they decided to leave for the Californian goldfields. He wanted such men to pay back their free sail to the colony before they left. Indeed, the more he thought about it, the more he thought it reasonable to insist that *all* bounty men, including Parkes and a number of his associates, should also reimburse the government their free fare—even if they were going to stay in the colony. Lowe had turned upon the very people who had elected him, Parkes complained to anyone who raised the matter at his Hunter Street toyshop, where his wife was now doing the lion's share of the work while Parkes sulked about in his new 'obscurity'.

But it was his absurd stoush with the popular philanthropist Dr William Bland that proved the last straw for Robert Lowe. Their disagreement began when the Legislative Council was discussing the colony's first university and suggesting nominations for the senate of that institution. Someone proposed the name of Lowe's old nemesis, Dr Bland, the man who when he first arrived in the colony had told Lowe he would lose his eyesight. Ever since that erroneous diagnosis, Lowe had been on Bland's heels, condemning him as a 'has-been' who was no more than a wag to Wentworth's tail. The notion of Bland on the university senate so appalled Lowe he went so far as to use the 'c' word in council. Even as the room hushed and nervous looks were exchanged, the forthright demagogue insisted that the appointment of an emancipist would sully the name of the colony and tarnish the very institution of education.

It was one thing to condemn a common criminal but the doctor was a gentleman who had been transported for duelling with another man thirty years ago. Since then he had been a benevolent presence in the colony, often stopping on the street to dispense pills and free medical advice. When Bland learnt of Lowe's comments he exploded with an apoplectic rage that was matched only by the collective shock of the townspeople. And when Lowe heard that the aggrieved doctor was thinking of challenging him to a duel he had Bland charged with breaching the peace and violating Parliamentary privilege. It was a farce that volleyed back and forth across the papers and courts throughout the spring of 1849. As it did so 'the deformities' of Robert Lowe's body and mind were repeatedly cited as the reason for the 'vile albino's cowardice'. The whole episode was too much, even for Lowe's most loyal supporters and thereafter few could bring themselves to invite the brilliant lawyer and his wife to any of their social gatherings.

The isolation of the Great Gyrator was now complete. Since arriving in the colony in 1842 he had crossed swords with several governors and many of his own sort. He had lured and lulled the settlers one moment only to mock and shock them the next. He had made many friends but discovered in each some fault he felt compelled to expose publicly. He had coaxed the mechanics and hypnotised the Cabbagers, then thought nothing of turning upon the very men who had hauled that carriage all the way up George Street. But now, the remarkable Robert Lowe had dared to break the one taboo that bound all classes in the colony. He had dared to suggest that a rehabilitated man should be forever condemned for his convict past—that there could be no redemption for a felon. The sting of that slur was felt by all who shared the doctor's past, as well as their children. No one wanted such a man among them and so, very quickly and quietly, the colony came to a decision: Robert Lowe must go.

The same paper that carried news of Dr Bland's successful legal outcome against Robert Lowe also carried the advertisement for Gill's Family Hotel and the George Street properties. On another page there was also a complete version of Mrs Lynton's elegy to John Kinchela Junior. William had opened the paper looking for their advertisement but once he had read the widow's poem he went in search of his father. He found Martin Gill talking with a man about San Francisco. Will showed his father their advertisements and then the florid poem. Both men stumbled over the stiff rhythm and awkward phrasing of the eulogy, until they came to the third stanza, which particularly captured Gill's attention:

He died, deserving to be mourn'd
As witness all the tears we gave—
My God! That He who life adorn'd
Should die, and fools in folly live.

Gill raised his eyebrows and made a sort of clucking sound. 'Well, well, well,' he said giving his son a tight sort of a grin. 'I wonder which living "fool" is going to inherit all the family fortune now, eh?' he finished, chuckling to himself as he rubbed his hands together. And with that Martin Gill disappeared into the almost empty hulk of a hotel, leaving a bewildered William looking after his father and wondering what sort of new madness he had just unleashed upon the world.

CHAPTER TWENTY

Under the Hammer

Martin Gill was keen to meet with James Butler Kinchela. He had put the word about town, but those who were willing to help had nothing useful to tell him about the gentleman felon's whereabouts. Others who might have known were not prepared to encourage further mischief in that regard. Kinchela might be all the things that had been determined in the courts last year, but his brother had just died and people felt compelled to respect the solemnities of that occasion.

On one hot and windy afternoon just before All Hallow's Eve, it was not, however, Martin Gill who first laid eyes on the man in question, but his eldest daughter. Mary Ann was coming through the kitchen, carrying a mortar and pestle that her mother had requested, when she stopped in the doorway completely stunned by the sight of James. He was dressed in mourning garb and leaning against his cane as he stood in the queue before the shipping agent. She must have gasped in shock, for most of the people in the room, including Kinchela, turned to see the young woman standing at the threshold of the kitchen, wearing a blue-green jacket over her full skirts, her braided hair free of a bonnet, and a large kitchen object in her hands. She blinked several times. It was like seeing a ghost, she thought, her mind racing. It had been several months since their altercation at the Monster Meeting and since then she had torn up each and every unread correspondence in Kinchela's handwriting that had arrived at the hotel. Since she had convinced herself of the Louisa Aarons matter she had quite successfully managed to dismiss her former suitor as the very worst sort of man.

But now there they both were, standing in almost exactly the same positions as two autumns ago when they had first set eyes upon one another. Only this time, instead of leaning against the bar looking out through the window, the gentleman settler was standing in the queue that splayed out before Robert Ogilby. And, from the particular angle Kinchela had assumed, he was not only looking straight into the kitchen but also directly at Mary Ann.

Kinchela couldn't help but smile. It might have been his nervousness or the fact that he was delighted to see her, or even her expression—eyes blinking, face awash with rage. He found it impossible to suppress the steady grin that took possession of his face. She looked more womanly than he remembered her from their chance encounter at Circular Quay—and certainly much more so than the very first time he had seen her standing almost in the same spot, more than a year ago, when she had been such a slight young thing. There was a new gravity to her bearing as well as a certain insouciance he found arresting to say the least. James Butler grasped all this within a few seconds as the room seemed to swell about him and then fall to a hush and it felt, to both of them, that they were alone in the room, looking at one another.

And then Martin Gill came striding into the front bar in the company of William and the portly dray man, who was trotting a little behind them both. Straightaway Mary Ann's brother picked up that something was wrong but before he could do anything Martin Gill seized the moment. 'A word, sir,' he growled to the gentleman with the cane, pointing his thumb in a slightly menacing manner towards the back room. All those with some knowledge about who was whom took a collective gasp and turned to look at Mary Ann.

Kinchela was taken aback, but not entirely. Two weeks had passed since he had attended his brother's memorial in the Bathurst district and since then he and his mother had undertaken several significant conversations about his future. His new financial circumstances changed matters considerably, even though his brother had left their brother-in-law with an unpaid debt of some £4000 which would have to be honoured. Even so, the profit from the sale of Hawkwood would now come to him and after years of living in his brother's shadow James would soon have all the money he needed to do whatever he wished. And yet, John's sudden passing had been a source of considerable suffering for Kinchela and as he reflected upon all that had been he realised that he must quickly acquire some of his brother's certitude and do something about his future before it was too late.

Kinchela decided to visit the hotel and face Miss Gill and her father. He had of course toyed with the idea well before he had encountered Mary Ann and her brother at the Monster Meeting in mid-June. During the perilous journey back from Hawkwood he had plenty of time to rehearse what he would say. And yet, Kinchela was ever the tentative country Irishman when it came to such matters and had preferred to write with the hope that this might smooth the path towards reconciliation. But several months of silence and his brother's recent death had brought him to the conclusion that matters were now close at hand. Coming to the hotel was a risk and anything could happen. But as he had been riding back from his brother's memorial with Jim Davidson he had learnt about the rumours of Mr Gill's encroaching bankruptcy as well as the unsuccessful attempts that had been made to match Mary Ann off with one of the rich old gulls in town. Perhaps he might be able to reason with Gill at last, Kinchela thought, arriving at the decision that he must act immediately.

'Bold and resolute,' he told himself as he guided his mother's tilbury to the side of the street and tied up in front of Gill's Family Hotel. He assumed that the family was in trouble, from what Davidson had said, but he had not expected a shipping agent to be selling fares to California in the once grand dining room. He hardly recognised the room where he had taken so many pleasant suppers the year before. As he made his way past the staircase where he and Mary Ann had previously conspired to meet each evening he stopped for a moment and then looked about for someone who might help him find her. Suddenly he became aware that people were looking at him. Having grown conscious of unwanted attention and the snide asides that followed wherever he went he slipped into the shipping agent's queue and adopted a certain stance with his cane while he tried to work out what to do. And that was where he had been standing when Mary Ann appeared at the kitchen doorway.

Mary Ann could not believe what she was seeing. Kinchela was just standing there with that foolish look upon his face. The nerve of it, she fumed. Of all the places he could go to buy his passage to California. And why was her father having an audience with the very man whose ruin he had been determined to bring about? Then she panicked, trying to recall if her father had his pistols with him. Her father had little to lose these days, and might be keen to finish the job he had started the year before that early morning out at the Homebush race-course. For all her loathing towards Kinchela, Mary Ann did not wish for that. And so, after watching the two men disappear into the back of the hotel, she waited a moment and then crept after them. Minutes later she was joined by William, who she beckoned to hush as they both bent to listen at the door.

Gill was already behind his desk when Kinchela stepped inside that small, rather dark room. The younger man insisted upon standing, even after Gill produced two glasses and a bottle of good Irish whiskey and beckoned Kinchela to sit. He poured two stiff drinks and pushed one glass towards his perplexed guest. 'She looks better these days, don't you think?' Gill started. 'It is interesting to see what time does to a woman,' he continued, watching Kinchela carefully as the younger man finally took a seat but left the glass before him untouched. 'So you are planning to take Mr Ogilby's *Cheerful* to California, Mr Kinchela?' Gill asked after a period of awkward silence. James Butler shook his head, recalling with disgust how Gill had spat at his feet outside the Supreme Court. 'Not the *Cheerful*, sir,' he said curtly. 'I will, however, be leaving for San Francisco in a little over a week.' 'Mmmm,' Gill finished his glass and gestured to Kinchela to drink. 'And would I be right to assume that you now have plenty of money to take with you?' he asked, perhaps a little too roughly for Kinchela, who looked incensed by what he considered a vulgar line of questioning from a man he could hardly call an intimate acquaintance, let alone a friend. Still it was the Irish way, Kinchela knew, for a father to ask after the money.

Undeterred Gill persisted. 'Is it the gold that most attracts you, Mr Kinchela?' he asked rather abruptly, 'or the promise of a fresh start elsewhere?' Kinchela gave a slight nod and put his hand to the back of his neck. The Gills were direct people, Kinchela mused. He considered the man before him as it gradually dawned upon him that they were engaged in marital negotiations. Despite all that had been, Kinchela decided, it was in his best interests to remain courteous. 'There is a lot of land out there, Mr Gill, from what I have read, and plenty of mouths to feed. Someone who knows about cattle could make do very well,' he said formally, before pausing to look about the room, 'and, yes, after all that has happened, a fresh start does look to be for the best.'

'I see,' Gill said, knocking back his second drink in a single gulp before putting it down on the table and refilling it again. He coughed and fixed the younger man with a look as he sized him up. 'Tell me, Mr Kinchela,' he asked, chin slightly raised, 'would you take my daughter with you as your wife?' Kinchela almost choked on his drink. It had been his intention to raise this very matter with the girl's father when, or indeed *if* he could secure such an agreement from Mary Ann, but he had never imagined such a proposal would come from his old adversary. The man's financial standing must be even more precarious than the rumours suggested, Kinchela thought as he recovered sufficiently to reply. 'Mr Gill,' he swallowed, 'you have given me the clearest possible indication on numerous occasions that such an idea is one to which you are ill disposed,' he finished, feeling that it was quite within his right to sound haughty.

Gill looked to be enjoying himself. He filled both their glasses and chuckled to himself. 'This is true, Mr Kinchela. I did,' and then he followed with a tone that he typically reserved for situations requiring the utmost charm, 'but I suppose there is no use in any of us drowning in regret over all that has been.' Kinchela arched his eyebrow and looked away. He thought about the trouble Gill had caused and felt his hackles rise in a way he imagined would have been all too familiar for his older brother. He could imagine John wanting to put this up-start old hand in his place. His brother would have been keen to bring out his riding crop to do so, he thought, but still Kinchela could not muster such a passion. He was curious about what had made Gill change his mind, and could also see that it would help his cause to allow the older man to continue. 'You will be aware, no doubt, from what you have heard around town, that my family's circumstances have changed,' Gill coughed, 'and not, as you can see, for the better.'

Despite the poor blood between them Kinchela could not help but feel a pang of pity. He remembered his own father's shortcomings in this regard and the shame of seeing his family's furniture dragged into the town square back in Kilkenny. His father had not been a particularly proud man but that moment had almost broken him. Kinchela wondered how a much more energetic patriarch like Martin Gill might manage under these circumstances. In such a moment he knew his brother would not only take the upper hand over a man like Gill, but also relish his position. Kinchela didn't have the same taste for it. Instead he found himself offering, rather kindly, 'These things can get the better of us all, Mr Gill.'

Gill looked at him in surprise, and blinked twice as he wondered how to proceed. He realised he had never spent a moment alone with the man who he had refused, point blank, as a possible suitor for his daughter. Now, however, as he sat before that man, Gill realised that what he *did* know about James Butler Kinchela was that which he had decided for himself. A nabob from the interior, he had assumed, and no doubt the sort of man who had lived around St Stephen's Green in one of the houses where the young Gill had been caught with the hand griddle. And yet, here he was—the gentleman settler from Moreton Bay—prepared to undertake a conversation with the very person who had shot at him twice and then exerted considerable energy to have him imprisoned. What type of a man was he? Gill wondered. He was not quite the same young buck he had seen enjoying himself in the front bar of his hotel the year before. Then, the settler had looked every bit the sort who would put him in his place as many had done when he had first arrived in the colony, not yet twenty years of age and skinny as a rat. Now?—Gill was not so sure.

The hotelier rubbed his throat for a moment and thought. He had sought this meeting to secure the business transaction he had been unable to line up with old Alexander Moore and that fool Samuel. He had hoped to settle the matter of his daughter and create a few financial opportunities for himself before he left the colony. But he suddenly found himself in a different situation. Gill ruminated for a moment but then tired of chasing his own thoughts. He placed his hands flat on his desk and looked frankly at the gentleman sitting across from him. 'My daughter has no future here, Mr Kinchela,' he said firmly. 'We both know that. In fact, I am fast coming to the conclusion that neither of us do.' Then he looked at the man he had all but destroyed and did him the honour of speaking straight. 'You wanted her once, Mr Kinchela,' Martin Gill continued steadily, 'and so I am asking you now, as a father who needs to see this matter settled,' he swallowed hard, 'if you would take her again.' Thirsty from this effort, Gill grabbed his whiskey and threw it down his throat.

All this could have been avoided from the very start, Kinchela thought to point out. If from the start, Gill had just given him a moment instead of assuming the worst. Various phrases passed through Kinchela's mind about the cost to all concerned, particularly the shame to Mary Ann and the loss of his family's name, but each sentence seemed to fall short. John was dead and life had irrevocably changed. The whiskey continued to warm his innards and as it did Kinchela found it harder to think why he would want to waste his time, particularly given the purpose of his visit. He also thought of Mary Ann standing in the threshold of the hotel kitchen. She was no longer some young thing with whom he had whiled away a few hours.

Just to look at her—it was clear that she now had accomplishments. He recalled that afternoon at Keck's gaol when she had surprised him with a visit, holding herself with the right portion of reserve and wit, looking so smart in her bonnet. That look in her eye. He could see that whatever agreement he might come to with her father, it would prove no substitute for that which he was truly seeking. 'The episode has been extremely costly, sir, for your daughter,' Kinchela began after several moments, 'and I sense she no longer harbours any good will towards me.' Gill flurried his hand through the air with a gesture of impatience. 'Well, Mr Kinchela, I have heard it said that some members of my family are in the fashion of blowing a little hot and cold,' he gave a rather disarming smile before adding, rather matter-of-factly, 'but you know, Mary Ann is my daughter and the point I have been insisting upon all along is that she is bound to marry who I choose.'

'No, sir,' Kinchela firmly shook his head, 'I will not have it thus.' The two men stared at one another for some time until eventually Kinchela continued, this time a little more lightly, 'You know, I cannot help but think, sir, that over the past year your daughter has been striving to make a similar matter apparent to you. It seems to me that your Mary Ann will have her own head regardless of what either of us might seek to say or do.' The two men locked eyes and then after a rather uncomfortable minute, Martin Gill allowed a wry smile. 'Aye, Mr Kinchela, you might have it there,' he agreed, shaking his head as he finally resigned himself to the fact that he might end up with an Irish son-in-law after all.

Gill scratched behind his ear and considered Kinchela, trying to imagine what sort of life his daughter might have with such a gentleman. What accomplishments his eldest daughter might hold for a country settler like Kinchela he did not care to guess at, but it seemed that the matter might work to his advantage if he let it go its own way. 'Well,' he said in a perfunctory tone, 'if you can secure her consent,' Gill said, 'in whatever time you have before you leave this colony, I would ask that you also buy a passage for her and her brother to ensure she travels the right way.' And then in an act that took Kinchela entirely by surprise, Martin Gill got up from his chair and presented the gentleman his hand. 'And on those terms,' he finished with a curt nod, 'I would be pleased to see the matter settled.'

The following Monday, Margaret Gill closed the door on Gill's Family Hotel and locked it for the last time, placing the key inside a small velveteen bag. William watched his mother climb into the coach piled high with the last of their possessions. She took her seat and put the heavy-looking mortar and pestle firmly in her lap. They were heading to the weatherboard cottage Thomas McCormick had taken on Kent Street. That humble worker's cottage would give the family a place to sleep while they worked out what to do next. Old McCormick had organised the entire thing and was also keeping a room for himself and Mary Riley just in case the creditors came looking for Margaret's keepings as payment for her husband's debts.

No sooner were Margaret and William Gill halfway up the street than Martin Gill slipped back inside the Pitt Street hotel via the cellar door. An hour or so later he and George Page the dray man had hauled out the most expensive furniture from the superior guestrooms. If Mr Samuel thought he could set the town against Martin Gill then he didn't know who he was dealing with, Gill muttered as he unloaded the solid bedheads and side tables into the back storage area of Moore's auction rooms. The long-awaited plan had finally come to him that morning and when it did it was almost too good to be true. He was still delighting at the sheer chicanery of it. Poor old Moore would not be able to help himself, he knew. The moment he saw all the elegant bedsteads and good quality possessions, the old auctioneer would be so keen for the commission that he would push hell and high water to get the furniture moved as quickly as he could. And then, with the proceeds Gill made from the sales of Mr Samuel's furniture to Alexander Moore, Martin Gill was going to buy himself a passage out of this rotten place and have the last laugh—all the way to California.

Once he had finished with the last of the hotel furniture he could take from the guestrooms Martin Gill went back into the hotel alone. The evening was closing in and the light gradually dissolving. He lit a candle and began looking about. He was sure that there would be items his wife and children had overlooked. He still needed more ready cash, not just for his passage but also to ensure that he was able to start his new life according to the standing to which he was now accustomed. He walked into the bedroom he once shared with Margaret and picked up an old washstand and a small looking glass that he knew were dear to his wife. Well, if she was fool enough to leave them here, he thought, they are good for the taking.

In William's room there were papers, some with his writing scrawled over them but others blank. There is a market for paper, too, Gill noted as he added these to the pile. There were a few wooden toys that must have come from the Hunter Street shop. The children had left them scattered across the nursery floor and Gill decided they might fetch a few shillings, so he bundled these under his arm, too. In Mary Ann's room he found a feather mattress, which he dragged out onto the landing. She wouldn't need these where she was going. As he was heading out of this room, Martin Gill spied the wardrobe door ajar and noticed the two dresses he had purchased for his eldest daughter—one lilac, the other deep red. He took the rich, heavy fabrics and slung them over his shoulder, struggling to carry the rest of the objects downstairs into the empty hotel. Those dresses, he thought, they would fetch a sufficient price to get him a good cabin. Even if he had to get his hands dirty, Martin Gill was going to leave the colony on his own terms and in the appropriate style.

～

On the first morning of their stay in the Kent Street cottage, William Gill was woken suddenly by a sharp rapping on the front door. He was still in his nightshirt when he opened the door and found himself face-to-face with a furious-looking Mr Samuel and several of his associates. 'Where is your father?' the irate gentleman asked, shoving the young man to one side before marching down the corridor and into the kitchen where Margaret and Mary Ann were preparing a breakfast of johnnycakes with warm ham. 'It has come to my attention, Mrs Gill,' Samuel began, fairly frothing at the mouth, 'that certain items belonging to my brother and I have disappeared from the hotel.'

Margaret gave her accuser an irritable look. She was in no mood for this sort of bluster. She rose slowly from the table, and looked her unwelcome visitor firmly in the eye. 'Are you asking to inspect my father's home, Mr Samuel?' she asked. 'If so, perhaps you would like to try some more of my cooking, first?' There was a snort of indignation from one of Mr Samuel's men followed by a snigger from Thomas McCormick, who was sitting in the corner drinking his tea. Next thing the old man was up and standing beside his daughter Margaret. He raised himself to his full height as he addressed the group of gentlemen who had crammed into the small cottage kitchen. 'What precisely do you mean by coming into my home and disturbing my peace at such an hour?' McCormick asked, voice full of thunder. Several of the associates looked about nervously and Mr Samuel took a step back. McCormick was still a big man and looked as though he would know how to wield a fire poker if it came to that. Samuel adjusted his tie. 'I am looking for your husband, Madam,' he said, preferring to address Margaret. 'I believe he may have confused some of my personal items for his own.' Margaret looked at William, who was standing in the doorway. 'Do you know where your father is, then?' she asked dully.

An hour later, the entire party was making their way towards W.G. Moore's auction rooms where William had a feeling he might find his father. William took them on the most circuitous route he could think of, hoping that his father's business might be done by the time they arrived. When, however, the irate group finally appeared in the grand foyer of the George Street auction rooms, it was clear that an auction was in progress and that many of the goods displayed on the front stage were associated with the sinewy Dublin businessman in the front row. Samuel's party forced their way through the auction crowd and down the aisle, making such a commotion that Martin Gill turned to see what was what. He was immediately confronted by his wife and two eldest children storming towards him. His father-in-law was fast behind them and right on their heels were a party of serious-looking men in suits. 'The auction must be stopped,' Lewis Samuel bellowed, waving his walking stick at the podium where a brightly clad gentleman was calling items numbered 22 to 58.

'What is all this about then?' Gill asked, rising from his chair and making his way over to the stage with the intention of concealing a number of things he hoped to hide from his wife. But Margaret shoved her husband to one side and quickly took possession of certain goods she knew to be her own. 'You can't prove a thing, Samuel,' Gill growled, 'and I am in no mood to be wasting my time with you again.' Mr Samuel's eyes grew wider and his face turned a pinkish colour. His mutton-chop whiskers bristled and he wagged his finger at Martin Gill, as he struggled to catch his breath. 'You are trying to sell my hotel goods from under me,' he finally exploded. Martin Gill simply raised his eyebrows and smugly crossed his arms. 'But these objects are no longer in my possession, Mr Samuel,' he explained coolly. 'They belong to the auctioneer and his customers, most of whom have already left with their purchases.'

The next moment Alexander Moore burst onto the stage with a wad of papers in his hand. 'I will not be accused of misconduct,' he flamed at Mr Samuel with whom he felt no little grudge regarding certain rumours that the latter had put about in relation to himself and Gill's eldest girl. He shook a fist of sheets in Samuel's face. 'I have all my records, each certificate of purchase right here,' he said, slapping bits of paper onto a host of objects displayed on the stage.

At that moment, Mary Ann saw her two dresses upon the stage where they had been draped over a velvet chaise longue. 'Mr Moore,' she said, stepping forward to address the unfortunate auctioneer who was now dabbing his sweaty brow with a giant handkerchief. 'The two dresses on your stage, you may recall that these belong to me,' she darted a disgusted look at her father before turning calmly to her one-time suitor. 'I am sure my father would want the proceeds from their sale to come directly to me,' she said, opening her gloved palm. Moore looked from Mary Ann to the dresses and then to Martin Gill with an increasingly perplexed expression.

With that, Mr Samuel seized his chance, 'We will take you for every penny,' he threatened, 'every penny, sir. You and your wife.' But Martin Gill simply appraised them all with a satisfied expression as he slowly surveyed the scene. There was his wife and father-in-law loaded up with looking glasses, cushions and washstands, Alexander Moore still clenching his papers, and Mr Samuel brandishing his walking stick about him in a most unwieldy manner. The Dublin emancipist gathered himself and addressed the party with an insolent smile. 'Well,' he said, 'you may all go to hell and find your money there, for all I care.' With that the bold entrepreneur folded the wad of pound notes he had secured from his day's efforts and stuffed them into his waistcoat pocket, before sauntering down the aisle of the auction rooms and out its front doors.

CHAPTER TWENTY-ONE

All That Glitters

What with the wretched drought and all that followed in its wake there were now hundreds, even thousands of colonists desperate to leave New South Wales. Smart elites and old hands, as well as artisans and mechanics, were all considering their options. Would they leave by sea or take their chances along one of the ramshackle roads that led out of the colony?

No sooner had the Legislative Council nominated Dr William Bland, rather than Robert Lowe, to a seat on the senate of the University of Sydney, than the People's Idol promptly resigned from his elected seat. Days later the industrious Georgina Lowe began sorting through their pretty home beside the cliffs of Bronte, preparing goods for auction as she eagerly envisaged her life as the wife of the future Viscount of Sherbrook. The years she and Robert had dwelt among the colonists of New South Wales had been lucrative but lonely and the Lowes were eager to return home. News that Robert's older brother had secured an excellent inheritance with a peerage also signalled that it was time for them to return to England and resume their rightful position. By early November 1849, the Lowes' departure had become a matter of when, not if, and few in New South Wales were sorry to hear of it.

Henry Parkes was contemplating Geelong, a populous portside town about a day's ride south-west of Melbourne. His Hunter Street business was looking grim, although not quite as grim as his over-worked and neglected wife. Parkes would do well to devote less time to the affairs of the colony and more to his family and business. But he could not quite bring himself to shift his focus. One of his remaining associates, Angus Mackay, had dropped *The Atlas* and was trying to convince Parkes to open a general store down south. Only, Parkes felt rudderless. The discreet departure of the *Hashemy* for a less contro-versial mooring up north, at Moreton Bay, had taken the wind out of his sails and Robert Lowe's recent conduct had also left a nasty taste in his mouth. The rocking horse vendor had risen to the challenge of a good campaign and experienced the thrill of bringing the people with him. Indeed he was now recognised as the most effective campaigner in the entire colony, but where had that got him? Thanks in large part to his efforts, there was now legislation before the British parliament concerned with granting New South Wales responsible government. This had been what he had wanted, but that only made the infernal new Bill even more vexatious. By the look of the draft, this new Act would give the squatters even greater power and could well cost the middling set more than if they had left the colony in the care of a remote Home Office and an indifferent governor. No wonder the idea of running a successful business and owning a newspaper was starting to look like his best path forward, even if that path did lead Parkes down the Great South Road to Port Phillip for a time.

Since news of gold had come to the colony last Christmas, close to three thousand colonists had tossed their bags upon their shoulders and boarded a boat bound for California. It had not been a full-scale rush, however, and departures to the American west coast had occurred in fits and starts during the first six months of 1849 with only fourteen vessels leaving from Sydney for San Francisco. In fact, most of the boats undertaking the voyage across the Pacific during that time carried stock rather than humans, thanks to a few canny businessmen who recognised that a burgeoning township like San Francisco would need everything from candles to canvas, bully meat to brandy.

It was only after an official United States Army Report confirmed

the sort of finds that were being made around Sacramento that a verit-
able exodus began among those colonists who had been contemplating
the new 'Gold Land'. Suddenly men, for it was mostly men, and mainly
from the middling set—skilled labourers and urban artisans, generally
between the ages of fourteen and sixty—were leaving New South Wales
in such numbers that the Legislative Council began grumbling that the
colony was little more than a 'halfway house for California'. Concerns
about the 'pecuniary loss' to the local labour market had become such
that the governor commissioned a report about this 'growing and
serious evil'. Now officials were stationed about the harbour determined
to deter the departure of anyone with legal constraints or other pressing
financial obligations. Some said it was like shutting the gate after the
horse had long bolted for, already, the flamboyant Ben Boyd had sailed
out of Port Jackson on his private schooner, the aptly named *Wanderer*.
In his wake Boyd had left at least £80,000 of debt, a collapsed bank, and
a string of flabbergasted shareholders and spoiled speculators, not to
mention the 20,000 sheep and 10,000 cattle he had abandoned on his
vast, drought stricken pastoral holdings. If the authorities were unable
to stop a prominent colonist like Ben Boyd, surely Martin Gill also
stood a chance of slipping through the net? Or so he was hoping.

Seventeen-year-old Mary Ann had been in a state of considerable agitation since she and her brother had eavesdropped at the door of their
father's office and overheard his conversation with Kinchela. Her heart
burned with the knowledge that the affection, which had been so frequently thwarted over the past year or so, was in fact reciprocated. What
she had heard was enough for her to put aside her concerns and decide
that her future lay with Kinchela. And yet. Mary Ann could think of
no way to act upon this new understanding. From that conversation
she had learnt that James would be leaving within days and despite her
brother making discreet enquiries, neither had secured any idea as to
Kinchela's whereabouts. Nor could she work out how he might find her
since the family had taken up their modest Kent Street cottage.

Will was also feeling desperate. The same conversation had filled his head with all sorts of glittering possibilities. He now wanted nothing more than to get on any one of the blasted boats out in the harbour and join the great flight of forty-niners. He wanted freedom and fortune. He also wanted to see his eldest sister happy, although he couldn't see how this was going to happen with Kinchela likely to depart any day now, and nobody knowing where that gentleman was residing, let alone what boat he was going to take out of Sydney. But with the hotel closing and the extraordinary events at the auction rooms less than a week ago, William Gill was sufficiently fed up with his family's circumstances to take matters into his own hands. He had, after all, been serving as a go-between for his parents since their 'rupture' in early June, and was one of the very few who knew his father's current whereabouts.

After his triumph at Moore's auction rooms, Martin Gill had been hiding out along the Punchbowl road, in his father-in-law's old farm-house, to be precise. This had been vacant since McCormick and Mary Riley had moved into town as they had, thus far, failed to attract a tenant. Gill hated the place but it was far enough out of town to put him at arm's length from Mr Lewis Samuel & Co. He could bide his time and raid McCormick's vegetable garden for supplies while waiting for the right opportunity to present itself. As things stood, Gill knew he was facing the debtor's prison or worse if he was caught in Sydney. He had also come to the realisation that it would be impossible for him to buy a berth to California in person. Nonetheless, his recent victory and the wad of notes secreted away about his person imbued Martin Gill with confidence. Something would turn up.

And so it did, that very afternoon, when his eldest son arrived at his grandparents' farmhouse. He and Mary Ann had heard everything at his office door, Will explained once he had greeted his dishevelled looking father. He knew his father was planning to skip town for San Francisco, he said right off, and that he would need to do so very shortly if he was to keep out of the courts. Will was prepared to buy his father's passage, but in return, he insisted, his father would buy two other passages: for himself and Mary Ann.

Gill rubbed his chin as he thought it through. He wanted to keep the money for himself and had been hoping Kinchela would assume the financial costs associated with his eldest children. Given all that occurred between himself and Mary Ann, he could not see how they could possibly undertake such a voyage together. Truth be known, Martin Gill had also come to the realisation that he wanted to arrive in California unencumbered by family. He was, after all, a man who knew how to survive—whatever the stakes. He would be better without any hangers-on. He wanted to be on his own.

'There has been a cooling off between your mother and I that is true,' Martin Gill responded as he started feeling about for a loophole through which he might yet wriggle. 'But,' he said with a forced sigh, 'I can't see fit to take your mother's eldest children away.' Will shot his father a look of disdain and shook his head. 'She wants us out of her hair,' he replied, 'or bringing in money of our own, and, as things stand,' he continued, 'you know as well as I that Mary Ann is unlikely to find any work in Sydney, let alone a husband. So you see,' the young man continued, 'the best we can do is make our own way and, as we can't find Kinchela to cover our fares, it looks like you will have to pay our way.'

Gill fixed his jaw and the two men sat in silence while the father continued to look for a way to untangle himself from his son's clever stratagem. After a while Will spoke again. 'Look at it this way, we can settle Mary Ann with her gentleman and as soon as we find our fortune we can send money back to Sydney too.' Martin Gill scowled. He didn't much like the idea of being stuck with his son or, even worse, sending money home to his estranged wife and father-in-law. Still, he could see the sense of the girl's match and a family connection with a gentleman might secure some advantages, particularly in a new territory where no one knew him. But before his father could come to his own mind, Will stood up abruptly, 'I am your only chance,' he said impatiently, 'and I need the money today,' he finished, thrusting forth his hand.

'All right,' Martin Gill finally conceded as he removed one of his boots and extracted from it a good wad of notes, 'but mind you book us a proper cabin—and don't be too clever making up a name—there are times when it is cannier to tell the truth, especially when no one thinks you would dare.' Will nodded. 'I've looked at the shipping lists,' Gill continued, 'there are six boats leaving for San Francisco in the next month,' he added returning his boot to his foot, 'and only the *Bee* and the *Sabine* still have berths, so you will need to make haste.'

And that was precisely what William did. He made his way back into town along the pockmarked Punchbowl road as fast as his pony would allow. It was growing dark by the time William Gill arrived on York Street but he dedicated the last of the daylight hours to making enquiries as to the whereabouts of James Butler Kinchela. He went to the Adelphi but they could tell him nothing, so he visited several of the better hotels, where Will had a feeling his sister's suitor might be, but no one knew anything. Eventually, Will headed back to the Kent Street cottage feeling increasingly anxious about how to proceed.

He knew he would have to square his new plan with his mother before he presented it to Mary Ann. Margaret had made it clear she didn't think much of Will keeping in cahoots with her husband, 'a lot more trouble than he is worth,' she had recently cautioned him, 'and likely to make even more trouble for us all if he can.' Will knew his mother would rise at the mere mention of her husband, especially once she realised that Will had been with him. It might be best to keep their bargain to himself. He also had an inkling that Mary Ann would say no if she knew where the money was coming from—let alone that she would have to travel with her father.

When he arrived home Margaret made her son wait until their meal was finished and the table cleared. Whatever he had to say would be heard by all in the room, she insisted, signalling to her parents to brace themselves for some new horror. Will looked about his family, both grandparents as well as all his five siblings and his mother were all crammed into the small hot room. He suddenly felt acutely aware of their reduced circumstances. He had been selfish to imagine that he and Mary Ann could leave their family at such a time. He would say nothing, he decided, and instead use his father's money to help those he loved right in front of him. But then he looked at Mary Ann who was wiping the last of the dinner dishes dry. She had been even more restless since the family had moved to Kent Street. And withdrawn. He recalled the shine to her eyes when they had eavesdropped at their father's door. There was something he had to do. Will took a deep breath and began.

Well before he could finish, however, Mary Riley chimed in. 'Well Margaret,' she said firmly, 'I'm thinking it is the only way for the two of them, at least for Mary Ann wouldn't you say?' Margaret sniffed but said nothing as she turned to her father. McCormick mused, 'Well, you know, some are saying it is better to be Irish there than here. And who knows,' he said pointing his chin at Will, 'perhaps Dick Whittington, here, might yet make us all rich.' Then McCormick considered Mary Ann. Margaret looked at him and sighed before turning to her eldest daughter. 'Well?' Margaret asked. 'Is this how you would have it?' There was a touch of lightness to her otherwise stern voice. 'Sailing off to meet a man who has already caused you such a world of trouble?'

Mary Ann flashed her brother a look of profound relief before replying. 'Yes,' she said with surprising certitude, 'it is. If you would have it yourself?' she asked, but then without waiting for a response she rushed on, 'There will be Will and I to keep an eye on one another and, you said yourself that we are not much use to you here.' The room was still and all eyes were on Margaret. After a moment Mary Ann continued with a wry smile, 'After all, I am now also of the understanding that none of my father's previous suitors wish to court me, so perhaps at last I might be finally free to marry Mr Kinchela.'

The following morning William Gill made his way down Pitt Street, past the family's old hotel where a FOR LEASE sign had been nailed to the front door demanding that 'all enquiries be made directly to Mr S. and L. Samuel'. The fifteen-year-old boy pushed through various passengers bustling about the quay. After talking to a group of lightermen busy unloading kegs from a small boat, Will learnt there were three different rigs set to depart for California in the next day or so. He had no idea which one might be Kinchela's sail, so he wandered about the dock, sizing up each vessel.

The *Phantom* was a small, square-sterned cutter with one deck and a single mast and no figurehead. She must have been one of the smallest on the quay. Will looked at her uncertainly. Surely Kinchela wouldn't take his chances on something like that, particularly now that he had come into money. So he walked on to find the *Gleaner*, docked at the next quay. She was much bigger and a schooner, too, and as Will watched passengers milling about he got a sense that she couldn't be taking more than thirty passengers. So he stopped one fellow, a well-looking tradesman, and asked him if he knew any of those who would be sailing with him. The man shook his head. He had not heard of a gentleman named Kinchela, but then that didn't mean much, he added, for he was travelling steerage, and such a man was likely to have himself a cabin. He would want to be about it, the man added, for the boat was set for the evening tide. Will thought he should wait, but he also knew he would have to put his father's money on their own passages and look to the *Lady Howden*. So he stood awhile, straining to see who might be about the deck of the *Gleaner*, but, when he had nothing to show for his efforts after an hour, made his way to where the *Howden* was anchored.

The *Lady Howden* was a large, 300-ton brig that had sailed into Sydney Harbour from Van Diemen's Land in mid-September, allowing its master, the well-groomed Henry Chalk, to enjoy a leisurely spring season as he drummed up business for his next voyage. His ship was capable of taking just under a hundred passengers and was certainly one of the bigger brigs docked at the quay. Will sized up the two tall masts and solid sails as well as the way the *Howden* sat in the water. It was probably the sort of ship a gentleman like Kinchela would prefer, he thought, although there was no sight of him. He learnt from one of the crew that all passengers had been required to board two days earlier, for the *Howden* would be sailing out on the morning tide.

Surely Kinchela must be somewhere on the quay, Will thought. But after waiting around for most of the afternoon, he reluctantly decided to head into town and buy their own passage otherwise he knew he would risk finding all the berths booked. Casting several last-minute backward glances, William Gill made his way up to Macquarie Place where a man named Wilkinson was selling freight and passage on a fast-sailing American brig named the *Sabine*. With £35 of his father's money the young man purchased a first-class cabin for 'Mr and Mrs Gill and Son'. As his father had instructed but with a little twist to confuse the creditors, if necessary. Then Will made his way back to the Kent Street cottage to report upon his various successes and disappointments.

The *Gleaner* was scheduled to sail that night and the *Howden* on the morning tide, Will explained to Mary Ann, who was busy ironing a stack of napkins Margaret had salvaged from the old hotel. He could not say which boat had Kinchela on board although he had a feeling it was the *Howden*. He had, however, booked their cabin, he said with much satisfaction. 'Now nothing can stop us leaving on the first Friday in December,' he added cheerfully. 'We will be drinking tea with Mr Kinchela in San Francisco early in the new year,' he grinned before looking up and noticing that Mary Ann was maintaining a steady focus on the task before her. 'Even if we can't find Kinchela before he sails tonight or on the morrow,' he rushed on, 'we can put a letter on both vessels. If that doesn't find him, it will be delivered to whatever post office has been set up in San Francisco.' Will trailed off, as he noticed how Mary Ann kept pushing the heavy iron across the square cuts of cloth, 'Yes, Will,' she said with a quiet voice, 'that would be well enough'.

⁓

A moment later, however, Mary Ann gave up the dreaded pile of ironing and sat down to compose two letters of similar length for Will to take down to the *Gleaner* and the *Lady Howden*. Once the letters were sealed and Mary Ann was just about to hand both to her brother, she decided that she must venture down to the quay with William, just in case. So brother and sister stepped out of their weatherboard cottage on that late afternoon in early November. Even though an afternoon sea breeze filtered up from the harbour and through the town streets, the air was still sticky and humid. The pair walked together in haste, travelling quickly down Kent Street and then onto Sussex and King, before hurrying past all the familiar stores on Pitt Street. On they walked, hardly talking to one another as they pushed closer towards the quay. When they got there, Will pointed out where the *Howden* was anchored, and took one of her letters before sprinting off towards the *Gleaner*.

And then Mary Ann began to walk in the direction of the other vessel. Her heart was thudding, and she felt somewhat breathless, not only because of their fast walk down to the quay, but also because she had, by now, come to associate a curious sense of dread with that particular gentleman settler from Moreton Bay. As she looked about for the boat she could not help but recall the painful disappointments she had already suffered because of him. Try as she might she was unable to banish certain recollections—their dashed encounter at the Sportsman's Arms, the wretched note she received the following morning when she learnt that she was done for, her agonising appearance in court and the shocking humiliation she suffered from Kinchela's counsel, and of course, the incident with Miss Louisa Aarons. Mary Ann felt completely overwhelmed. She stopped and shook her head, looking behind her anxiously as she considered turning back.

But then, there he was. Standing on the deck of the *Howden* eating an apple. He was still in his mourning garb and had a tall, rather weather-beaten companion with him—Jim Davidson—who had come to bid his friend good fortune for this forthcoming adventure. The two men were chatting in a leisurely manner and Mary Ann watched the pair—heart pounding as she tried to work out what to do. And that was where she was, looking up at the *Howden*, seemingly rooted to the spot, when Kinchela casually cast his gaze along the quay and suddenly dropped his half-eaten apple into the harbour.

CHAPTER TWENTY-TWO

A Tuppenny Damn

How it got there neither Mary Ann nor William could say. And that was the truth of it, but when brother and sister returned home from Circular Quay late that evening, Margaret Gill and McCormick were waiting for them in the kitchen, wanting to know if either of them knew anything about the matter. Both looked grave as they sat in the half-dark room, and for a moment neither child could make any sense of what was going on. Indeed, Mary Ann was so giddy and had such a sheen to her cheek that she had to settle herself before she could properly listen to her mother and grandfather. She was also, Margaret noticed, clutching something in her hand and seemed intent upon keeping it to herself. When both children continued to look at both of them with an expression of utter bewilderment, their grandfather pointed to *The Sydney Morning Herald* and told them to turn to page three.

And there it was—a 'NOTICE to all persons', declaring that M. Gill 'would not be answerable for any claims or orders drawn without my signature'. Will was reading it out loud but his voice trailed off when he came to the next sentence so Mary Ann leant forward and read the rest in silence. 'I advertise in consequence of Mrs Gill having left her home without any just cause', the notice continued, 'and I will not', it finished, 'be answerable for any of her debts.'

Both children looked at their mother. 'What does this mean?' Mary Ann asked quietly. 'Is he planning to put those debts upon you, do you think?' Margaret's complexion was grey. She bowed her head but said nothing. Eventually, both she and her father turned to look at William. 'I had nothing to do with this,' the young man said, shaking his head vehemently until his grandfather waved him down. 'I wouldn't have helped him put such a thing in the paper,' Will insisted. 'He means to make your mother insolvent, I would say,' McCormick offered, 'and to clear off and leave her with his debts.' 'Aye,' Margaret continued in a dry tone. 'Worse than that,' she sighed, 'he doesn't just want to reduce my circumstances, he also wants to make me look the sort of woman who would leave her husband without just cause.'

Mary Ann sucked in her breath. Every colonial woman knew the cost of such a slight upon her reputation. It was as good as a divorce and no woman, let alone a respectable Roman Catholic woman, could expect to recover from such a blow. With this notice Martin Gill had doomed his wife and children to the sort of penury that had little hope of restoration. It was reprehensible and brutish. Will must have been thinking the same, for he erupted in a passion. 'We won't go,' he blustered. 'We can't leave you like this,' he repeated, looking around the room and turning at last to his sister with a look of considerable distress.

The room fell silent and Mary Ann looked about the modest room at the people with whom she was closest in the entire world. How could she and Will possibly leave their family in such circumstances and with their mother's reputation so discredited? With the signet ring she had received from Kinchela growing warm in her hand, Mary Ann nodded at her mother. 'No, Will,' she said solemnly, 'we shall not leave our family at such a time.'

What an agony November was for Margaret Gill and her six children. They kept close to one another, rarely straying from the tight confines of their small hot cottage up the working end of town as Saul and Lewis Samuel advertised for a new tenant for their former hotel and rumours about the notice Martin Gill had placed in *The Herald* began to circulate. The first suggestions of the summer might have encouraged men like Mr O'Neill from George Street to advertise their new stock of lightweight fabrics and George Chisholm to boast of his new assortment of 'Bohemian Muslin dresses' but Will and Mary Ann could feel nothing for such matters, let alone any enthusiasm for the forthcoming advent of the railway or Mr Norrie's new 'photographic art', which promised portraits taken 'at very short notice'. For whenever brother and sister dared to look upon the news-sheets all they saw were the various brigs preparing to depart for California, including, of course, the *Sabine*.

And while other confectioners were selling their stores of raisins and dried fruits, it was painfully apparent that there would be no Twelfth Night cake for the Gills this year, nor for the villain who remained holed up at the farm out on the Punchbowl road. Since Robert and Georgina Lowe were set to make an 'immediate departure for Europe' they were also likely to be denied certain festive extravagances. They had put their 'unique and charming' property up for public auction and this 'enchanting seaside residence' with its 'extensive and romantic grounds' was attracting considerable interest from those who wanted to see if what had been described in *The Herald* was real. Much to the Lowes' disdain all sorts of colonists were trekking out to their property, inspired, no doubt, by the paper's fanciful encouragement. 'Let the visitor seek out the beauties of its palms and flowers—rendered like unto a fairy land by its sparkling waterfall and sylvan scenery', the advertisement for the auction enthused. 'Let him climb the hills' and 'take in the splendid views, which meet the gaze at every turn' and they will not fail to be 'enraptured by it!' Well, no wonder it looked like Lowe's land was going to fetch a good price.

'Indeed,' thought Martin Gill, casting an eye over a purloined copy of the news-sheet. He had been growing increasingly tetchy over the past fortnight or so as he had been fending for himself from McCormick's vegetable garden and waiting for his son. He had assumed Will would return promptly with good news about his forthcoming passage out of Sydney. But several days had gone by and then a week and then another and still there was no sign of Will. 'What to do?', Gill wondered as he stomped about the wretched garden now fast going to seed.

Throughout this time Mary Ann kept close to her mother and made sure that she was at hand whenever the older woman needed assistance. It was clear to everyone, however, that the eldest Gill girl was suffering. On the one hand the seventeen year old was still savouring the few, fleeting moments she and Kinchela had snatched together before the *Howden* sailed, but then, on the other hand, she was also fuming with frustration about how her glorious promise of a better future had been dashed—yet again—by her father. Her resentment was unbridled, and this time it was shared by all in the Kent Street cottage.

But if Mary Ann and William were filled with despair and bitterness, this resignation was not shared by their grandparents. Instead, each night Thomas McCormick and Mary Riley stepped out onto the patch of green behind the cottage for their evening walk and used their time together to talk freely about how they might improve the current circumstances. McCormick had also seen the extravagant advertisement for Robert Lowe's property and it had given him an idea. The various goods Margaret had rescued from the hotel coupled with the sale of the Punchbowl farm might just give them enough to lease another city hotel, McCormick suggested to Mary Riley one evening, but they would need to sell, not lease, the old farm. A new hotel would get Margaret back on her feet, he was sure, but they must put the lease under his name, Mary Riley cautioned, so the creditors could not come after Margaret. McCormick had a feeling they could make it work. 'The two eldest can look through the papers and keep an eye out for an establishment that's been on the market a while,' McCormick explained to Margaret the following night. 'We need something that the owners want off their hands and then,' he said sounding pleased with himself, 'and then, we will be back in business.' Margaret looked at him sceptically. 'Come now girl,' McCormick finished, 'the people of Sydney won't give a tuppenny damn about your debts when they're scoffing down your turtle soup.'

Despite their current disdain for the news-sheets, Mary Ann and Will took to scouring the papers for the sort of establishment their grandfather had described. 'It needs to be just as grand as the Pitt Street hotel,' he advised, 'only way to put a stop to all the rumours,' he added shrewdly. The same day McCormick took their salvaged possessions to an auction room far enough out of town to not yet be tainted by Sydney gossip. He planned to head out to the Punchbowl farm the following day and asked Will to come along and help him spruce up the place before it went on sale. Will swallowed and nodded.

✦

Grandfather and grandson arrived at the Punchbowl farm the following morning, their cart loaded with rakes and hoes and spades. McCormick grabbed a heavy-looking spade when he thought he spied a person disappearing into the garden shed. He pushed the old shed door and looked about. There, crouching under the rough bench was his son-in-law, bare-footed and in a filthy shirt without a collar. Straight away McCormick fired into a rage and before he knew it, he had thrust his spade up against Martin Gill's throat. The pair were locked in that position—glaring at one another—with McCormick towering over the diminutive Dubliner when Will appeared at the door. His grandfather drew back a little and lowered the spade. 'You'll leave this place now, you vermin,' McCormick growled, 'or I shall create such a hell for you, you will wish you'd ne'er left Dublin.'

Will's disgust for his father was now mingled with guilt about his family's situation and it made him particularly agitated. He stepped forward with a wild look in his eye. 'I am ashamed to know you sir,' the young man spat on the ground at his father's bare feet, 'ashamed to call you my father.' Martin Gill gave his son a contemptuous look and tried to push past him. But Will blocked his path, and when Gill made no effort to move, the young man put both hands on his father's shoulders and shoved him hard to his knees. For the longest moment the three men were locked in this position with Martin Gill muttering curses at both men as they stood over him, arms crossed, refusing to let him leave. Eventually, however, McCormick and then Will stepped back so that his father could struggle to his feet. Martin Gill was a filthy mess but no sooner had he put his hand on the handle of the shed door than he turned back to his son and sneered, 'Well my boy,' he said, 'now you have decided where you stand—why don't you tell your grandfather who is paying for you and your sister to get to California?' And with that the one-time hotelier slammed the door and disappeared.

It was an awkward afternoon out at the Punchbowl farm and grandfather and grandson worked in silence. When it was time to head back to town the two men rode together in the cart without exchanging a word between them. When, however, they were on the outskirts of town McCormick asked his grandson to explain himself. The fifteen year old did so in an anxious rush, describing how he had wanted to put everything together for Mary Ann and his mother, adding several times that he had nothing to do with the 'vile notice' in the newspaper. His grandfather listened, keeping his eyes on the path as he gave the matter his consideration.

The following morning as Mary Ann was toasting bread at the kitchen fire and Mary Riley was ordering Thomas and his younger sister into their day clothes, McCormick made a series of raps on the table to motion the family to hush. 'Now look,' he started. Will felt the colour drain from his face dreading that his terrible allegiance with his father was about to be exposed. 'We know we have been worse off before and that we've a habit of coming out on top,' he acknowledged his daughter with a nod. 'I can't see the point of us all being cramped up in this hot little room for the rest of our lives.' The young children stopped their play. 'I want your eldest two out of here,' he said firmly to Margaret, 'you know—getting forward with things that might well make it better for us all in the long run,' he continued, 'and in the meanwhile I am sure we will make do together.'

Mary Ann glanced over at Will, who had been leaning forward on his chair with his head between his hands. She was not quite sure what was going on. She watched her brother lift his head and look up—first at his grandfather and then his mother before turning to look directly at her. 'Young Will has shown a certain flair for fixing things,' McCormick said, tossing his grandson a quick look, 'even if he has done so in a most unusual manner.' McCormick considered Mary Ann. 'But for all the trouble they have both given us, I still think we should let the two of them have their heads and see if they can't make their own way for a while.' Then he added gruffly, 'Heaven knows, Margaret, it might be the only way we'll get some peace.'

Margaret furrowed her brow and sniffed uncertainly as the old tailor continued. 'I want to see them off to California—with all our blessings—that way they will be back soon enough with great big nuggets of gold for all of us.' Mary Riley watched Margaret play with the rim of her tea cup as she considered her father's words. Will and Mary Ann looked at one another, not sure if they should believe what they had heard. 'As for your wretched husband,' McCormick finished, 'I am of the opinion that there will be no more trouble from him, so I think it is high time we all start making our way in the world once more.'

Thomas McCormick had spoken just in time: it was a desperate rush to get the two eldest children prepared. Margaret and Mary Riley fussed about collecting shoe brushes and linen bags, packing these and a set of carefully wrapped silver servers from the old hotel into a trunk. After several frantic hours, Mary Ann and Will were packed. In haste, the entire family bustled into a coach and headed to Circular Quay. No one wanted to be left out. Mary Riley and Margaret both took a child on their laps, Mary Ann held Isabella on hers while Thomas insisted on taking his own place on the bench next to William.

They should have boarded a day earlier, they were told by the churlish master who stood at the bottom of the gangway, checking his shipping list. They were in time, though only just. Next minute one of the crew, a large South Sea Islander, took their trunk and carried it up the gangway. And then there they all were—Mary Ann and William Gill standing before the American brig, with their four younger siblings, their grandparents and their mother. The family stood about awkwardly until Mary Riley came forward and put a small tin of something for seasickness in William's pocket. Then Mary Ann reached out and folded her mother's hand inside her own and two of the younger children grabbed at Mary Ann's skirts. 'No more fuss,' McCormick growled as he brought his two grandchildren into a rough embrace. 'We will be seeing you both for Christmas in a few years,' he said rubbing his large hands together. 'Just mind yourself,' he patted them both, 'and make sure you bring back plenty of gold.' One of the crew called out it was time to go. The young woman and her brother exchanged a quick look and then made their way towards the boat, only once daring to glance back to where their family was standing on the dock.

⌇

First light. Friday 7 December 1849. Mary Ann and Will were both on deck to witness the *Sabine* catch the early tide and push out onto the harbour, then beyond the Heads where both would be travelling further than they had before. The morning had a sharp breeze to it, but otherwise all was still and dark. As the town slowly emerged from the night shadows, Mary Ann began to pick out some movement along the quay—men already about their work, some lugging lengths of wood, others rolling barrels from ship to warehouse.

This was the town she had lived in all her life. She knew the stench of the Tank Stream in high summer and the way her clothes turned wet with sweat when she ran errands during the day. She knew the taste of the air—something like fetid fruit mixed with grit and the stench of the nearby factories. Soap, candles and tanneries. The heavy sweetness of the hotel kitchen and how it had clung to her clothes for as long as she could remember. Sounds too. Not only the distant hiss of the factories but also the male voices in the front bar—rising and falling as tempers flared and jokes were told. All the shop owners and people about town. The click and whirr of carriage wheels. And of course, the horses—the clink of their bridles and that warm grassy smell.

From here, however, everything looked different. Mary Ann watched the morning lift over the factories and warehouses and then the weatherboards and brick buildings further up town. It all seemed curiously small from the deck of the *Sabine* and it made Mary Ann feel queasy. She cast about for a few familiar things. The windmills she had watched from her window and the line of gumtrees which curved around the harbour. Coaches, like old Somerville's, already lined along the street, waiting for passengers, she thought. And, of course, Pitt Street, rising in a slope away from the quay before it disappeared into town. Next moment, Mary Ann heard the heavy clunk and clatter of the second anchor being hauled up. The crew began calling to one another, and then the boat began to slip away.

As the vessel pushed further out of the harbour, William craned his neck over the other passengers milling about the deck. He wanted to be the first to see the Heads, to point them out to his sister. But then he stopped in shock. It could have been a play of the light, he thought, so he shut his eyes and opened them again. But there was no doubt to it—standing just apart from the rest of the passengers, hands shoved in his trouser pockets and chin set at a determined angle. His father. He looked quite dapper, Will noted, and certainly better groomed than the bedraggled creature he had encountered in his grandfather's shed a few weeks ago. 'So he found a way to slip through the officials after all,' Will thought, with just a little admiration. But then he remembered his sister and looked about anxiously, keen to warn her about their fellow passenger.

But, at the moment Mary Ann was nowhere close at hand. As the brig pushed into the Harbour she had begun walking towards the stern, eager to catch a last look at her hometown. She had been walking in that direction when a flickering shimmer of reflected sunlight had caught her eye. It was coming from the rise of Pitt Street, she was sure. So she moved quickly along the boat, all the while scanning the hill and chasing the light, straining for a final glimpse of the sudden blaze that she was certain she had seen coming from a certain window on the third floor of their old hotel.

CHAPTER TWENTY-THREE

The High Seas

That first class, fast-sailing American brig, the *Sabine*, was about half the size of the *Lady Howden*, but this allowed it to travel quickly through the unpredictable waters of the Tasman and arrive at the North Cape of New Zealand less than ten days after Mary Ann and William Gill left Sydney in the company of their ubiquitous father. The *Sabine* sailed into the vast whaling cove at the most northern tip of New Zealand and anchored next to a Hobart vessel named the *Eliza*, which had arrived only a few days earlier. The crew on board Mary Ann's vessel had made a previous journey to 'Gold Land' and were full of stories about the new 'Emporium'. *Bell's* had recently published a lively piece about the 'Latest from California per brig *Sabine*' detailing all sorts of tempting facts. And days before the brig's departure *Bell's* had also enjoyed recounting how two crewmembers had come to grief after flashing glimmers of gold around one of the rougher hotels in The Rocks.

As the *Sabine* lay anchored beneath those jagged New Zealand cliffs, Captain McLeod of the *Eliza* came on board with even more interesting news. He and his crew had been at Mangonui—just a day or two away—where they had discovered three men and two schoolgirls who had been abandoned by a party of pirates who gave them no more than a brace of muskets and a few bags of flour and sugar. Thanks to the assistance of several 'friendly Maori' the rescued party were now safely on board the *Eliza*, McLeod reassured his audience, but the 'piratically seized vessel' previously known as the *Helen* was still at large and said to be heading for California.

This news created considerable trepidation among the passengers and their crew, although it did not deter them from their journey—for a day or so later the *Sabine* weighed anchor and set a north-west course towards San Francisco Bay. Seventeen-year-old Mary Ann and her fifteen-year-old brother were now sailing across the Tasman and into the Pacific, watching the colours of the water change and feeling the winds lift and shift as the summer temperatures became increasingly tropical. It took the two a little time to grow accustomed to the slow pace of ship life as well as days at sea without sighting land. However, the proximity of forty-two other passengers on board was not so different from their childhood experience in their parents' various hotels. There were also familiar faces on board and all sorts of conversations to be had about gold and California, so Mary Ann and Will soon began to enjoy their first taste of freedom even if this was marred by the presence of Martin Gill, who preferred, for the time being, to keep his distance from his eldest children.

Thanks to poor winds the *Sabine*'s journey through the South Pacific was slow going and after several weeks of a listless sail the enterprising Captain Barmore decided to make port at Upolu in Samoa to replenish supplies. Brother and sister were on deck to notice how the steady slope of volcanic rock rose out of the crystalline waters of the ocean and then formed a series of cliffs and ridges that disappeared into low-lying cloud. They marvelled at the great cliffs of weathered olivine basalt and how they jutted out at wild angles before melting into dense green foliage. The shallows before them were scattered with azure lagoons and light blue reefs and the *Sabine* carefully navigated its way through these before anchoring at the mouth of the Vaisigano River. There the passengers were rowed to shore and Mary Ann and Will set foot upon land for the first time since leaving Sydney more than a month ago.

Together, the young colonists walked the broad sandy walkways of that village where the British Consul George Pritchard had recently established himself with his family. Both brother and sister were familiar with the Samoan sailors around Circular Quay, but had never seen a Samoan woman in her native-dress let alone the domed huts that sheltered the 300 or so inhabitants of that small village. The tropical sights and smells were intriguing to them both, but not so for Martin Gill who could still remember his convict ship stopping at some such place on his voyage to New South Wales in 1820.

Captain Barmore dedicated two days to resupplying the ship. Even then, he and his two partners were keen to press on with the voyage to California, as every extra day in port added to the cost of feeding their forty-five passengers. Having considered the weather the ship's pilot recommended that the crew and passengers 'spend another day or two with the kanakas at the bowling alley' waiting for the right breeze, but the Captain and his partners were determined to set their Baltimore clipper upon its course. And so, on 26 January 1850 a boat was sent out to tow the *Sabine* past the shallows, where a dead calm had stirred up a shore-based rip which was strong enough, the pilot suspected, to drag the boat leeward. He again advised against proceeding, but once more the Captain insisted it was time to leave. Indeed, he and his partners were now so determined, that after several hours of waiting unsuccessfully for the boat to take the winds, they requested another vessel tow the *Sabine* out to sea.

Even with this second tow, the brig continued to drift in the shallows and after half an hour of desperate work the vessel suddenly struck into a shelving ledge. Next moment the brig heeled broadside and huge waves began crashing overhead. Soon all the passengers were soaked to the skin and the *Sabine* began to take water. The brig rocked and groaned against the pounding surf as Captain Barmore stood astride the poop deck with a pistol in each hand, threatening to shoot anyone who dared to leave before the women and children. Mary Ann was then ushered into a lifeboat along with the other women and children and she bade farewell to William and her father before being lowered onto the sea and rowed through the treacherous surf.

Despite these perilous conditions, the *Sabine*'s passengers and crew were all safely returned to Upolu. A rescue party even managed to salvage several dray wheels and a pianoforte—as well as at least twenty cases of wine and six of beer, although all of these were badly damaged. The *Sabine* now lay in the tropical waters, hauled to one side and entirely wrecked. The forty-five passengers who had been determined to get to San Francisco as quickly as they could were now stranded on this isolated island in the Pacific Ocean.

For several days Mary Ann and Will wandered about the small village until, on their third day, a strange-looking ship with 'The Pilot' painted—somewhat amateurishly—upon its side, sailed into Upolu with an American captain at his helm. Those on board the *Sabine* had already informed the British Consul about the extraordinary news they had heard at North Cape concerning a ship known as the *Helen* which had been captured by a group of pirates led by a restless young man named John Wilson, who came from Massachusetts and had a curious habit of tilting his head—just a little—to one side.

It was the son of the British Consul who came up with the cunning plan about the whaleboat race. A group of men from the island were told to hide their weapons 'under each man's thwart' before partaking in what appeared to be a friendly boating competition across the bright blue waters of the harbour. The *Pilot* would be their starting point and they would ask the young American captain to arbitrate upon proceedings. Will and Mary Ann gathered on the beach with the other passengers to watch the race.

Off both boats set—only to make not one, nor two, but ultimately three deliberately bungled false starts—each requiring them to return to the *Pilot* and allowing them to take careful note of how many men were on board the seized vessel and how well armed they might be. On their third start the two boats set off, to much cheering from the shore. On their return journey, they were rowing neck-to-neck and appeared to be locked in a dead heat as they approached the *Pilot*. No sooner had both crossed the finishing line and Captain Wilson declared one the victor, than the Consul's son and his men stormed onto the pirate ship, arresting all on board and reclaiming the stolen vessel.

So far so good, but now George Pritchard was faced with the dubious reality that he had no prison on the island in which to incarcerate the *Pilot*'s pirate crew. The Consul had little choice but to put Wilson and his men on parole and release them onto the island while he waited for a colonial warship with a prison below deck. And so, for the following week, Mary Ann and Will supped with the local Samoans, a crew of pirates and the British Consul—although during this time half of the *Pilot*'s crew, including the young blue-eyed Captain, managed to escape.

The restoration of the pirated vessel provided the crew of the *Sabine* with a ship to recommence their journey. But when they finally did set sail out of Upolu, Mary Ann found herself bound, not for California but Sydney. Captain Barmore and partners were legally obliged to inform authorities of the *Helen*'s seizure to ensure immediate action was taken to find the escapees and bring them to justice. After all the frustrations she had already encountered regarding her romantic aspirations, Mary Ann was once more forced to suffer another exasperating delay. She had been away from Sydney almost two months, every day edging closer to James Butler as well as the beginning of her new life, and now—yet again—she had been thwarted, and this time by pirates.

⁓

Since Margaret Gill had farewelled her eldest children she had been having a terrible time of it. On the first day of 1850, Saul and Lewis Samuel commenced action against Martin Gill, determined to sequester whatever goods he or his wife might have in payment for the £75 that was still outstanding on the Pitt Street hotel rental. Mr Samuel had also been successful in encouraging other men about town to pursue costs and once it was clearly established that Martin Gill had managed to 'defeat and delay' his creditors by absconding the colony, Margaret Gill was summonsed to court to answer for her husband.

Such were the times that while Martin Gill was free to publicly refuse to honour his wife's debts, Margaret had little choice but to stand in court and answer for her husband's.

As January and then February wore on, Margaret Gill faced the insolvency court, and repeatedly insisted that she and her father had only ever been intent upon retrieving certain personal possessions—a bedstead and a feather mattress as well as a washstand and a small looking glass—that her husband had taken up to Moore's auction rooms without her permission. The whole business was murky however, for Alexander Moore was claiming that Martin Gill had authorised the return of certain goods to his wife, but only because he wanted 'peace and quietness'. Week after week, auctioneers and dray men were called to give evidence and together they told a winding tale about goods that had been taken from the Pitt Street hotel to the auction room and money that seemed to change hands between Martin, Margaret and even, at one stage, Mary Ann.

There was also the question of the Saracen's Head which Margaret's father had taken possession of a few weeks after these hearings began. Rather than do so surreptitiously, however, Thomas McCormick proudly announced to readers of *The Herald* in mid-January 1850 that 'with the assistance of his daughter, the recent hostess of Gill's Family Hotel', the new proprietor was delighted 'to ensure a portion of the public favour' and that he would do so by providing the same 'genuine comforts' of that previous establishment. There would be 'nothing wanting', his advertisement promised, 'to contribute to their comforts', and sea captains could also enjoy 'a glass of "first-rate" English ale' with their luncheon.

As tropical waves crashed over the heads of those on board the *Sabine*, and Mary Ann was supping with Captain Wilson and his band of rogues, Margaret Gill continued to front Sydney's insolvency court protesting that nothing but 'papers and a lot of old clothes' had gone to Moore's auction rooms with her consent. As her two eldest children sailed back to Sydney, the Samuel brothers' legal counsel persisted with a line of questioning that eventually provoked their mother to protest that she had never claimed to anyone that she had 'removed all the things from their hotel to prevent the creditors getting any of it'. Nor had she bragged that she would avoid prosecution by having her father take a new hotel for her in his name. And yet, while Margaret Gill made such vehement remonstrations, she was not, the affidavit confirms, prepared to swear to any of them. By the first week of March 1850, several claimants had become suspicious that Margaret Gill was in cahoots with her husband. There was a growing feeling that she might, in fact, be playing them all. But throughout the interrogations Margaret remained staunch. There had been a 'rupture' with her husband, she insisted. He had departed the colony and left her 'with no more than seven farthings'. The entire matter was increasingly farcical and seemed to have confuddled even the judge who eventually decided to let the matter drop, even after allegations were made that there were still a number of items from the Pitt Street hotel stored at the Kent Street cottage.

Meanwhile, Thomas McCormick continued to 'respectfully' inform 'friends and the public' that he had taken 'splendid rooms' on the corner of King and Sussex and that he and his daughter were well-equipped 'to accommodate families of the highest respectability' at the Saracen's Head. And so they should have been for the advertisement from the year before, when the owners were seeking a new tenant for the property, listed extensive 'household furniture, bar fittings, license and other effects' from this establishment. These included elaborate furnishings for six guest bedrooms, each containing a four-poster bedstead, while the 'Bar and Dining Parlour, Drawing room and little Parlour' were all variously furnished with eight-hour clocks, mahogany sideboards and silver decanters, as well as horsehair sofas and seats, bell ropes and window blinds. With eleven guestrooms, the Gills' Pitt Street hotel may have been slightly larger than this new establishment, but just as McCormick had insisted, the Saracen's Head was every bit as grand.

About this time—on 20 February 1850 to be precise—the *Lady Howden* sailed into San Francisco Bay with James Butler Kinchela peering through the notorious fog of that harbour so he could catch his first glimpse of 'Gold Mountain' or *Gum San* as it was known to the thousands of Chinese also flocking to California at this time. Already the town was surprisingly well established with lines of two- and three-storey buildings advancing in an orderly fashion from the busy harbour up towards the central plaza, where there was a bank and a post office as well as several hotels and a number of stores.

Kinchela disembarked at Clarkes Point, the oldest part of San Francisco and the only place where ships could discharge directly onto land. It may have been eerily familiar to him, for a large number of Australian colonists were working on the wharf as sailors and boatmen and had also taken residence in the nearby boarding houses, ensuring that the area greatly resembled The Rocks around Circular Quay. Such was the infiltration of colonists around Clarkes Point that the area was already known as Sydney Town (sometimes Sydney Valley). It was reputed to be a great 'rendezvous of scamps', renowned for 'constant scenes of lewdness, drunkenness and strife' among the 'most daring, depraved and reckless men'. Some of this may have been hyperbole created by American businessmen keen to resist an 'invasion' from the worst 'sweepings of British jails', but there were already sufficient accounts of vice and violence in this part of San Francisco to suggest that Sydney Town was populated by colonial 'men and women' energetically devoted to 'drinking, swearing, fighting and thieving'.

In 1848 there had been little over a thousand people in San Francisco—some Mexicans who had stayed after the end of the Mexican–American war, the *Californios* (Spanish-speaking Californians), a group of Irish immigrants who had fled the 1848 famine as well as a number of American military men, a smattering of American and European entrepreneurial sorts and a handful of Chinese men. There were also some African-American slaves who had been brought to the territory before it was declared a free state in the Compromise of 1850.

Before the arrival of Europeans there had been as many as 700,000 Native Americans living throughout the region. By 1850, however, their numbers were already rapidly diminishing not only from European diseases and the way gold mining ravaged their natural water and food supplies, but also the frontier conflict that followed on the heels of European settlement. Some Native Americans, such as the Maidu, worked with settlers like the German-born Swiss timber mill owner, John Sutter, who had built a fort in 1839 at the junction of the American and Sacramento rivers. A huge population of Native Americans also lived in the Great Basin east of Sierra Nevada and west of the Rocky Mountains, where they defended themselves from vigilante attacks and also engaged in their own acts of retaliation. The Native Americans had little cultural interest in gold but quickly recognised its trade value and became adept at finding the coveted mineral. Such proficiency attracted its own problems, however, for within a year or so of the gold rush, the first governor of this state declared the territory a 'battleground between the races' and offered rewards to any Europeans who 'exterminated or removed' those whose traditional life had been so disastrously disrupted by the invading gold seekers.

And it was correct to describe it as an invasion, for once James Polk the American President verified that gold had been discovered in early December 1848, thousands of gold seekers hauled their covered wagons along the Siskiyou Trail and over the Appalachian Mountains or took the treacherous sea route from the Atlantic to the Pacific. Thousands more sailed into the foggy port from Hawaii, China, England, Europe and, of course, the Australian colonies. Thanks to this great explosion there were more than 25,000 people living in San Francisco by 1850 and thousands more out on the goldfields of Sierra Nevada and up north. And so, by the time Kinchela was making his way from Clarkes Point into town, it was no longer possible to pick up nuggets on the street. The first stage of the rush was over and a new era of mining was about to begin.

In addition to this, the majority of this new immigrant population was male and desperate for gold. Within a year or so San Francisco had utterly transformed from an isolated town to a rapidly expanding, multicultural port city that was yet to develop the significant social structures and legal systems required for civil society. Such conditions meant that at best, the mood about town was improvised and exciting, at worst, extremely lawless and dangerous and whenever allegations of theft, violence and arson were made, the finger was pointed at the rough colonists living up around the lighthouse on Sydney Town.

Many of these men were bounty migrants who, like Henry Parkes, had received a free passage as a way of addressing the labour shortage that blighted New South Wales in the late 1830s and early 1840s. Before these working class men left England they were issued a 'duck shirt' of rough blue material and many were still wearing this when they stepped ashore at San Francisco. This harsh duck fabric earned them the appellation of Sydney Ducks but they soon became notorious for other reasons. Among this cohort were a number of men who shared a penchant for pyromania and easy plundering and by the time Kinchela arrived in early 1850, the Sydney Ducks had already set a number of fires raging through the streets and settlement camps of San Francisco.

During the Christmas festivities of 1849, for example, a great conflagration had burnt down a fine two-storey 'palace' on the west side of the town plaza before engulfing the town in a 'tornado of flame and smoke'. It had been the real Tom Sawyer, on whom Mark Twain would loosely base his fictional boy adventurer, who pushed forward with other brave crusaders to fight this blaze. Sawyer and his friends had rallied before the swirling chaos of sparks and burning embers, but by the time they were done the fire had devoured most of the timber buildings and the town had been reduced to piles of smouldering rubble.

Town entrepreneurs were always quick to rebuild their establishments so they could recommence trade with those coming in from the goldfields, but nonetheless, San Francisco was in a constant state of mayhem and by the early 1850s there were reputed to be as many as sixty deaths a week, of which a good many were buried in pauper graves having taken their own lives rather than die of starvation and shame. Already, the promise of a fast fortune had become a cruel joke and an atmosphere of sullen despair was said to permeate the town, so much so that one colonist condemned it as a 'city of sordid selfishness, heartless profligacy, violence, disease and despair' before wiping the dust off his boots and returning to Sydney.

As Kinchela walked the streets he sensed this volatile mood, and also noticed the hostile attitude reserved for those from the Australian colonies. Indeed, at the very time he arrived, the atmosphere was particularly tense, for the blame for the most recent blaze was being attributed to the Sydney Ducks and the town was now baying for colonial blood.

By extraordinary good fortune the *Helen*, still bearing 'The Pilot' on its side, returned to Sydney just five days after the legal dispute relating to Martin Gill's debts had been resolved. Samuel and Co. were not going to recover their money, but they could secure a new tenant for the Pitt Street hotel. Gill had managed to avoid the ignominy and inconvenience of these recent proceedings and was now returning to find his family in much better financial conditions than he left them.

The end of the bankruptcy proceedings must have boosted Margaret Gill's confidence for the advertisements that featured in the press after the bankruptcy proceedings assume a new bravado. In late April, for example, 'Mrs Gill, pastrycook and confectioner' was apprising 'her friends and the public' that she was 'prepared to undertake any orders to supply refreshments on the most elaborate scale', for 'public dinners, balls and routs' and that with 'sixteen years in the trade', she was willing to 'flatter herself' that she was more than capable of giving 'every satisfaction'. Again in mid-May, 'Mrs Gill' informed readers that she was conducting the above establishment for her father and that 'families from the country' would find the Saracen's Head 'equal to her old establishment. Dinners and Balls' could be 'got up in her usual style' she pledged, before adding in a slightly reprimanding tone, 'but not in twenty-four hours for a thousand people'.

A week later an even more curious advertisement appeared from 'Mrs Gill and family' who wished to express their gratitude for the 'deep sense of the kindness and support' they had received from all who relied upon her 'efforts to supply them with the best accommodation in the city'. This advertisement went on to describe Mrs Gill's 'well-established reputation', which originated from her 'time in Dublin with . . . the pastry cook to the Lord-Lieutenant of Ireland'. This, the advertisement continued, had been further refined during the five years she had attended upon 'the nobility of Sydney', including no lesser personage than 'Sir Richard Bourke and family'. There was also an unusual N.B. at the end of this advertisement. While Mrs Gill would supply routs, balls and public assemblies in her 'usual style', the advertisement concluded, 'Mr Gill' was also available to 'attend at the private dwellings of gentry in and near Sydney'.

So, things had clearly changed. Mrs Gill was now cutting her own dash and boldly asserting her expertise as the head of this business while her husband was relegated to an inferior position and her father not even mentioned. Far from earning the disapproval of the Victorian public for her status as an independent businesswoman, Margaret Gill appeared to be attracting greater favour. In June the Saracen's Head was chosen by the Attorney General to provide the refreshments for 'The Railway Ball and Supper' and to dress a 'real Green Land Turtle . . . the largest that has ever been in Sydney at six hundred weight' for that occasion. At this time the hotel was also immortalised in a satirical poem in *Bell's* which celebrated the opportunity to 'head off to the Saracen's Head for our gin, and our pipes and our porter'. But then, in mid-August of the same year, Margaret Gill's ascent came to an abrupt halt. Or perhaps it simply shifted gears. For, quite suddenly, *The Herald* announced that the Saracen's Head—with 'beer engine and spirit fountain, kegs and gas fittings' was 'To Let' and the only explanation given in regards to this change was that the present proprietor was 'going to another business'. Was this another insolvency for the Gills or had Margaret decided to dedicate her culinary talents to elite private parties rather than the unreliable rabble of the city hotel trade?

When precisely Mary Ann Gill left Sydney for San Francisco again remains unknown. It is certain however that Martin Gill was in Nevada by July 1852, where he was listed as a baker. Did father and daughter travel together on this second voyage with Will once more in their company? It seems likely that Mary Ann left Sydney in early February 1851. Before then she may have been on hand to assist her mother with what must have been one of Margaret Gill's proudest professional accomplishments, perhaps even the beginning of a new, independent business venture. The day was 'the celebration of the anniversary . . . to commemorate the foundation of New South Wales'. Of all the various amusements' available on 26 January each year, it was 'the Regatta upon Sydney Harbour' that 'deservedly' took 'precedence', or so Henry Parkes, now the editor of *The Empire*, proclaimed in an article he devoted to the occasion. However, the weather on this particular Foundation Day was 'extremely inauspicious', Parkes observed. There were strong southerly winds as well as a cloudy sky from which heavy showers frequently descended upon the hundreds of 'holiday folks' who 'tramped' to Fort Macquarie in their 'gay attire'. Rather than surrender to the 'sunless sullenness', however, Sydney-siders dangled from 'housetops and windowsills' delighting in 'the bellows that blasted about them' and watching the crowd 'pour' into Circular Quay and its surrounds.

The harbour was 'literally studded' with vessels of all shapes and sizes, Parkes noted. There were giant, 1000-ton burthens as well as small skiffs and sloops and even the *Thistle* steamer upon which James Butler Kinchela had sailed back and forth between Sydney and Moreton Bay on numerous occasions. Some were carrying lively freights of party-goers while other vessels had a jovial band performing gay tunes upon their polished decks. For all of this, Parkes could not help but remind his readers that they should be extremely proud that there were no longer any vessels 'tainted with the stigma of having brought convicts to our shores'. More than a year had passed since Parkes had made his defiant stand against the *Hashemy*, but the success of that campaign was clearly still on his mind, particularly on that day of self-conscious colonial celebration.

Sprawled upon the outer lawns of Fort Macquarie were summer booths supplying refreshments for the huge crowds. From these there issued the noisy 'clamour' of fruit vendors and those selling 'hot saveloys'. At noon, the governor, 'Sir Charles', arrived on foot and without any of the formal regalia customarily expected of the governor upon the anniversary of the colony's foundation. The crowd cheered as he took to his Flag Ship and pulled up beside an amateur club of 'Jolly Young Watermen' who afforded him more than a little 'aquatic' amusement. Finally at one o'clock, the Governor of New South Wales signalled for a salute of seventeen guns to herald the formal celebrations of the day. A few moments later, those who had been 'privileged with a special entrée into the interior of Fort Macquarie' were ushered into that imposing stone edifice where they received, *The Empire* was pleased to note, a most 'excellent luncheon' that had been prepared for them by none other than Mrs Margaret Gill.

CHAPTER TWENTY-FOUR

Natural Justice

Mary Ann probably left Sydney with her father and brother in February 1851 and arrived in San Francisco in early June of the same year. By then there had been a dramatic decline in the number of ships heading to America as numerous colonists had returned to Australia with tales of horrendous hardship as well as the vilification they had experienced in San Francisco. Between the time James Butler Kinchela arrived in February 1850 and the Gills set foot upon Clarkes Point in June the following year, there had been several more great conflagrations in San Francisco. The local Night Watch was now also particularly vigilant for they had been warned that the town was about to be attacked by '500 Sydney men' who were coming to San Francisco for the sole purpose of burning and plundering the town. The public were thirsty for vengeance and there was a sense that something had to be done. In early 1851 as the Gills were probably boarding their second vessel for California, a group of men came together of their own accord to answer these complaints and form what became known as the Committee of Vigilance. This Committee comprised San Francisco's most prominent businessmen, merchants, bankers and mechanics and within a few months over a thousand men had signed up, intent upon bringing a group of villainous colonists to justice and then running the rest of the reviled Sydney Ducks out of the town.

It seems fair to say that the Gills found themselves in the wrong place at the worst possible time. At the very moment that Mary Ann and her emancipist father were making their way through the streets of San Francisco, the spirit of 'Judge Lynch' was not only presiding over the town but also specifically intent upon spilling colonial blood. William Gill would have had more luck finding gold a few hundred miles from home as Edward Hargraves had recently returned from California and having observed that certain portions of rural New South Wales resembled the American goldfields he went looking for and soon found gold. No sooner had Hargraves begun boasting of nuggets than hundreds of men and women abandoned Sydney for the new Australian goldfields. Unfortunately, however, William Gill had sailed to San Francisco at the very time that the mining of gold was becoming more demanding and less rewarding in America and when his accent identified him as public enemy number one. Martin Gill may also have borne a few of the well-known signs that marked him as an emancipist. For all his dash and pluck, he may have had a certain shuffle to his gait that would have aroused suspicion during that feverish period in San Francisco in 1851.

Even if the Gills somehow managed to avoid overt discrimination themselves, they were still likely to have had some sort of encounter with the vicious expression of American justice that took place between June and August of that year when the Committee of Vigilance undertook four public lynchings, all of which involved the brutal execution of Australian colonists. The first of these occurred in June to a Sydney man who had stolen a safe in broad daylight. His public hanging was attended by a crowd of approximately 2000 people even though it occurred at two o'clock in the morning. The second involved James Stuart, another Sydney immigrant, who confessed to assault, robbery and murder when he was rounded up by a group of 500 armed Committee members. In early July he was hanged from the mast of a ship docked at Clarkes Point.

During the last of these 1851 vigilante executions the Committee broke into the city's police gaol, where two 'Sydneyites' were being held before their trial for a spate of crimes that included robbery and arson. The two men—Sam Whittaker and Robert Menzies—were dragged from their cells, quickly tried and then hanged at the threshold of the building where the Committee held its meetings. There the colonists' corpses attracted 'a great, dense, agitated crowd' of over ten thousand men, while a further five thousand local inhabitants filed past the two dead bodies over the following days.

Would Mary Ann and her family have seen the ghoulish corpses of these Sydney migrants bloating in the San Francisco sun? As more than half of the town's population either witnessed the execution or viewed the dead bodies it would have been impossible for the Gills to remain untouched by this horrific incident. What might Kinchela have thought of such an event? His elder brother had shown a taste for taking the law into his own hands—was this something he also deemed necessary in this unpredictable frontier environment? Surely Kinchela did something to earn the title 'Judge' he apparently acquired in California, although exactly what this was and when, remains unknown.

～

We do however know that Mary Ann Gill and James Butler Kinchela were married on Saturday, 16 October 1852 and that this took place 'by special licence' before the Reverend Father Scanlan, who solemnised their union at St Mary's church in San Francisco. On that fine autumn day, the weather was one of the 'pleasantest days' of the season. It was a 'bright, clear day', the *Daily Alta* claimed, 'without a particle of wind or dust and just warm enough to be comfortable'. The atmosphere was so surprisingly clear that the hills of the Contra Costa seemed within a 'stone's throw of the city' and 'the trees in the ravines and the buildings in the valley' could be seen 'with the naked eye'. Already there was much general excitement about the forthcoming federal election and the shop windows and theatre doors were posted with cartoons of the various candidates standing for the election of the fourteenth president of the United States. Out on the harbour the number of steamers anchored about the bay had quadrupled and the hotels were brimming with more bodies than they had beds.

Early in the morning, the town fire alarm had rung out and six or so water wagons rushed through town determined to tame a blaze that had started in one of the residential areas. Within hours the fire was settled and calm restored, but for a party of Chinese men, who caused a stir by hiring a carriage and riding up and down the main street. So much for California's busy gold town. It was, the news-sheet claimed, a rather uneventful day.

Perhaps on that morning Mary Ann walked to the church in the company of her father and brother, negotiating her way along the wide streets as carts and pedestrians went about their business and one or two men stumbled out of one of the more notorious gambling dens. Or perhaps it was decided that the bridal party should maintain a semblance of respectability by taking a carriage to the church? Did William accompany James Butler—just in case he had another episode of cold feet? If so, Mary Ann would have made her way through the city streets with only her father as her chaperone.

If she was unable to have a dress made for the occasion, Mary Ann would have found some way to furnish her costume with a little lace or a shawl or perhaps even some fabric flowers that would have helped to create a sense of occasion. In keeping with the fashion, whatever dress she wore would have had a tight waist and full skirts, perhaps even a generous bustle. If, however, she had organised to have something tailored for the occasion it is most likely that it would have been bone and ivory with floral embroidering about the bottom of the skirt. With arms and décolletage covered and buttons to her throat, Mary Ann would have been a modest bride. Kinchela would have probably carried his best top hat, such a universal fashion item at the time, and also worn one of his better waistcoats and jackets. Perhaps he also carried his father's cane with him.

What would Martin Gill have thought as he stood before the altar preparing to give his twenty-year-old Roman Catholic daughter to the forty-year-old Protestant gentleman who he had once tried to murder before successfully convicting and incarcerating him for the abduction of his daughter? More than four years had passed since Mary Ann had first defied her father by slipping out of the third-storey window of their Pitt Street hotel. Since then there had been so many interludes and intrigues that perhaps Martin Gill was finally relieved to see the matter done.

And James Butler Kinchela? Mary Ann's arrival in San Francisco had been delayed by as much as a year, perhaps even two. When she did not arrive on the *Sabine* in early 1850 he must have wondered if a shipwreck had taken his future wife, or if perhaps she had changed *her* mind. More than two years had passed since he had left Sydney and during that time we might assume that he had not only learnt the lie of the land but also found a way to secure a foothold in this new society. James Butler was to do well in California and perhaps as he stood before the altar at St Mary's he felt a new sense of confidence about himself and his future.

Those few moments at the altar must have been profoundly satisfying for Mary Ann, who had persisted with her affections for James Butler in the face of the most devastating discouragement. She had suffered social humiliation and ostracism as well as the wrath of her parents and the highly erratic conduct of her father. Her suitor had been imprisoned, her family bankrupted and she had set sail to San Francisco only to be forced to return to Sydney on a pirate ship after her own vessel had been wrecked. Despite all these delays, she had set sail again, no doubt with the promise of her future husband and her new life firmly in her thoughts—only to find herself in a city that was every bit as capricious as her hometown and perhaps even more so.

Her journey to the aisle had taken more than four years, and during this time all had seemed lost so many times. But here she was—no longer a furtive fifteen-year-old runaway romancer intent upon defying her father, but rather a twenty-year-old woman standing in the church of her faith, about to marry her gentleman settler with her parents' blessing.

CHAPTER TWENTY-FIVE

What Mary Ann Did Next

Mary Ann and James Butler Kinchela were married for twelve years and lived most of this time on Kinchela's ranch, which was, an advertisement in the *Sacramento Daily Union* stated, located a mile east of Sutter's Fort, 'out on the old Johnson Road'. Mary Ann had what she'd always wanted, even if she had to move to another hemisphere to get it. She was now the wife of a gentleman settler and had already seen more of life than many of her female contemporaries in New South Wales. She also enjoyed a degree of wealth, freedom and respectability. We might imagine this period of her life—between the ages of twenty and thirty-two—as halcyon, a time when she was rewarded for the persistence she had shown in the face of so many romantic frustrations.

Mary Ann's and James Butler's ranch would have been near the Sacramento River and close enough to town to enjoy a certain amount of society. They would have survived the devastating floods in the early 1860s, and seen many of their neighbours perish from the cholera epidemics that followed. The Kinchelas would have also witnessed the expansion and consolidation of Sacramento as the town grew to accommodate a population of over 10,000, including thousands of Chinese immigrants who survived various attempts to run them out of town.

James Butler Kinchela would have brought his experience of colonial frontiers in Australia to his life as a pastoralist in America, engaging not only in daring acts of enterprise but probably other sorts of 'encounters' with the Maidu and Nisenan people of the Sacramento region. In a state where the governor had proclaimed the need to 'exterminate and remove' Native Americans as early as 1850, a man like Kinchela was likely to have played a role in the tragic genocide that took place during this period. Indeed, James Butler was probably the sort of man who perceived such activities as not only necessary for the protection of his family but also part of his civic duty.

The Kinchelas would have used the steamships and then the First Transcontinental Railroad to transport their goods to and from San Francisco. When the new Transcontinental Telegraph was introduced in 1861, Mary, as he preferred to call her, and James would have found themselves much more connected to the rest of the world which would have allowed them to follow the news regarding various antagonisms between the northern and southern states of America and then the declaration of the Civil War in 1861.

Mary Ann probably gave birth to both of her children in their homestead—James John, who was born in 1857 and Edith Ann who was born a year later in 1858. The land around their homestead must have been much like the rest in this region—bountiful with canopies of oaks and cottonwoods as well as grapevines, and an air that had been described as smelling 'like champagne'. Although, probably not in the areas of Sacramento that had been devastated by gold-mining. Mary Ann and James Butler may have had access to the ten-acre orchard belonging to John Sutter, the German-Swiss miller who built his fort here in 1839. They may even have taken cuttings from these orchards to start their own grove of citrus and stone-fruit trees. James and Mary Ann made their money in cattle, and it is likely that Kinchela continued to drive his herds to local auction yards throughout the 1850s and early 1860s and that as he did so this Irish gentleman and sometime Australian overlander resembled an American cowboy.

Did other family members, such as Mary Ann's mother, ever visit the Kinchelas during this twelve-year period? Did Martin Gill ever impose upon their hospitality or did he prefer to take his chances baking for the miners of the Sierra Nevada? Or was the wife of Judge Kinchela content with the company of the other ranch owners and whatever town society was available in Sacramento? Perhaps Mary Ann added a Californian drawl to the flat, nasal tones of her native-born accent. What did she think of the abolition debates that raged throughout America during those years? Harriet Beecher Stowe's influential novel *Uncle Tom's Cabin* sold over 300,000 copies in the year that she and Kinchela married. It soon became the most popular novel of that era in England as well as America. Surely she and Kinchela had a copy in their home, although we are unlikely to know their attitudes to it and the important question of slavery.

Mary Ann would no doubt have enjoyed watching her only son grow from infancy to early childhood as she marvelled at the way he resembled each of them in different ways, although the records suggest that he had blue rather than brown or hazel eyes. When in February 1860 Edith Ann died at the age of seventeen months, Mary Ann may have buried her only daughter beneath one of the great American oaks on their ranch, watching as her baby daughter's coffin was lowered into the winter ground. Then, a few years later, Mary Ann would have tended to her husband as he too became ill—with cancer of the mouth. We do not know how long Kinchela's illness lasted, although the records confirm that he was in his fifties when he finally died of this disease in the spring of 1864.

And what of Kinchela's death? What would it have meant for 32-year-old Mary Ann, who had already been separated from her own family for over a decade and had also quite recently lost her daughter?

Mary Ann's obituary claims that after Kinchela's death she returned to 'her parents' in Sydney and, shortly after that, embarked upon a voyage to the French penal colony of New Caledonia, where colonial speculators had begun investing in cattle and cane in the mid-1860s. By then the papers regularly contained vivid descriptions of the various crops that could be grown by colonists keen to 'turn a pretty penny' in cane and cattle. Whether Mary Ann travelled there with a family member or by herself is unclear, although it seems unlikely that she would have been joined by her sometime companion, William Gill, for he had returned from America sometime before 1856. He married that year in a part of the Bathurst district, where eventually gold was found.

By this time Thomas McCormick and his second wife Mary Riley were both dead and Margaret and Martin were once more living together in Sydney. There are no records with which to trace this final stage of their working life together, but we might imagine the Gills running a private catering business and hoping to enjoy some of the comforts of their eldest daughter's fortune. Alas, this was not to be, for not long after returning to Sydney, Mary Kinchela sailed to New Caledonia, probably in a clipper like the *Friend* or the unfortunately named schooner *Black Dog*, which regularly made this short but treacherous voyage throughout the late 1860s.

At this time New Caledonia was generally no more than two days sail from Moreton Bay and the French convicts who had been imprisoned there since 1863 had become a great source of moral alarm for Australian colonists, who appear to have been equally horrified by the close proximity of French citizens as they were of convicts. The public were somewhat reassured, however, that the voyage was known to be a treacherous sail and that the island was 'girdled with coral reefs' which ran along the 400 miles of coast, forming an outer barrier, against which the ocean 'broke in thunder', and through which only a carefully timed vessel might find a gap into the smooth waters of the harbour.

As Mary Ann's boat sailed within sight, she would have observed the low chain of hills that ran the entire length of the island and sometimes climbed as high as 2000 feet. They were said to look well suited to cultivation. Did Mary Ann share with other passengers a sense of excitement about the possibilities of the island, or was she filled with dread about this next stage of her life? Her vessel was one of the hundreds that miscalculated the reef and her obituary describes how the ship was violently wrecked upon the coast and that this 'ill-starred arrival' soon became 'a forerunner of the great financial wreck that was to follow'.

When 'Madame Kinchela' eventually found her feet on dry land on *Nuevo Caledone*, she may have been struck by how much the French settlement resembled the Sydney of her childhood. This was yet another port town with a bay of clinking ship masts, narrow roads cut into impossibly steep hills and streets lined with wooden cottages. Like Sydney in the 1830s, there were also convicts. More than 20,000 in total, and Kinchela's widow may have been startled by her proximity to these diminished French men and women, as well as the 'shabbily clad' Indigenous inhabitants who also lived about town. There were, in fact, some 'twenty-seven rival tribes' settled about various parts of the island. These included a considerable number of rebels who hid out in the mountains committing arson attacks and guerrilla warfare upon the wealthy settlers who had arrived before the convicts, and were known to exact exceedingly vicious reprisals upon the 'cannibals' of the island.

By the late 1860s, 'tropical storms and shipwrecks' had caused Mary Ann's plantation investment to entirely collapse and she had little choice but to return to Sydney. There in 1869, she married again—this time to a man thirteen years her junior. At the time 24-year-old Charles Augustus Beatty married the 37-year-old widow he was five feet nine with a dark complexion, with dark hazel eyes, and dark whiskers and moustache. Their courtship may have begun during one or another of Mary Ann's short visits to Sydney during her time on New Caledonia. The wedding took place at the Free Church of England and Mary Ann's sister Harriet was there to witness the marriage between the 'esquire' and his 'lady', as they were listed in the certificate. It is possible that the union was one of convenience that helped Mary Ann navigate the financial hardship after New Caledonia for there is little evidence that the pair enjoyed much intimacy.

Not much can be found about Charles Augustus, although it does appear that he may have been another gentleman settler from the Darling Downs, for it was there he disappeared in 1888 when his wife placed a notice in the *Police Gazette* seeking the whereabouts of her husband. This note indicates that Beatty might have been working in the 'north of Queensland' as a station manager, for he had previously held a similar role at Chinchilla Station near Dalby. Like Banjo Paterson's poem 'Clancy of the Overflow', Charles Beatty had 'gone to Queensland droving'. A few months later the *Police Gazette* concluded this episode by noting that Mrs Beatty, as she was then known, had been informed that her husband was working in Queensland's Mitchell district. And perhaps that suited them both.

By that time, Mary Beatty had been living in the rural town of Corowa on the New South Wales side of the Murray River for more than thirteen years. She had moved there with her widowed mother Margaret Gill in 1875 and taken possession of a large one-storey weatherboard building—just a little distance from the banks of the Murray. There she established a seminary that became known as 'Mrs Beatty's Boarding & Day School for Young Ladies'.

By the 1870s Corowa was a thriving port town that had benefited from the discovery of gold in the nearby towns of Beechworth and Rutherglen. This in turn had encouraged the expansion of pastoral interests throughout the region making the town both populous and reasonably affluent. The area had something of the Australian bush feel to it. It was at a large sheep station just outside Corowa that Tom Roberts painted one of his most well-known Australian works, *Shearing the Rams*, which he completed in 1890, when Mary Ann was still in charge of her seminary. There was regular strife along the river throughout this period as a result of the different tariffs that were charged on goods as they were shipped back and forth across the Murray. These conditions encouraged the growth of both the Australian Native Association (ANA) and the Federation League—two patriot organisations intent upon resolving inter-colonial differences through the creation of a Federated Nation.

Given her early years in Sydney, these political debates may have been of particular interest for Mary Beatty, especially when she learnt that a good number of the country's most important politicians were to converge upon Corowa for the Agricultural Show of winter 1893. These men were determined to secure agreements from both the ANA and the Federation League so they could further the cause of Federation.

The now ancient 'White Beard' of Australian politics, Henry Parkes, was meant to attend this event. Mary Ann would certainly have been aware of his public persona well before this, for by the early 1890s the one-time bone turner had served as the Premier of New South Wales several times and was already declaring himself the future 'Father of Federation'. Mary Ann may have been curious to see her childhood neighbour again. A long time had passed since she and her brother had stood at Circular Quay in 1849 and watched the fiery bounty migrant striding back and forth upon the 'triumphant car of defiance'. Such was Mrs Beatty's standing in Corowa by the 1890s that she may have been granted permission, as a number of women were, to sit in on the debates at the Globe Hotel in Corowa, on the explicit proviso that they didn't interrupt. There she could have watched a young Edmond Barton encourage others to embrace their vision of a united nation. Sadly, however, Henry Parkes had suffered an episode of ill health shortly before the Corowa Convention and was unable to attend this event, so it is unlikely that Mary Ann encountered her previous neighbour, the one-time rocking horse vendor, ever again.

What must it have been like for Mary Ann to be in charge of the education of the young women of the area, the majority of whom were probably the daughters of wealthy and well-known pastoralists? No doubt these girls were well fed, having Margaret Gill to supervise in the kitchen while she supported her eldest daughter's new business venture. Her eldest daughter had certainly achieved a degree of respectability and domestic comfort but there may have been some sadness, too—for both of Mary Ann's own children were now dead and her extended brood of nephews and nieces lived some distance away. In total, eight nephews and nieces had been born to William and his wife Elizabeth, although they were living about 500 miles further north, while her younger brother Thomas Edward had ten children with his wife, Mary Jane Trasey, but they were living in Melbourne where Thomas was working as a milliner.

Mary Ann had been a headstrong and defiant adolescent, who had been determined to pursue her own romantic ambitions and disobey her father if necessary. Would Mrs Beatty of Corowa have recognised a similar spirit in some of the young ladies in her care, or would age, experience and responsibility have compelled her to censure such behaviour in a way that gave her a new appreciation of her father's discipline? Mary Ann's obituary suggests that she was 'endowed with a keen sympathy for the afflicted'—and often 'foremost in the promotion of charitable relief' particularly when it came to 'deserving cases' such as those associated with the Corowa Hospital and other 'public movements'. Was Mary Ann Beatty more interested in public life than the domestic sphere? Or did she simply share her parents' entrepreneurial instinct, as well as her father's desire for public recognition and her mother's particular ability as an independent businesswoman?

Mary Ann did not entirely shirk her familial responsibilities, for in the early 1880s she adopted one of her nephews, a son to her brother Thomas who had died. This young boy, Frederick James, was the youngest of ten surviving siblings and must have been under five years old when Mary Ann assumed his care. Many years later F.J. would describe his aunt as cold and his time in her care as harsh and unloving, but Mary Ann was raising her nephew in a school for young ladies and no doubt concerned about the presence of a young boy in such an establishment. F.J. would go on to work as a jeweller and a diamond trader. He acquired property in Rutherglen then Victoria's western district, where he also became a town councillor. He earned a reputation for being a charming if somewhat erratic adventurer, travelling to Papua New Guinea in his late seventies to visit the Ok Tedi mines. He was known to have put himself before his children on several occasions, not unlike Martin Gill. Perhaps Mary Ann detected this in her adopted nephew and was intent upon curbing his headstrong disposition. Again and again, this portion of the story raises more questions than the archives answer. Nonetheless, we might return to the documents to consider what they do reveal and allow them to guide Mary Ann's story to its conclusion.

~

On 11 May 1883, Margaret Gill died of Bright's disease aged sixty-nine. She was buried—after a short service that morning—in the Roman Catholic section of the Corowa cemetery. Her death certificate identifies her as the mother of twelve children; of whom three men and three women were still living, while two males and four females had all died within a year or so of birth. The certificate notes that Margaret was born in Dublin and that her father had been a farmer and that she had come to the colony more than fifty years ago. No other details were present with which we might connect the deceased to her life as a successful hotelier in Sydney, let alone her earlier years as a transported felon.

Mary Ann died nineteen years later. She had endured more than ten months of bowel cancer, but eventually on the morning of 2 March 1902, she slipped away 'so peacefully', the obituary claimed, that none of those around her bedside noticed 'for some little time'. Mary Ann's remains were interred in 'the old cemetery' alongside her mother. The two women share a gravestone, modestly engraved with their names, as well as the dates of each woman's birth and death; each of them were sixty-nine when they died.

Together, the lives of these two women span from the Napoleonic Wars to the Federation of Australia. Margaret had come to the colony a young convict in 1828 and died fifty-five years later, as the mother of a respectable school mistress. In that time she not only bore twelve children but also gained a reputation as a hotelier who catered for banquets, balls and routs, as well as the colony's most distinguished gentry. She reinvented herself, from convict to respectable colonist, from deserted wife and mother to successful businesswoman.

Like her father and mother, Mary Ann took risks. She had been so determined to marry the man of her own choice that she had defied her parents and flouted social convention. In so doing she had earned the ire and perhaps even a little admiration from the colonial newspapers, including one which commented upon her ardent determination to become 'the Mistress of her own Actions'. Such daring conduct came with consequences, however, and Mary Ann was compelled to travel far from her home and family. Rather than watch the world from the confines of her bedroom window, Mary Ann climbed down the drainpipe of the Pitt Street hotel determined to pursue her romantic ambitions and embrace adventure. In so doing, she witnessed events that must have far exceeded her childhood imagination. She had been the wife of a gentleman settler—perhaps more than once. She had been in San Francisco during the craze of the gold rush and at the very time fellow colonists were violently lynched. She had lived in New Caledonia when it was rife with French convicts and in a state of constant guerilla warfare. She had suffered shipwrecks, encountered pirates and experienced not only the loss of a great fortune but also the deaths of two children and a much-loved husband. Like her mother, Mary Ann—Madame Kinchela, Mary Beatty—reinvented herself several times, so successfully that during the final decades of her life she was able to enjoy considerable respectability.

The theme of reinvention resonates throughout this book, but while we might expect nineteenth-century men such as Martin Gill and James Butler Kinchela to enjoy social mobility, it was less usual for colonial women to so successfully marshal and manipulate the social conditions of the period to their advantage. It took pluck and guile as well as imagination and determination. As it was in life, perhaps also in death, for Mary Ann's last will contains a few final clues regarding her ability to engage in self-fashioning.

In this document Mary Ann's mother is given a maiden name that conceals her connection with her convict father, Thomas McCormick, while the occupation of Mary Ann's father, the emancipist Martin Gill, is listed as that of gentleman. This thin web of half-truths is too flimsy to conceal what we now know about the Gills' convict past, yet this concealment is precisely what Martin and Margaret's descendants needed if they were to have any chance of achieving respectability for themselves in Australia at the beginning of the twentieth century. So perhaps this final act of concealment, of concealing the convict taint in the family's history, was the best parting gift Mary Ann could leave her great brood of nephews and nieces, including F.J., the young boy she adopted.

And yet, as I scan the sundries that were put to auction upon Mary Ann's death, certain curiosities appear that suggest links between Mary Beatty and Mary Ann Gill. At the time of her death, for example, the mistress of the Corowa Seminary was £500 in arrears on her rent, a debt that far exceeds that which brought about Martin Gill's financial ruin in 1849–50. These outstanding costs made it necessary for all of Mrs Beatty's remaining items to be sold at auction.

Among the hundreds of goods sent to A.A. Piggins and Co. Auction House were a steam cooker and several flower pots, two quills, a number of jugs and decanters, several rocking chairs and a wheelbarrow. Modest items indeed, and nothing in keeping with the considerable means Mary Ann must have enjoyed as the daughter of two Sydney hoteliers and the wife of one, possibly two gentlemen settlers.

Among the items there were also two picture frames—which probably held the portraits of her husbands—now sadly gone. There was a sausage machine and also a gun worth £2.4, which may have once belonged to Judge Kinchela. The list also includes a number of horsehair chairs, a washbasin and a small silver looking glass. Were these perhaps the very things that Margaret Gill rescued from the George Street auction rooms in November 1849?

All of these items are now long gone. The Piggins' auction very likely dispersed Mary Ann's unremarkable possessions among private homes and perhaps even one or two historical societies and country museums. To such very ordinary remnants of an extraordinary life we must add the distorted memory of an adopted nephew. And of course, a faded newspaper clipping from *The Sydney Morning Herald* in 1848 when a fifteen-year-old currency lass stepped into the witness box of Sydney's Supreme Court and was for several moments, 'too agitated to speak'.

Afterword

> . . . a space, a window through which
> the reader has the capacity to wonder,
> to imagine and discover the past for
> themselves.
>
> Mark McKenna, *Writing the Past*, 2005

This is a book of thresholds, of windows and open spaces through which the reader is free to wander and imagine and perhaps even discover the past for themselves. When I began writing I felt as if I too was slipping, furtively, out a window in pursuit of my own adventure. I wanted to write Mary Ann's story in a way that made it as exciting as fiction—that revealed how precarious life was for colonial Australians, that there were eccentrics and opportunists as well as ordinary flesh and blood people who were surprisingly similar to those in the novels of Charles Dickens, William Makepeace Thackeray and Elizabeth Gaskell.

I have had plenty of time to wonder and imagine myself, for I began researching this book in 2007. I became increasingly inquisitive about why Mary Ann and James Butler, Martin and Margaret behaved as they did. The more I explored this question the more I found the

answers in the particularities of their world. These people were creatures of their time. They thought and acted as they did because of the
circumstances they found themselves in and the resources—mental
and actual—they had to respond to obstacles and opportunities. As I
learnt more about these people I realised that I would need to become
intimately acquainted with their everyday life if I was to gain any sense
of how they thought and felt. From the beginning then, I have striven
to recreate the sounds and smells, textures and tastes of their time,
believing that this exterior world would provide a pathway into the
interior world of these ordinary colonial subjects.

In so doing I have, like Mary Ann, flouted certain conventions.
Mine are concerned with unsettling the role of objectivity and imagination in historical writing, rather than defying the existing mores
associated with marriage. I did this because the story has demanded it.
It is after all, a romantic tale of sense and sensibility in which feelings
are integral. It is also a woman's history and as such it serves as a foil to
the various histories of this period that are concerned with the develop-
ment of Australia's distinctive brand of democracy. If, for example,
Peter Cochrane's impressive 584-page *Colonial Ambition* dedicates one
sentence to 'Miss Gill's abductor', *The Convict's Daughter* is concerned
with this domestic drama and uses the political agitation of the 1840s
as a backdrop.

We see this world not through official documents and the eyes of
the men who made them, but from the perspective of a young woman
who was preoccupied with everyday as well as grander intimacies.
We spend more time with middling orders than the influential set,
with ambitious emancipists and their native-born children than the
members of the Legislative Council. And when we do dwell among
the elite, we discover their flaws and foibles, including the fact that
the settler classes were often diminished by debt and doubt. And yet,
while such men were hardly the heroic pioneers of many previous
triumphalist histories, nor were they all as morally bankrupt and
malicious as some more recent frontier accounts might have us
believe.

By retrieving a little-known woman from historical anonymity I have wanted to contribute to our understanding of the colonial era. As an urban native-born woman Mary Ann Gill belongs to a demographic that has attracted less historical interest than her female convict predecessors and male native-born contemporaries. After reading this book I hope you have a sense that women like Mary Ann were vital to their society and often exercised considerable influence upon both their immediate families and future generations. Indeed, I like to think that in her own way, Mary Ann was as much of a nation-builder as her father, the convict-made-good, her husband, the gentleman settler, and her neighbour, Henry Parkes, the bounty migrant who became premier.

Mary Ann's story takes us into less familiar parts of the nineteenth century and in so doing provides us with new insight into what it meant to be Australian at this time. We learn that colonial Australia was not only locked into relations with England and the Colonial Office; there were all sorts of connections throughout the Pacific and America. There may be easily recognisable elements to Mary Ann's story, her convict parents and gentleman romancer, but there are also unfamiliar aspects such as her mother's ability to operate as a successful businesswoman after she was deserted by her husband, and Mary Ann's ability to travel to America and New Caledonia and eventually thrive despite the death of one husband and the disappearance of another.

Mary Ann's story was one that demanded to be told. My curiosity was first piqued by the newspaper clipping my mother showed me after I expressed an interest in the native-born women who lived in colonial cities before the gold rushes. I soon found an obituary from the *Corowa Free Press* concerning a woman, then known as Mrs Beatty, who died in Corowa in 1902 having encountered all sorts of hardships in both America and the Pacific. Sometime after that I discovered an extensive collection of material, including an abundance of newspapers and three surprisingly detailed legal depositions. Still dusty and tied in their faded pink legal ribbons when I unearthed them in the State Records of NSW, these yellowing documents are punctuated with contradictory eyewitness accounts from the key characters as well as Mary Ann's tear-blotched signature. Discovering these sources was extremely exciting and it represented the real beginning of my research journey.

As well as undertaking research throughout Australia I conducted several trips to Ireland and England where I learnt much about the history of two families with very different religious and social positions within Irish society. As part of what is now referred to as the Anglo-Irish elite, there was an abundance of material associated with the Kinchelas, including a parcel of family letters as well as several portraits and photographs which Annette Miller, a descendant of James Butler's sister, generously shared. In contrast, there was no comparable epistolary or visual material associated with the Gills. I well recall the futile afternoons spent at the National Archives and traipsing the windy streets of North Dublin where not only Martin Gill but also Margaret and Thomas McCormick had once lived. Despite such frustrations, Ireland did yield other insights about the Irish heritage of these people, including contemporary legends such as Ellen Hanley and Captain Rock as well as ancient lore like the *tochmarca* tales.

With only a few exceptions, the majority of the primary material concerned with Mary Ann's story is associated with the prominent male members of both families. There was a wealth of official correspondence about the Kinchelas in New South Wales and it was also relatively easy to trace the entrepreneurial ascent of Martin Gill in the colonial press. Later, I would also be able to find surprising detail about Margaret Gill's phoenix-like rise from the ashes in 1850.

The uneven nature of these primary sources points to the fact that it is often much easier to 'retrieve' well-established historical characters than those from the 'middling' and 'lower orders' as well as male figures from their female counterparts. Mary Ann's scandal ensures that she is something of an exception to this, and we can certainly learn more about her than many other native-born women from this period. And yet, there are no daguerreotypes or photographs of Mary Ann. Nor have I uncovered a private diary or personal correspondence with which to study the secrets of her interior world. In addition to this, the records associated with her life tend to cluster around the years of 1848 and 1849 where, consequently, much of this book has been focused.

In writing the biography of this little-known native-born woman I have been presented with the task of recreating a life that is only partially documented. I have approached this challenge in three ways: The first involves drawing upon the existing primary sources to recreate what is already known about Mary Ann. Where there is sufficient material I have done this with considerable accuracy, down to the detail of the carpetbag Mary Ann 'stole' from her mother for her elopement and what she and James Butler said to one another at the window of her father's hotel. The elopement and later court proceedings are therefore all closely drawn from the newspapers and deposition files. I have, however, added embellishments. I don't know, for example, the colour of the gloves and bonnet Mary Ann wore when she stepped into the witness box in 1848, but I do know the fashionable colours of that year and the importance of stagecraft in nineteenth-century courts, particularly when it came to romantic scandal.

To bring context and colour to this world, I have also referred to a vast array of primary and secondary sources. For example, the convict and prison records frequently include details regarding height and skin complexion, eye and hair colour. Such records confirm that Martin Gill had black hair and hazel eyes, while Margaret had brown hair as well as 'freckles across her broad nose'. While I have no records regarding Mary Ann's appearance, I have assumed that she had light freckled skin, brown hair and hazel-brown eyes. Similarly it is well known that during Mary Ann's childhood, native-born Australians were often referred to as 'cornstalks' because of the way they were said to 'shoot up' in the fresh air of a new country and quickly become taller and healthier than their parents. This encouraged me to imagine fifteen-year-old Mary Ann standing nose-to-nose with her father who, the records reveal, was no higher than five foot five.

During this period native-born men and women were often referred to as currency lads and lasses because they were considered a local currency of lesser value than their 'sterling' immigrant counterparts.

In 1844, at the very time that Martin Gill was managing a confectionery stall at the Royal Victoria Theatre on Pitt Street, an Irish convict named Edward Geoghegan wrote a frothy musical farce entitled *The Currency Lass; Or My Native Girl*, which he smuggled off Cockatoo Island while still serving his sentence and organised to have performed at the Vic. *The Currency Lass* represents the first theatrical performance to be specifically concerned with local characters and its namesake was a young native-born woman like our heroine. I have found it reasonable to speculate that Mary Ann, who was approximately twelve years of age at this time and working within the family business, witnessed a performance of *The Currency Lass*.

In a desire to weave Mary Ann's story through particularly evocative and illuminating episodes of this era I have made similar creative assumptions about the presence of these characters at events such as St Patrick's Ball in 1840 and the two Monster Rallies held at Circular Quay in 1849. I do not know if these characters were present at any of these occasions, but the possibility seems reasonable. Similarly, while I have no evidence that Mary Ann ever visited Kinchela at Darlinghurst Gaol, she certainly demonstrated sufficient pluck to embark upon such an adventure and if she had done so on election eve in 1848 she certainly would have encountered a fire at Hyde Park as well as dangerous mobs throughout the city streets.

I have sought to sew these characters into the fabric of their society by weaving them into both the everyday and the eventful of the colonial world. For this reason I have implicated Kinchela in the brutal reprisal that took place in the Upper Burnett in early June 1849, in response to the murder of the Pegg brothers by Aboriginal warriors. While I cannot confirm Kinchela's presence at this conflict, the records indicate that at least fifty settlers from the district were involved. There are records which suggest that Kinchela engaged in such activities if not then, then most probably another time. Again, while I do not know if Kinchela ever met Edward Hawkins, there is evidence that Hawkins and Thomas Archer were both settlers from the Upper Burnett and that the two men travelled together to Californian goldfields.

There have been occasions when the trail of clues associated with Mary Ann's tumultuous romance petered out and I have found myself perched upon the stepping stone of one fact—needing to make something of a leap in order to land safely upon the next set of solid facts. On such occasions I have drawn upon the conventions of the romantic and social fiction that was popular during this period, as well as my long association with these characters, to make certain assumptions about what these people may have said and done and why. In several such instances I have imbued these historical characters with the sort of interior world their fictional counterparts enjoyed and in so doing I have woven a thread of fiction into a book that is otherwise solidly grounded in historical research.

Sometimes this has been necessary because the facts associated with this story appear stranger than fiction. The incident involving Kinchela and Louisa Aarons, for example, seems utterly unlikely but was true. Even more incredible is the fact that despite the numerous hostilities and disappointments that occurred between James Butler, Martin Gill and Mary Ann some sort of reconciliation was eventually achieved. Again, I have found no records that cast light upon how and why this occurred, but the facts are irrefutable; Mary Ann travelled to California and married Kinchela there in 1852, with her father's blessing.

To provide some explanation as to what might have happened I have drawn upon Irish courtship practices in the first half of the nineteenth century and imagined the sort of conversation that might have taken place between Martin Gill and Kinchela. My research of contemporary Irish abduction cases also encouraged me to assume that, like many other Irish fathers of this period, Martin Gill may have sought to match his daughter with a wealthy businessman as a solution to familial and financial shame. While Alexander Moore and Lewis Samuel both feature extensively in the deposition records associated with Martin Gill's insolvency, and Samuel does occasionally demonstrate personality traits similar to those I have attributed to him, there is nothing to suggest that either man was engaged in any sort of marital machinations with Mary Ann. That is pure imagination on my behalf, but not,

I think, entirely implausible. For readers who would like to learn more about how I used primary and secondary sources I have included both Notes and a Bibliography.

Rather than confess all my inventions and speculations, perhaps it is best to finish by saying something about why I wrote this book. I certainly loved Mary Ann's defiant streak and her determination to pursue her romantic ambitions, come what may. I also admired her resilience and her capacity for reinvention. The ancestral connection provided a strong hook, although, I firmly believe that the differences between historical subjects and ourselves are as important as any elements we might have in common. It seems careless to project our sensibilities upon people whose actual peccadillos and particularities often prove more interesting than what we might like to assume about them.

Much as the personality of Mary Ann fascinated me it was the story that drew me on and in this I am reminded of the great power of narrative not only to heal and reveal but also subtly convey argument. If there is an argument to this book, it is that women were a vibrant part of the colonial world and that they often exercised astonishing influence as well as character and courage. The healing power of narrative relates to the act of retrieving Mary Ann from anonymity. Her story is one that reveals the complexities and contradictions of her age, and in so doing will, I hope, add depth and dimension not only to her world, but also to our own.

Glossary

barque: A sailing vessel with three or more masts.

Black Maria: An enclosed prison vehicle. During this period, it comprised a carriage and pair.

bone turner: A person who carves bone and ivory, typically into household items or toys. Most often a poor man's trade.

bosky: A Regency term for being drunk.

bounty migrant: A free British immigrant whose passage was paid by the colonial government under the 'bounty scheme'.

brig: A sailing vessel with two square-rigged masts.

Bright's disease: A nineteenth-century term for kidney disease.

brown beaver: A brown felt top hat, made from beaver fur, worn by many British immigrants.

bully meat: Salt-cured canned or corned beef.

Cabbager: A nickname for a member of the lower orders, as they often wore a broad-brimmed, cheap hat made from cabbage-tree leaf that was considered better suited to the colonial climate than the brown beaver hats commonly worn in England. Also cabbage-tree hatter.

carpetbag: A travelling bag made of carpet, commonly oriental rug.

Chartism: A nineteenth-century working-class movement for political reform in Britain.

clipper: A fast sailing ship with three masts and a square rig.

cornstalk: Early nineteenth-century term originating in New South Wales for the native-born, due to the manner in which those born in Australia to free or convict stock grew rapidly, like cornstalks. Also currency lad or lass.

Cortess and Pisarro: Two Spanish explorers of the new world, more commonly known as Cortés and Pizarro.

currency lad or lass: The first Australian-born generation of Europeans; the term derives from the local currency issued by Governor Macquarie in Sydney in 1812. As the local pound depreciated against the sterling, the word 'currency' implied the inferiority of locally born Europeans. Also cornstalk.

cutter: A small, single-masted boat.

darg: The distinctive mark each convict etched into every stone brick they made to keep a tally of their work.

Drapers' Purse: A horse-racing event funded by local drapers.

dusky warrior: A colonial term for an Aboriginal Australian.

Elysium: An ancient Greek notion of the afterlife repopularised in the nineteenth century.

emancipist: A convict who had served out their sentence or received a conditional or absolute pardon.

flashman: A colonial criminal or rogue (often an ex-convict).

greengage: A common green plum used in cooking and confectionery.

Gretna Green: A village in southern Scotland that became famous for runaway weddings in the late eighteenth century.

gunyio: An Aboriginal shelter made from bark and leaves, probably a derivative of gunyah. Also known as a humpy.

half-mount: An eighteenth- and nineteenth-century Irish term for Irish gentlemen who had lost their fortunes or position and were forced to borrow horses from wealthier associates.

Hibernian: Of Irish descent. From Hibernia, the Classical Latin name for Ireland.

honey-fall: A Regency term for good fortune.

horse bazaar: An auction house and stable specifically for horses.

Jenny Lind: A nineteenth-century drink named after a famous Swedish opera singer.

Jimmy Grant: Colonial nickname for an immigrant.

johnnycake: Cornmeal flatbread; also johnny bread or journey cake.

kanaka: Derogatory nineteenth-century term for a Pacific Islander, typically (but not exclusively) one employed in the colonies.

keeping a close hand: A card-game term that implies secrecy.

kerseymere: A fine-twilled woollen cloth popular for waistcoats in the Regency era.

Klaberjass: A German card game invented in the 1820s.

lackland: To be landless, typically referring to younger sons without an inheritance.

lag: A convict or ex-convict.

leatherjacket: A type of fish.

licensed victualler: A person who is licensed to sell alcohol and other provisions.

lighterman: A worker who operates a lighter, a type of flat-bottomed barge used to transfer goods from a large vessel to shore; also lighters.

loose tin: Slang for money, particularly loose coins.

lower orders: A nineteenth-century term for the poorest social groups in society.

madeira: Portuguese fortified white wine popular in the nineteenth century.

mechanic: A nineteenth-century term for a manual labourer.

middling sort: Middle classes, generally lower rather than upper; also middling set.

mutton-chop whiskers: Sideburns that are narrow near the ear and broad and rounded near the chin. Popular in the nineteenth century.

muzzle-loader: A gun that is loaded through its muzzle.

nabob: An Anglo-Indian term for a conspicuously wealthy man who made his fortune in 'the Orient' or 'the Sub-Continent'. In the colonial context it referred to a similar class of men who made their fortune through corrupt practices and at the expense of others.

native-born: Another term for currency lads or lasses.

new chum: A colonial nickname for a newly arrived immigrant.

old gull: A dupe, fool or simpleton.

old hand: A term for an emancipist convict.

omnibus: An enclosed, horse-drawn, passenger-carrying vehicle.

phaeton: A sporty open carriage popular in the late eighteenth and early nineteenth centuries.

play with a straight bat: A cricketing term that refers to a batsman playing with a vertical bat and means 'honest or honourable behaviour'.

porter: A well-hopped beer that is brown in colour.

public assembly: Regency-period activity in a large room where middle to upper-classes socialised as part of match-making preparations.

Regency era: A period in the United Kingdom from 1811 to 1820 when King George III was unfit to rule so his son the Prince of Wales ruled by proxy as the Prince Regent.

Rockite: A follower of the Irish rebel Captain Rock.

rout: A crowded party, akin to a modern cocktail party.

salt junk: Salted beef or pork.

schooner: A sailing vessel with fore and aft sails on two or more masts.

scurvygrass: A perennial herb popular in Georgian gardens.

shandygaff: A beer mixed with a non-alcoholic beverage such as ginger beer.

snuff: A fine-ground tobacco commonly inhaled or sniffed into the nose; very popular with the upper classes in the eighteenth and nineteenth centuries.

Spanish dollar: The first distinct currency in Australia; made from a Spanish coin with the middle punched out and stamped with a sunburst. Also called a Holey dollar.

squireen: Like a half-mount, the squireen was an Irish country gentleman. He was often a young landowner, hence a squireen and not a squire.

sterling: Term for a free settler in New South Wales. Whereas *currency* alluded to the Australian-born and the children of convicts and emancipists, *sterling* became a synonym for the free, generally wealthier British immigrant, as it referred to the more valuable British money.

Swan Drop: A type of ammunition that differed from bullets and powder.

swizzler: A sort of colonial rum punch.

Sydney Duck: A derogatory term used in America to describe an Australian who went to California during the gold rush. It is likely this referred to the hard-wearing 'duck frocks and trowsers' worn by many colonial working-class immigrants.

tallow: A rendered form of beef and mutton fat used to make candles, soap, dip and grease.

ticket-of-leave: A document of parole issued to convicts, which allowed restricted freedoms. Emancipists were also known as ticket-of-leavers.

tilbury: A light, open, two-wheeled, horse-drawn carriage with or without a top.

tochmarca: An ancient form of Irish story concerned with illegal, illicit and unorthodox love.

tuppenny: Another name for twopence or tuppence.

turnkey: A prison guard or gaoler.

Twelfth Night cake: A Twelfth Night cake was made with dried fruits and spices. According to the author of Jane Austen's Christmas, 'these represented the exotic spices of the East and the gifts of the Wise men'. It was typically a large cake that was used for a number of festival games.

waddy: An Aboriginal hunting stick or war club. Also nulla nulla.

whaleboat: A long rowing boat with a prow at both ends, used for whaling.

Young Ireland movement: An Irish political and social movement that promoted independent Irish nationalism and led to the 1848 rebellion. Members were called Young Irelanders.

Acknowledgements

This book began as a PhD in 2007 and has benefitted from many crucial conversations as well as numerous acts of generosity. I must start by acknowledging the Writers Centre at the University of Melbourne. They had the good sense to pair me with a mentor, and I found in Jennifer Kloester a rare and wonderful spirit who genuinely champions others. Jen's honesty and sheer life force have been crucial throughout the process of writing this book. In 2015 I was awarded a Hawke Fellowship from the Hawke Research Institute (HRI) at the University of South Australia. I truly appreciate the support of Anthony Elliott, Denise Meredyth and my colleagues at HRI. Those employed within archival institutions deserve due acknowledgement for all they do to preserve the sources with which we tell our stories. I am indebted to the NSW State Records, the Mitchell Library, the National Archives in Ireland and the British Library. A special thanks to Angus Trumble from the National Portrait Gallery for his prompt and personal assistance.

I am grateful to David Goodman and Joy Damousi, who supervised my PhD and taught me much about rigorous research. My fascination with colonial history began during my Masters and I thank my supervisors, Kate Darian-Smith and Michael Cathcart, for their past encouragement and ongoing friendship. I was extremely fortunate to have Alan Mayne as my Head of School when I was first employed at the University of South Australia. I treasure the friendship I share with him and his wonderful wife, Jude King. I have also had the good fortune to be mentored by Jo Cys and to enjoy the hearty collegiality of both Rosie Roberts and Stephen Atkinson.

In 2012 I had a conversation with Penny Russell that proved crucial to the way I conceived this book. Penny's scholarship and exquisite prose is matched only by her professional generosity. Many other academics were also generous with their ideas and research. Peter Cochrane's impressive 2006 *Colonial Ambition* has been close at hand for much of the last ten years. Jonathan Richards and I share a fascination for New Caledonia and his genial generosity was greatly appreciated. Likewise Cameron White shared his excellent unpublished article about the Sydney Ducks in San Francisco and in so doing demonstrated a degree of trust that deserves acknowledgement. The architectural historian Miles Lewis provided me with insights about Georgian architecture in Sydney while Babette Smith shared her experience with me at a crucial crossroad.

Family stories often only survive thanks to those who keep them alive. These are the people who hunt down records, restore old photographs and maintain contact with distant relatives. Annette Miller plays a crucial role in preserving the history of the Kinchela family and I am indebted to her for the time and resources she shared with me, including the portrait of John Kinchela, which has never been published before. Victor Miller was the first to track me down and he has maintained affable and informative contact with me throughout. He also introduced me to Alicen Miller who gave permission to publish the portrait of Anne Bourne. In my own family, Pat Cameron did some extensive early digging which got me off to a healthy start with the Gills.

For a book to be published you need a pitch and a publisher. Jen Kloester, Sybil Nolan and Emma Balazs offered considered feedback on my early pitches. Throughout the writing process I have enjoyed long skype conversations with Emma which have been vital to sustaining my spirit. My publisher at Allen & Unwin, Elizabeth Weiss, combines consummate professionalism with common sense. I appreciate her initial faith in me and the way she allowed the project to evolve. Angela Handley has been responsible for guiding the book to publication and has done so with good grace and creative flair. There have been a number of friends who have read drafts and offered advice. Emily Harms, also known as Gwennie, has a superb eye for detail and her comments ignited many creative sparks. Alecia Simmonds shared her sharp intellect and greatly appreciated enthusiasm just when it was most needed.

I underwent a period of profound personal change during the decade that I worked on this book. I was able to rise, phoenix-like from the ashes, because of the love and support I received. I would like to thank Bob Slater for the first glimmer of hope. Aviva Kipen and Philip Kreveld for a safe place to land, Karen Soo, Jane Freemantle, Jenny Holmes, Hartley Mitchell and Naomi Lawrence for their wisdom and insight. It was, however, Katrina Carling and her family, who endowed me with a new sense of possibility. I am particularly indebted to Katrina for her character and courage and, of course, that fantastic laugh.

My brother Tim has been a true travelling companion, offering practical support, as well as lots of laughs along the way. As I wrestled with questions of grammar and sought urgent answers to obscure questions my father was also a constant and loving presence. Then there is my darling Brye, from whom I have learnt so much about unconditional love. Thank you for our deep happiness. And finally, there is my mother, to whom this book is dedicated. My dear friend, you have been there from the beginning, always believing, always curious, always learning. Mary Ann's story has given us both a world of conversations and a lifetime of memories and this book is, therefore, as much yours as it is mine.

Notes

These notes are included for readers who seek information about which parts of *The Convict's Daughter* are factual and which are imagined.

Chapter One: High-Growing Fruit

The convict records for Martin Gill and the McCormick's convict records provide this chapter with much of its detail. They are supplemented by shipping records, government and medical reports, and birth, baptism, marriage and death certificates. Colonial archives and newspapers detail the rise of the Gills. The Pitt Street hotel appears in newspapers, Sydney directories, maps and Joseph Fowles' *Sydney in 1848*. Gill had a booth at the Royal Victoria theatre where *The Currency Lass* was performed. I quoted verbatim from this play but Mary Ann's presence there is imagined, as is the vista from her bedroom window. All references to food come from newspaper advertisements and secondary sources.

Chapter Two: Decline and Fall

There are extensive primary sources for the Kinchelas. For Ireland, I referred to mayoral papers, land grants and local newspapers, while the West Indies is based on government documents supplemented by secondary sources. The *Historical Records of Australia* (HRA) and colonial newspapers contain much about Kinchela's professional activities and debts. *Mudie v Kinchela* (1840) details can be gleaned from newspapers and legal documents. Family letters describe the various overland expeditions taken by the Kinchela brothers between 1838 and 1840, including the last expedition, which James led with cousin William Thornton. These letters hint at tensions with Thornton and a later obituary suggests that the party had 'several smart brushes with the blacks'. The letters refer to James Butler's liver damage and John Kinchela borrowing £4000 from his brother-in-law, Thomas Gore. I imagined Mary Ann's first encounter with Kinchela, but he was staying at the Pitt Street hotel at the times indicated and the pair orchestrated regular 'chance' meetings.

Chapter Three: The All-Seductive James

The account of early Moreton Bay and Dundali come from newspapers and secondary sources. The Kinchela brothers purchased Hawkwood in 1845; it was in what is now the Upper Burnett Region and a place named Hawkwood still exists there. My research into Irish countrymen of Kinchela's class led me to suggest that he was more comfortable with horses than women. In the *Regina v Kinchela* (1848) deposition Margaret insists she asked Kinchela to leave. The same deposition mentions that Martin Gill threatened his daughter with pistols and also threw furniture at her when she visited her grandparents' farm.

Chapter Four: The Parramatta Romance

This chapter draws on the *Regina v Gill* and *Regina v Kinchela* depositions and extensive newspaper coverage. The dialogue is quoted verbatim, as are the sequence of events and characters therein. *Regina v Kinchela* suggests Kinchela was drinking on the night of the elopement. Secondary sources were used to recreate Mrs Kelly's brothel and other establishments. Margaret may have been looking for work for Mary Ann as she posted ads to this effect, but I have imagined tension in their relationship and that they took tea each day. Ellen Hanley's death in 1819 was well known in Ireland and considered a cautionary tale about love across the classes. I imagined Mary Riley recounting this story to her granddaughter and Mary Ann cutting herself on the drainpipe.

Chapter Five: Shooting With Intent

The descriptions of European unrest come from colonial newspapers and secondary sources. The same papers include commentary about the 1848 New South Wales (NSW) elections and local court intelligence, which I have quoted verbatim. My depiction of Sydney's social and political climate is based on secondary reading. To recreate the trial I quoted directly from the *Regina v Gill* deposition and newspaper reports. These sources confirm that Martin Gill employed Robert Lowe, who was in the habit of carrying a crop and wearing pinstripe trousers and floral waistcoats. Kinchela disappeared after the shooting and had to be summonsed to court. I imagined that R.G. Nichols went to visit Kinchela and that Gill spat at Kinchela's boots after his acquittal.

Chapter Six: The Deposition

I assumed Margaret Gill managed the hotel during her husband's absence and also borrowed his bail from her father. I created the scene with Margaret and Mary Ann taking tea and Martin Gill bathing when he returned from gaol. The deposition confirms that Rebecca, the Gill's family servant, delivered the carpetbag to Kinchela before the elopement but I have imagined her returning its contents to Mary Ann and the admonished woman crying herself to sleep. I do not know what happened at the police station when Mary Ann went to give evidence against Kinchela, but the ink splotches under her signature in *Regina v Kinchela* encouraged me to imagine she gave evidence under duress. All references to Irish abductors in Ireland and Australia are based on extensive primary research.

Chapter Seven: To Court

Newspapers confirm that when Darlinghurst Court House was being built in the 1840s it was used for fairs and events, such as the St Patrick's Day ball in 1840. There is nothing to confirm that the Gills or the Kinchelas attended this event, but if they had done so it is likely that they would have seen Irish dancing. All information about the Wakefield case (1827) is based on primary research. I used my knowledge of the stagecraft associated with this case to suggest that Lowe and Gill conspired in similar theatrics for Mary Ann's attire. I have also imagined Lowe's attitude to Martin Gill and this case.

Chapter Eight: A Sporting Affair

Numerous biographies were used to sketch the influential personalities in this chapter, although I did imagine that Holroyd's experience in Kororareka was traumatic. I drew closely on *Regina v Kinchela* and newspaper coverage to ensure that the court proceedings are almost entirely verbatim. From such records it is possible to read certain traits into characters, such as Henry Webb's lack of confidence, Holroyd's inability to read the local audience and Lowe's spectacular timing. I do not know who came to watch this trial although the papers indicate that the court was crowded. I imagined Kinchela carrying a cane with a whiskey compartment.

Chapter Nine: The Gloves Come Off

The legal depositions and newspapers make it relatively easy to recreate Mary Ann's testimony. Several newspapers mention that when she first stepped into the witness box she 'sobbed bitterly' and was 'too agitated to speak'. These clues encouraged me to recreate this episode as one in which she felt torn between duty to her family and a desire to save herself and her lover. Most of the questions and responses here are verbatim. I don't know how Mary Riley and Margaret felt about the outcome of the case and there is no evidence that Nichols ever gave Mary Ann a sweet treat.

Chapter Ten: The Thoughtless and the Giddy

Details about the colonial newspapers, the elections and the economic conditions of NSW during this period come from the newspapers and secondary sources. During the 1843 election Gill signed petitions in support of Wentworth but there is nothing to indicate he supported Wentworth in 1848. I used direct quotes from the newspaper articles associated with the 'abductions' of Mary Ann Gill and Mary Ann Challenger. I have nothing to indicate how Martin Gill felt towards Mary Ann after the trial or to suggest she was made to read the newspapers to her father. Mary Ann would have been more literate than her parents and Margaret was probably a better reader than Martin. Details of Darlinghurst Gaol and the trial of John Knatchbull are based on secondary sources. Irish *tochmarca* tales can be traced back to the medieval period. By the early nineteenth century it was still common for such stories to be told by wandering teachers, who regularly adapted them. It is likely that the McCormicks knew such stories. Cormac O'Grady published a version of this particular story in 1873.

Chapter Eleven: A Story Without a Hero

Henry Keck was the governor of Darlinghurst Gaol in 1848 and sources confirm that he was both colourful and corrupt. Prison records reveal that Kinchela was incarcerated after the trial but the ambiguous nature of one particular source makes it impossible to confirm where. Conversations with archivists led me to determine it was most likely Darlinghurst Gaol and this allowed me to imagine Kinchela enjoying certain latitudes from a fellow Irishman. This chapter uses the subtitle of Thackeray's *Vanity Fair*, first published in serialised chapters of *Punch* in 1847–48 and, as the exchange between the couple suggests, the leading characters in this story bear some resemblance to James Butler and Mary Ann. I imagined Mary Ann making her intrepid visit to the gaol on election night. If she did she would have witnessed the fire in Hyde Park, angry mobs in the street and Robert Lowe being hauled along George Street in a carriage 'driven' by his campaign team. I placed Lowe on the carriage rooftop cracking a stock whip.

Chapter Twelve: The Manly and the Unmanly

Kinchela's appeal was heard before a full bench of the Supreme Court, including Roger Therry, who defended John Kinchela in the Mudie incident. This legal decision was published in *The Sydney Morning Herald* (*SMH*) and I have quoted it directly, adding only one phrase from an abduction trial Therry presided over in 1851. Although Manning did condemn the defendant for his 'unmanly defence' there are no records to indicate how Kinchela responded. He was incarcerated in Parramatta Gaol and the prison book lists his personal appearance. Given Martin Gill's future financial conditions it is likely he was experiencing financial hardship in

1848. There is nothing to suggest Gill tried to match his daughter with a 'monied gull'. Nor do I have any information that Alexander Moore was unfortunate in his appearance or that Lewis Samuel was as depicted. However, both Moore and Samuel were well-known colonists who featured prominently in Gills' 1850 insolvency trial, and their colourful responses inspired me to imagine that their indignation towards Gill may have been due to more than mere money matters.

Chapter Thirteen: A More Exalted Position

The story of the *Hashemy* can be traced through the *HRA* and secondary sources. Of these, Peter Cochrane's *Colonial Ambition* provides the most detailed insight into the campaign mounted by Henry Parkes and his associates. Primary sources confirm that John Kinchela returned to Sydney and became Superintendent of Schools in the Orange district at this time. There is no record of how he responded to James Butler's incarceration, and his meeting with Governor FitzRoy is my creation, as are all conversations between the two brothers. While I have imagined that John told his brother about the Irish Battle of Ballingarry and the discovery of gold in San Francisco, these events are factual. Thanks to the governor's prerogative, James Kinchela was granted an early release on 1 January 1849, but there is nothing to confirm John Kinchela negotiated this.

Chapter Fourteen: In the Soup

The luncheon scene with Alexander Moore is inspired by my reading of the 1850 insolvency trial of Martin Gill, and secondary sources concerned with the pecuniary focus of Irish marriage during this period, particularly when the woman had been involved in a scandal like abduction. On the day of his release Kinchela was arrested for the alleged abduction of Louisa Aarons, whose father was a shopkeeper, but not, as far as I know, a tobacconist on George Street. I quote directly from the newspaper coverage concerned with Kinchela's arrest in this and the following chapter. These articles suggest Kinchela went to the New Year's Day races. Many of the horses mentioned ran that day. I have no record about who Kinchela may have met that day and there is no record of his conversation with Captain Innes. There is no record about what actually occurred between Kinchela and Louisa Aarons.

Chapter Fifteen: A Gross Breach

The activities of Earl Grey, Governor FitzRoy, Parkes and his committee are based on primary and secondary sources. The *Hashemy* did lose convicts to cholera before leaving England. I have imagined John Kinchela's response to his brother's second abduction charge and how this might have affected Mary Ann. As indicated, the newspapers suggest the second abduction charge was dropped when no witnesses came forward to testify. I imagined Kinchela quitting Sydney after this episode. I also created the incident with Lewis Samuel in the Pitt Street hotel dining room as events preceding Samuel's pursuit of Gill during later insolvency proceedings and 'the rupture' between Margaret and Martin Gill.

Chapter Sixteen: The Thwarted Plot

Bell's newspaper published the articles listed, including the satirical study of Kinchela as a bushman 'without a hair on lip or chin'. There are no shipping records to confirm Kinchela went to Moreton Bay after the Louisa Aarons incident; however, records confirm Hawkwood was sold to John Walker in 1848–49. Given John Kinchela was working in the Orange district at this time, it is possible James negotiated the sale. I have imagined the exchange of letters between the brothers. While the scene with the Brisbane barfly is imagined, the details of the Blaxland party heading north in 1847 with the widow Pegg and her sons is accurate. Samuel was encouraging other men to also litigate against Gill. I have found no records to reveal what happened to Rebecca, the Gill's servant. I assumed she was 'let go' during the family's financial difficulties. I don't know which route the Kinchelas took when they travelled to Hawkwood, but Drayton was a newly surveyed township in 1849 (now known as Toowoomba) and the Bull's Head Inn was popular. Dr John Dunmore Lang did send several immigrant boats to Moreton Bay in 1849 to address the labour shortage in that region.

Chapter Seventeen: Defiance

All descriptions of the *Hashemy* protests are based on primary and secondary sources and the speeches have been quoted from newspapers. Originally, Lowe was reluctant to participate in the campaign spearheaded by Parkes but he did eventually join the rally at Circular Quay in June 1849. His speech was the most sensational of the day. The omnibus he spoke from was draped with a banner reading 'Defiance'. Governor FitzRoy was reputed to have trained cannons on the rally and put troops around Government House. I don't know if Mary Ann and Will witnessed the rally. I have listed the actual names of the men and the properties they owned in the districts around Hawkwood. In June 1849 the two Pegg brothers were murdered by Aboriginal warriors. Fifty settlers participated in the reprisal that followed and hundreds of Aboriginal people were murdered. Other than the Thompsons and their 'friendly trackers', I have no evidence that Kinchela or these other men were involved.

Chapter Eighteen: Lions After Slumber

I can't confirm if Edward Hawkins and Thomas Archer knew Kinchela, but these two Upper Burnett settlers went to San Francisco in 1849 and Walker bought Hawkwood from the Kinchelas. Governor FitzRoy's wife died in a riding accident and her husband was holding the reins of the vehicle. Those at the rally deputised Lowe, Parkes and four other men to present their petition to the governor, who left the large crowd waiting in the rain before issuing orders to return the following day. Official records and newspapers suggest that next day's meeting occurred as described. Most of this dialogue is verbatim and FitzRoy was reputed to have stationed troops in his pantry and mounted cavalry in his stables. The committee met at the Royal Hotel and recounted FitzRoy's response to followers. I imagined a committee member evoking the Peterloo Massacre and quoting Shelley's well-known poem.

Chapter Nineteen: The Camel's Back

The weather was sunny for the second rally at Circular Quay but I have no evidence Mary Ann and Will were among the 5000 or so present.

I imagined their encounter with Kinchela after he disembarked the Moreton Bay steamer. The advertisements associated with Gill's properties are verbatim from the *SMH*, as is Lowe's speech invoking Peterloo and the Boston tea party. Kinchela was rooming with Major Pitt D'Arcy at Joseph Walford's in July 1849. The Major had encountered the Rockites as a younger man and died of gout that night. John Kinchela died in October 1849 and his eulogy was published in the *SMH*, attributed to a 'J.L.' I have imagined this to be a widow named Mrs Lynton with whom Kinchela boarded while visiting the Orange district as Superintendent of Schools. The correspondence between FitzRoy and Earl Grey is in the *HRA*, while the dispute between Lowe and Bland comes from parliamentary records and newspapers.

Chapter Twenty: Under the Hammer

The record is silent about how Martin Gill, James Butler and Mary Ann reconciled their differences. I invented the scene where James Butler visits Gill's Family Hotel and sees Mary Ann for the first time in several months and negotiates her hand with Martin Gill, by drawing on secondary sources and oral history records concerned with nineteenth-century Irish marital negotiations. The family was evicted from the hotel in early November. They moved into a weatherboard cottage on Kent Street and this was leased by McCormick. The episode at Moore's auction rooms comes from the 1850 insolvency trial and Gill's response, 'You may all go to hell' is verbatim. The list of goods put to auction includes the washbasin and mirror Margaret Gill retrieved. The only exception is Mary Ann's dresses, which I imagined.

Chapter Twenty-One: All That Glitters

The social and economic conditions of NSW, including the departure of Ben Boyd and other colonists, come from colonial newspapers and shipping records as well as Cameron White's unpublished article and Charles Bateson's *Gold Fleet for California*. These confirm the three vessels departed 5–6 November 1849. Kinchela sailed on the *Lady Howden*. While I imagined Martin Gill holding out at the McCormick's farm, the shipping lists confirm 'Mr and Mrs Gill and son' were booked first class on the *Sabine*. I also imagined the reconciliation between Mary Ann and Kinchela before he sailed.

Chapter Twenty-Two: A Tuppenny Damn

Martin Gill published a notice against Margaret Gill in the *SMH* in early November 1849, which I quote verbatim. This and other newspaper quotes concerned with fashion, photography and Lowe's auction are also direct quotes. Thomas McCormick leased the Saracen's Head for Margaret Gill under his name. I imagined McCormick's visit to the out-of-town auction rooms and the confrontation with Martin Gill at the Punchbowl farm. Both the newspapers and shipping records confirm that Mary Ann and Will sailed first class on the *Sabine* and in the company of their father on 7 December 1849.

Chapters 23–25

The final chapters are written in a different style from the rest of the book and do not involve imaginative incursions. The shipwreck of the *Sabine* and the passengers' encounter with the pirates from '*The Pilot*' are gleaned from Bateson's *Gold Fleet* and the newspapers. The newspapers provide details of Margaret Gill at the time of the 1850 insolvency trial and her rise as an independent businesswoman who managed the Saracen's Head and catered for special guests at Fort Macquarie in 1851. The notice of Mary Ann's marriage to James Butler appeared in the *SMH* in 1853. To piece together the final portion of Mary Ann's life, I consulted extensive secondary sources as well as shipping records, colonial and Californian newspapers and archives, census reports, birth, death & marriage records, Police Gazettes, Mary Beatty's final will and testament and A.A. Piggin's auction of her personal goods in 1902.

Bibliography

PRIMARY SOURCES
ARCHIVES
AUSTRALIA
City of Sydney Assessment Books
City of Sydney Council, 2005: [CRS 15: 1848], [CRS 17: 1871], [CRS 18: 160/2/7]

State and Mitchell Library of New South Wales
Historical Records of Australia, Series 1 to 3.
Returns of the Colonial Census: [ML/CY/4/281]
Governors Dispatches to the Secretary of State for the Colonies [1128: 23:134/ML1/1212/
R545, 1128-1131]

State Records (SR) NSW
SRNSW: NRS 935, Copies of letters sent: Local and overseas, 1809–13 [4/3490B], Reel
6002
SRNSW: NRS 937, Copies of letters sent within the Colony 1814–27, items [4/3508], Reel
6010 [4/3509], 6011
SRNSW: NRS 898, Special Bundles 1794–1825, items [4/1718], Reel 6023, [4/1725,
4/1778], Reel 6040
SRNSW: Colonial Secretary NRS 897, Letters Received 1788–1826, items; Reel 6042, Reel
6061 [4/1804], Reel 6066
SRNSW: NRS 12210, Certificates of Freedom [4/4295], Reel 983 and No 36/0557 [4/4333],
Reel 996
SRNSW: NRS 907, Colonial Secretary Letters relating to Land 1826–1856 [2/7865], Reel
1131 [2/7899], Reel 1149

SRNSW: NRS 906, Colonial Secretary's Special Bundles [2/8015.1], Reel 1247

SRNSW: NRS 13480, Session returns of persons tried and convicted by the Supreme Court at Sydney and on Circuit 1846–1849 [X47], Reel 2756

SRNSW: NRS 12188, Convict Indents, Reel 395

SRNSW: NRS 880, Sydney Supreme Court Criminal Jurisdiction Depositions, [9/6345]

SRNSW: NRS 845, Depositions and other papers, Sydney and Country [2/10415]

SRNSW: NRS 2388, Parramatta Gaol Description Books, Reel 810

SRNSW: NRS 1291, Reports of Vessels Arriving NSW [4/5202], COD 24, Reel 1263

SRNSW: NRS 13654, Insolvency Files: Martin Gill, Pitt Street, Sydney, 23/1/1850 File No 2028 [2/8842]

SRNSW: Monthly Returns [4/1718], Reel 6023 see NRS 898 above

SRNSW: NRS 1155, Musters and Papers Convict Ships 1821–35 [2/8253], Reel 2420

SRNSW: NRS 10857, Police Reports of Crime for Police Information, Reels 3607, 3608

SRNSW: NRS 12202, Ticket of Leave: No 30/282 [4/4075], Reel 914

REPORTS

ENGLAND & IRELAND

Admiralty

Royal Navy Registers of Seamen's Services. Registers. 80601–81200. Name: James John Kinchela. Official Number 81007. Born San Francisco, 8 August 1857. [ADM 188/73/81007]

House of Commons Parliamentary Papers

Slave Trade. Return to an address of the Honourable House of Commons, 12 March 1827. Further reports made to His Majesty's Government by Thomas Moody Esquire and John Dougan Esquire or by any other commissioners appointed to inquire into the state of the slaves. Captured Negros at Demerara. Report of Commissioners Sir C.W. Burdett and Mr Kinchela (1827).

National Archives, Kew, England

Colonial Office: West Indies Original correspondence, Secretary of State from Governor of Barbados. 'Sir Charles Wyndham Burdett and John Kinchela, commissioners to inquire into the State of the Africans liberated from slavery and apprenticed in the West Indies', 2 December 1825, [70 folio: 428, CO 28/93/86].

Colonial Office and Predecessors: West Indies Original correspondence, Secretary of State. 'Commissioners enquiring into the state of the captured negroes', 1 January 1826–30 June 1826, CO 318/85-88.

National Archives of Ireland

Chief Secretary's Office, Convict Department, Transportation Registers: MFS 56/1–5

Chief Secretary's Office, Prisoners' Petitions and Cases: MFS 57/1-14

Chief Secretary's Office, Convict Department, State Prisoners' Petitions: MFS 58/1–6

Chief Secretary's Office, Convict Department, Convict Reference Files: MFS 59/1–77
State Papers, Register of Convicts on Convict Ships: MFS 60/3

Parliamentary Statutes

3 Henry 7, Chapter 2, *The penalty for carrying a woman away against her will that hath lands or goods,* 1487

4 & 5 Phillip and Mary, Chapter 8, *An Act for the punishment of such as shall take away maydens that be inheritors, being within the age of sixteen years, or marry them without the consent of their parents,* 1557

30 Elizabeth I, Chapter 9, *An Act for taking away of clergy from offenders . . . concerning the taking away of women against their wills unlawfully,* 1597

10 Charles I, Chapter 3, *An Act for the punishment of such as shall take away maydens that be inheritors being within the age of sixteen years, or marry them without the consent of their parents,* 1634

6 Anne 16, *An Act for the more effectual preventing the taking away and marrying of children against the wills of their parents and guardians,* 1707

9 Geo 4.c31, *An Act for consolidating and amending the statutes in England relative to offences against the person,* 1828

UNITED STATES OF AMERICA
The US National Archives and Records Administration
Census 1870: [M593: 000545574: 004259313: 00597]

NEWSPAPERS
AUSTRALIA & NEW ZEALAND
The Argus, The Atlas, Australasian Chronicle, The Australian, The Bathurst Advocate, Bathurst Free Press, Bell's Sporting Life, The Brisbane Courier, Colonial Times, The Cornwall Chronicle (Tasmania), *Corowa Free Press, The Courier* (Hobart), *The Empire, Evening News, Freeman's Journal, The Goulburn Herald and Chronicle, Government Gazette, The Herald, The Hobart Town Mercury, The Maitland Mercury, The Mercury* (Hobart), *The Moreton Bay Courier, The Morning Chronicle* (Sydney), *The New Zealander, The Perth Gazette, Police Gazette, The Queenslander, The Sentinel, The South Australian, The Sydney Chronicle, The Sydney Gazette, The Sydney Mail, Sydney Monitor, The Sydney Morning Herald, The West Australian Times*

ENGLAND & IRELAND
The Belfast Newsletter, The Bristol Mercury, Caledonian Mercury, Captain Rock in London, or, The Chieftain's Weekly Gazette, The Examiner, The Freeman's Journal, The Glasgow Herald, The Hull Packet, The Ipswich Journal, Jackson's Oxford Journal, The Kilkenny Moderator, The Liverpool Mercury, The Morning Chronicle, The Morning Post, The Newcastle Courant, The Poor Man's Guardian, Punch, or the London Charivari, The Times, Trewman's Exeter Flying Post

BIBLIOGRAPHY

UNITED STATES OF AMERICA
Daily Alta California, Los Angeles Star, Sacramento Daily Union

PUBLISHED
Baker, William, *Heads of the People*, Sydney, 1847

Bigge, J.T. (ed.), *Report of the Commissioner of Inquiry on the Judicial Establishments of New South Wales*, London: House of Commons, 1823

——, *Report of the Commissioner of Inquiry on the State of Agriculture and Trade in the Colony of New South Wales*, London: House of Commons, 1823

——, *Report of the Commissioner of Inquiry on the State of the Colony of New South Wales*, London: House of Commons, 1823

——, *Report of the Commissioner of Inquiry on the State of Agriculture and Trade in the Colony of New South Wales*, Adelaide: Libraries Board of South Australia, 1966 [1823]

Cannon, Richard, *Historical Record of the Thirty-Ninth or Dorsetshire Regiment of Foot*, London: Parker, Furnivall and Parker, 1853

Carleton, William, *Characteristic Sketches of Ireland and the Irish*, Dublin: P.D. Hardy and Sons, 1845

Cunningham, Peter, *Two Years in New South Wales*, London: Henry Colburn, 1827

Fowles, Joseph, *Sydney in 1848*, NSW: Ure Smith, 1973 [1849]

Geoghegan, Edward, *The Currency Lass, Or My Native Girl* (ed. Roger Covell), Sydney: Currency Press, 1976 [1844]

Griffin, Gerald, *The Collegians*, New York: JJ Harper, 1829

Haey, James, *The Only Genuine Edition: The Trial of Sir Henry Browne Hayes, Knight*, Cork: King's Arms Exchange, 1801

Harris, Alexander, *Settlers and Convicts*, Melbourne: Melbourne University Press, 1967 [1847]

——, *The Emigrant Family*, Canberra: Australian National University Press, 1967 [1849]

Hogan, James F., *The Irish in Australia*, London: Ward and Downey, 1887

Inglis, H.D., *Ireland in 1834*, London: Whittaker & Co., 1835

Low, Francis, *City of Sydney Directory for 1844–45*, Sydney: Ferguson, 1844

Maclehose, James, *Picture of Sydney & Strangers' Guide in NSW for 1839*, Sydney: J. Maclehose, 1839

Maxwell, W.H., *Wild Sports of the West of Ireland*, London: Simpkin and Co., 1892

Molesworth, Sir William, *Report from the Select Committee of the House of Commons on Transportation: Together with a letter from the Archbishop of Dublin on the same subject: and note by Sir William Molesworth*, London: Henry Hooper, 1838

Moore, Thomas, *Memoirs of Captain Rock*, Paris: A. & W. Galignani, 1824

Mudie, James, *The Felony of New South Wales*, Melbourne: Lansdowne Press, 1964, [1837]

Mundy, Godfrey C., *Our Antipodes*, Canberra: Pandanus Books, 2006 [1852]

O'Connor, Fergus, *A Series of Letters from Fergus O'Connor to Daniel O'Connell*, New York: Garland Publishing, 1986 [1837]

O'Donovan, J. with Eugene O'Curry & Co., *Ancient Laws of Ireland*, Dublin: Longman, 1869

309

O'Sullivan, Mortimer, *Captain Rock Detected*, London: T. Cadell, 1824

Pigot & Co.'s Provincial Directory 1824, Clonakilty: Pigot & Co., 1824

Pritchard, W.T., *Polynesian Reminiscences*, London: Chapman and Hall, 1866

Shelley, Percy Bysshe, *The Masque of Anarchy*, London: Bradbury and Evans, 1832

Stowe, Harriet Beecher, *Uncle Tom's Cabin*, Boston: Jewett and Co., 1852

Tennyson, Alfred, Lord, *In Memoriam A.H.H.*, London, Bankside Press, 1900 [1849]

Thackeray, William Makepeace, *Vanity Fair*, London: Thomas Nelson and Sons, 1906
   [1847]

Therry, R., *Reminiscences of Thirty Years' Residence in NSW and Victoria*, London: Sampson
   Low and Sons, 1863

Townsend, Joseph P., *Rambles and Observations in New South Wales*, London: Chapman
   and Hall, 1849

Townsend, William C., *Modern State Trials*, London: Longmans & Co., 1850

——, *Modern State Trials Revised and Illustrated*, London: Longman, Brown and Green,
   1850

Walsh, John E., *Sketches of Ireland Sixty Years Ago*, Dublin: McGlashan, 1847

UNPUBLISHED PRIMARY SOURCES

Annette Miller's personal archive: Kinchela Family Letters. From John Kinchela and Anne
   Bourne in Sydney to their daughter Matilda Miller in India: 2 July 1838–August 1838,
   25 May 1841–28 August 1842

SECONDARY SOURCES
PUBLISHED

Arensberg, Conrad M. and Kimball, Solon T., *Family and Community in Ireland*, 3rd edn,
   Clare: Clasp Press, 2001

Asbury, Herbert, *The Barbary Coast*, London: Robert Hale, 1933

Atkinson, Alan, *The Europeans in Australia*, South Melbourne: Oxford University Press,
   1997

——, 'The moral basis of marriage', *The Push*, 1978, 2: 104–23

—— & Aveling, Marian, *Australians 1838*, Broadway, NSW: Fairfax, Syme & Weldon
   Associates, 1987

——, 'Marriage and distance in the convict colony, 1838', *The Push*, 1983, 16: 61–70

Aveling, Marian, 'Gender in early New South Wales society', *The Push*, 1987, 24: 31–41

——, 'She only married to be free', *The Push*, 1978, 2: 104–23

Bateson, Charles, *Gold Fleet for California*, Sydney: Ure Smith, 1963

Beck, Deborah, *Hope in Hell*, Sydney: Allen & Unwin, 2010

Bitel, Lisa M., *Land of Women*, Ithaca, N.Y.: Cornell University Press, 1996

Brennan, Russell & Richards, Jonathan, 'The scum of French criminals and convicts',
   History Compass, 2014, 12(7): 559–66

Broeker, Galen, *Rural Disorder and Police Reform in Ireland, 1812–33*, London: Routledge,
   1970

Buckley, Maria, *Irish Marriage Customs*, Cork: Mercier Press, 2000

Burchell, Robert, 'The gathering of a community', *Journal of American Studies*, 1976, 10(3): 279–312

Burton, Brian, *Flow Gently Past*, Corowa: Shire Publisher, 1973

Byrne, Paula J., 'A colonial female economy', *Social History*, 1999, 24(3): 289

——, *Criminal Law and Colonial Subject: New South Wales 1810–1830*, Cambridge: Cambridge University Press, 1993

——, 'Women and the Criminal Law: Sydney 1810–1821', *The Push*, 1985, 21: 1–19

Campbell, Malcolm, *Ireland's New Worlds*, Madison: University of Wisconsin Press, 2008

——, 'Ireland's furthest shores', *Pacific Historical Review*, 2002, 71(1): 59–90

Clune, Frank, *Rascals, Ruffians and Rebels of Early Australia*, Sydney: Angus & Robertson, 1987

Cochrane, Peter, *Colonial Ambition*, Melbourne: Melbourne University Press, 2006

Colley, Linda, 'Britishness and otherness: An argument', *Journal of British Studies*, 1992, 31(4): 309–29

Connolly, S.J., *Religion and Society in Nineteenth-century Ireland*, Dudalk: Dundalgan, 1985

Connors, Libby, *Warrior*, Sydney: Allen & Unwin, 2015

Cosgrove, Art (ed.), *Marriage in Ireland*, Dublin: College Press, 1985

Costello, Con, *Botany Bay*, Cork: Mercier Press, 1987

——, 'The convicts: Transportation from Ireland', in Colm Kiernan (ed.), *Ireland and Australia*, Sydney: Angus & Robertson, 1984

Cullen, L.M., *The Emergence of Modern Ireland 1600–1900*, London: Batsford Academic & Educational, 1981

——, 'Catholics under the Penal Laws', *Eighteenth-Century Ireland*, 1986, 1: 23–36

Curthoys, Ann, and McGrath, Ann (eds), *Writing Histories: Imagination and narration*, Melbourne: Monash University Press, 2000

Damousi, Joy, *Depraved and Disorderly*, Cambridge: Cambridge University Press, 1997

Daniels, Kay, *Convict Women*, Sydney: Allen & Unwin, 1998

Dargan, Pat, *Exploring Georgian Dublin*, Dublin: Nonsuch Publishing, 2008

Davidoff, Leonore & Hall, Catherine, *Family Fortunes*, London; New York: Routledge, 2002

Devlin-Glass, Frances, Bull, Philip & Doyle, Helen (eds), *Ireland and Australia, 1798–1998,* Sydney: Crossing Press, 2000

Dixson, Miriam, *The Real Matilda*, Ringwood: Penguin, 1976

Donnelly, James S., 'Captain Rock', *Eire—Ireland*, 2007, 42(3 & 4): 60–103

——, *Captain Rock*, Wisconsin: University of Wisconsin, 2009

——, *The Land and the People of Nineteenth-Century Cork*, London: Routledge, 1975

——, 'Pastorini and Captain Rock', in Samuel Clark & James S. Donnelly (eds), *Irish Peasants*, Madison, Wis.: University of Wisconsin Press, 1983

—— & Miller, Kerby A., *Irish Popular Culture, 1650–1850*, Dublin: Irish Academic Press, 1998

Doyle, John, *An Historical Survey of St John's Kilkenny*, Kilkenny: J. Doyle, 1990

Drake, Michael, 'Marriage and population growth in Ireland, 1750–1845', *Economic History Review*, 1963, 16(2): 301–13

Evans, Ray, Saunders, Kay & Cronin, Kathryn, *Exclusion, Exploitation and Extermination*, Sydney: Australian and New Zealand Book Company, 1975

Fitzpatrick, David, *Oceans of Consolation*, Melbourne: Melbourne University Press, 1995

——, 'That beloved country that no place else resembles', *Irish Historical Studies*, 1991, 27(108): 324–51

Fletcher, Brian H., *Colonial Australia Before 1850*, West Melbourne: Thomas Nelson, 1976

Forth, Gordon, 'No petty people', in Patrick O'Sullivan (ed.), *The Irish in the New Communities*, vol. 2, Leicester: Leicester University Press, 1992

Foster, Robert & Nettelbeck, Amanda, *Out of the Silence*, Adelaide: Wakefield Press, 2012

Gibbons, Luke, *Transformations in Irish Culture*, Cork: Cork University Press, 1996

Goff, Victoria, 'Convicts and clerics', *Media History*, 1998, 4(2): 101–20

Goodman, David, *Gold Seeking*, Stanford: Stanford University Press, 1994

Graysmith, Robert, *Black Fire*, New York: Broadway Books, 2012

Grimshaw, Patricia, Lake, Marilyn, McGrath, Ann & Quartly, Marian (eds), *Creating a Nation: 1788–2007*, Perth: Australian Scholarly Classics Network, 2006 [1994]

Grimshaw, Patricia, McConville, Chris & McEwen, Ellen (eds), *Families in Colonial Australia*, Sydney: Allen & Unwin, 1985

Guinnane, Timothy W., *The Vanishing Irish*, Princeton: Princeton University Press, 1997

Heaton, J.H., *The Bedside Book of Colonial Doings*, London: Angus & Robertson, 1986

Hind, Robert J., 'We have no colonies', *Comparative Studies in Society and History*, 1984, 26(1): 3–35

Hirst, John, *Convict Society and Its Enemies*, Sydney: Allen & Unwin, 1983

——, *The Strange Birth of Colonial Democracy, New South Wales 1848–1884*, Sydney: Allen & Unwin, 1988

Holcomb, Janette, *Early Merchant Families of Sydney*, North Melbourne: Australian Scholarly Press, 2013

Hurtado, Albert, *Intimate Frontiers*, Albuquerque: University of New Mexico Press, 1999

Inglis, Ken S., *Australian Colonists*, Melbourne: Melbourne University Press, 1993

Irvin, Eric, *Dictionary of Australian Theatre 1788–1914*, Sydney: Hale and Iremonger, 1985

——, 'Australia's first dramatists', *Australian Literary Studies*, 1969, 4(1): 25–9

Johnson, Susan Lee, *Roaring Camp*, New York: Norton and Co., 2000

Jordan, Robert, *The Convict Theatres of Early Australia 1788–1840*, Sydney: Currency Press, 2002

Kelleher, Margaret & Murphy, James H., *Gender Perspectives in Nineteenth-Century Ireland*, Dublin: Irish Academic Press, 1997

Kelly, Veronica, 'Hybridity and performance in colonial Australian theatre', in Helen Gilbert (ed.), *(Post) Colonial Stages*, Hebden Bridge, UK: Dangaroo, 1999, 45–54

Keneally, Thomas, *The Great Shame*, Sydney: Random House, 1998

——, *The Commonwealth of Thieves*, Sydney: Random House, 2005

Kennedy, Robert E., *The Irish: Emigration, marriage and fertility*, Berkeley: University of California Press, 1973

Kercher, Bruce, *Debt, Seduction, and Other Disasters*, Sydney: Federation Press, 1996

——, *Outsiders*, Melbourne: Australian Scholarly Publishing, 2006

Kiernan, Colm, *Australia & Ireland, 1788–1988*, Dublin: Gill and Macmillan, 1986

Kiernan, T.J., *The Irish Exiles in Australia*, Melbourne: Burns and Oates, 1954

Kloester, Jennifer, *Georgette Heyer's Regency World*, UK: Arrow Books, 2008

Knight, Ruth, *Illiberal Liberal*, Melbourne: Melbourne University Press, 1966

Laidlaw, Zoe, 'Richard Bourke', in David Lambert & Alan Lester (eds), *Colonial Lives Across the British Empire*, Cambridge: Cambridge University Press, 2006

Lindsey, Kiera, 'A new stage for the stage Irish', in Ciara Brethnach & Catherine Lawless (eds), *Visual, Material and Print Culture in Nineteenth-Century Ireland*, Dublin: Four Courts, 2010, 234–46

——, 'So much recklessness', *Australian Historical Studies*, 44(3): 438–56

Linn, Rob, *Battling the Land*, Sydney: Allen & Unwin, 1999

Lloyd, Brian, *Rutherglen*, Wangaratta: Shoestring Press, 1985

Love, Harold, *The Australian Stage*, Kensington: NSW Press, 1984

Luddy, Maria, *Women in Ireland, 1800–1918*, Cork: Cork University Press, 1995

Lyne, Charles E., *Life of Sir Henry Parkes*, London: T.F. Unwin, 1897

MacCana, Proinsias, *The Learned Tales of Medieval Ireland*, Dublin: Dublin Institute of Advanced Studies, 1980

McConville, Chris, *Croppies, Celts and Catholics: The Irish in Australia*, Caulfield East: Edward Arnold, 1987

MacCurtain, Margaret, *Ariadne's Thread: Writing women into Irish history*, Galway: Arlen House, 2008

—— & O'Corrain, Donnchadh, *Women in Irish Society*, Westport: Greenwood Press, 1979

—— & O'Dowd, Mary, *Women in Early Modern Ireland*, Edinburgh: Edinburgh University Press, 1991

MacDonagh, Oliver, *Early Victorian Government, 1830–1870*, New York: Holmes & Meier Publishers, 1977

McKenna, Mark, 'Writing the past: History, literature and the public sphere in Australia', *Australian Financial Review*, 16 December 2005, 1–2, 8

McKenzie, Kirsten, *Scandal in the Colonies*, Melbourne: Melbourne University Press, 2004

McLaughlin, Trevor, *Irish Women in Colonial Australia*, Sydney: Allen & Unwin, 1998

Magee, Seán, *Weavers and Related Trades, Dublin 1826*, Dublin: Dun Laoghaire Genealogical Society, 1995

Mandle, William F. & Travers, Pauric (eds), *Irish Culture and Nationalism, 1750–1950*, London: MacMillan, 1983

Martin, Allan W., *Henry Parkes*, Carlton: Melbourne University Press, 1980

Meleisea, Malama, *The Making of Modern Samoa*, Apia: University of the South Pacific, 1987

Mitchell-Marks, Paula, *Precious Dust*, Lincoln: University of Nebraska, 1994

Molloy, Kevin, 'The commodification of texts for the Irish Colonial reader', *Australasian Journal of Irish Studies*, 2009, 9: 73–94

Molony, John, *The Native Born*, Melbourne: Melbourne University Press, 2000

Nasson, Bill, *Britannia's Empire*, Stroud, Gloucestershire: Tempus, 2004

Neale, David, *The Rule of Law in a Penal Colony*, Cambridge: Cambridge University Press, 1991

Neely, W.G., *Kilkenny*, Belfast: Institute of Irish Studies, 1989

Nord, Deborah E., *Walking the Victorian Streets*, Ithaca: Cornell University Press, 1995

O'Brien, John & Travers, Pauric, *The Irish Emigrant Experience in Australia*, Swords, Ireland: Poolbeg, 1991

O'Connell, Lisa, 'Dislocating literature', *Novel: A forum on fiction*, 2001, 35 (Fall): 5–23

——, 'Marriage Acts', *Differences*, 1999, 11(2): 68–111

——, 'Matrimonial ceremonies displayed', *Eighteenth-Century Life*, 2002, 26(3): 98–116

——, 'Scotland 1800', in H. Gilbert & A. Johnston (eds.), *In Transit*, New York: Peter Lang, 2002, 21–44

O'Curry, Eugene, *On the Manners and Customs of the Ancient Irish*, Dublin: Williams and Norgate, 1873

Ó Danachair, Caoimhín, 'Some marriage customs and their regional distribution', *Béaloideas*, 1974–76, 42–4: 136–75

——, 'An Rí (the King)', *Journal of the Royal Society of Antiquaries of Ireland*, 1981, 111: 14–28

——, 'Cottier and landlord in pre-famine Ireland', *Béaloideas*, 1980–81, 48–9: 154–65

——, 'Distribution patterns in Irish folk tradition', *Béaloideas*, 1965, 33: 97–113

O'Dowd, Mary, *A History of Women in Ireland, 1500–1800*, Harlow: Pearson Longman, 2005

O'Farrell, Patrick, *The Irish in Australia*, (rev. edn), Kensington: UNSW Press, 1993

—— & O'Farrell, Richard, *Vanished Kingdoms*, Kensington: UNSW Press, 1990

Ó Gráda, Cormac, *Ireland before and after the Famine: Explorations in economic history, 1800–1925*, 2nd edn, Manchester: Manchester University Press, 1993

Oppenheim, Helen, 'The author of *The Hibernian Father*', *Australian Literary Studies*, 1966, 2: 278–88

Outhwaite, R.B., *Clandestine Marriage in England, 1500–1850*, London: Hambledon Press, 1995

Perkin, Joan, *Women and Marriage in Nineteenth Century England*, London: Routledge, 1989

Philpin, C.H.E., *Nationalism and Popular Protest in Ireland*, Cambridge: Cambridge University Press, 1987

Reece, Bob, *Exiles from Erin*, Basingstoke, UK: Macmillan, 1991

——, *Irish Convict Lives*, Sydney: Crossing Press, 1993

——, *The Origins of Irish Convict Transportation to New South Wales*, Basingstoke, UK: Palgrave, 2001

Ricards, Sherman L. & Blackburn, George M., 'The Sydney Ducks', *Pacific Historical Review*, 1973, 42(1): 20–31

Richards, Jonathan, *The Secret War*, St Lucia: University of Queensland Press, 2008

Richards, Leonard, *The Californian Gold Rush and the Coming of the Civil War*, New York: Alfred A. Knopf, 2007

Robinson, Portia, *The Hatch and Brood of Time*, Melbourne: Oxford University Press, 1985

——, *The Women of Botany Bay*, Sydney: Penguin Books, 1993

Ronayne, Jarlath, *The Irish in Australia*, Camberwell: Viking/Penguin, 2003

Russell, Penny, *Savage or Civilised*, Sydney: UNSW Press, 2011

——, 'Travelling steerage', *Journal of Australian Studies*, 2014, 38(4): 383–95

Ryan, Mary, *Women in Public*, Baltimore: John Hopkins University Press, 1990

Sassoon, Anne S., *Women and the State*, London: Hutchinson, 1987

Shanley, Mary L., *Feminism, Marriage and the Law in Victorian England*, New Jersey: Princeton University Press, 1989

Shaw, A.G.L., *Convicts and the Colonies*, Melbourne: Melbourne University Press, 1977

Shunsuke, Katsuta, 'The Rockite movement in County Cork in the early 1820s', *Irish Historical Studies*, 2003, 33: 278–96

Smith, Babette, *Australia's Birthstain*, Sydney: Allen & Unwin, 2009

——, *Cargo of Women*, Sydney: Allen & Unwin, 2008

——, *The Luck of the Irish*, Sydney: Allen & Unwin, 2014

Staff, Kevin & Orsi, Ricard J., *Rooted in Barbarous Soil*, California: University of California Press, 2000

Stone, Lawrence, *Uncertain Unions*, Oxford: Oxford University Press, 1992

Sturma, Michael, 'Eye of the beholder', *Labour History*, 1978, 34 (May): 3–10

Summers, Anne, *Damned Whores and God's Police*, Melbourne: Allen Lane, 1975

Teale, Ruth, *Colonial Eve*, Melbourne: Oxford University Press, 1978

Temple, Philip, *A Sort of Conscience*, Auckland: Auckland University Press, 2002

Thorpe, Bill & Evans, Raymond, 'Frontier Transgressions', *Continuum*, 1999, 13(3): 325–32

Tink, Andrew, *William Charles Wentworth*, Sydney: Allen & Unwin, 2009

Travers, Robert, *Henry Parkes*, Roseville: Kangaroo Press, 2000

Wannan, Bill, *The Wearing of the Green*, Melbourne: Lansdowne, 1965

Ward, John Manning, *Colonial Self-Government*, Toronto and Buffalo: University of Toronto Press, 1976

Ward, R. Gerard & Ashcroft, Paul, *Samoa*, Apia: University of the South Pacific, 1998

Webby, Elizabeth, *Colonial Voices*, St Lucia: University of Queensland Press, 1989

Webster, David, 'Terminology, hegemony and the Sydney press in 1838', *The Push*, 1981, 10: 31–46

Weiner, Albert B., 'The Hibernian Father', *Meanjin*, 1966, 4: 446–64

Whelan, Kevin, 'An underground gentry?', in James S. Donnelly & Kerby A. Miller (eds), *Irish Popular Culture, 1650–1850*, Dublin: Irish Academic Press, 1998

Wilson, Sandra, 'Language and ritual in marriage', *The Push*, 1978, 2: 92–101

Windschuttle, Elizabeth, 'Women, class and temperance', *The Push*, 1979, 3: 5–25

Wright, Clare, *The Forgotten Rebels of Eureka*, Melbourne: Text Publishing, 2013

Yuval-Davis, Nira, Anthias, Floya, & Campling, Jo (eds), *Woman, Nation, State*, Hampshire: Macmillan, 1989

——, *Gender and Nation*, London: Sage, 1997

UNPUBLISHED SECONDARY SOURCES

Laurie, Arthur, 'Early Gin Gin and the Blaxland tragedy', read by Arthur Laurie, a Vice-President of the Historical Society of Queensland, 27 November 1952

Lindsey, Kiera, 'Taken: A history of bride theft in nineteenth-century Ireland and Australia', PhD thesis, Melbourne: University of Melbourne, 2011

McKinnon, Firmin, 'Early pioneers of the Wide Bay and Burnett', read at a meeting of the Historical Society of Queensland, 27 June 1933

Norrie, Philip Anthony, 'An analysis of the causes of death in Darlinghurst Gaol, 1867–1914, and the fate of the homeless in the nineteenth-century', MA (research), Sydney: University of Sydney, 2007

O'Connell, Lisa, 'Marriage Acts: The rise of love and birth of the novel in eighteenth-century England', MA thesis, Melbourne: University of Melbourne, 1992

Ridden, J.S., 'Making good citizens: National identity, religion and liberalism among the Irish elite, c. 1800–1850', PhD thesis, London: King's College, 1998

White, Cameron, 'The Sydney Ducks versus the San Francisco Committee of Vigilance: British–American rivalry in the Pacific, 1839–1851', publication forthcoming

CORRESPONDENCE

Cochrane, Peter, email communication, 29 October 2007

Lewis, Miles, email communication and phone conversation, 6 October 2015

Miller, Victor, email communication, 26 February 2011

WEBSITES

Australian Dictionary of Biography, <http://adb.anu.edu.au>

British Library, 19th century newspaper database, <www.bl.uk>

Colonial Case Law, Macquarie University Law School, <www.mq.edu.au>

National Library of Australia, Trove, <http://trove.nla.gov.au>

Patricia Downes, 'Michael Kennan c1797–1846: Soldier Settler, 39th Regiment of Foot, <http://members.pcug.org.au/~pdownes/keenan>

Index